I0879730

THE POLITICAL THOUGHT OF ANDRE GORZ

Since the late 1950s André Gorz has produced a unique and influential body of work, which has profound implications for politics, economics, sociology and social policy. This is the first book-length analysis of Gorz's thought and its enormous contemporary importance.

Gorz's intellectual foundation was the existential Marxism of post-war France, which he applied to his study of work and class in advanced capitalist societies. Adrian Little recognises the significance of his early writing, but argues that Gorz's seminal work was his *Critique of Economic Reason* which tied together the eclectic themes of his theory.

Adrian Little discusses all of these themes in detail in this book, but pays particular attention to Gorz's use of political ecology, his advocacy of utopian politics and his proposals for a socialist alternative to the existing systems of work and welfare. Little concludes that Gorz's work supplies a coherent theory of 'socialist individualism' that provides a new agenda for the Left in the approach to the twenty-first century.

Adrian Little is Senior Lecturer in Politics at Nene College, Northampton.

ROUTLEDGE STUDIES IN SOCIAL AND POLITICAL THOUGHT

1 HAYEK AND AFTER
Hayekian Liberalism as a Research Programme
Jeremy Shearmur

2 CONFLICTS IN SOCIAL SCIENCE
Edited by Anton van Harskamp

3 THE POLITICAL THOUGHT OF ANDRÉ GORZ
Adrian Little

THE POLITICAL THOUGHT OF ANDRE GORZ

Adrian Little

Routledge
Taylor & Francis Group
LONDON AND NEW YORK

First published 1996
by Routledge

2 Park Square, Milton Park, Abingdon, Oxon, OX14 4RN
Transferred to Digital Printing 2005
Simultaneously published in the USA and Canada
by Routledge
711 Third Avenue, New York, NY 10017
Routledge is an imprint of the Taylor & Francis Group, an informa business
First issued in paperback 2013

Typeset in Garamond by
Keystroke, Jacaranda Lodge, Wolverhampton

British Library Cataloguing in Publication Data
A catalogue record for this book is available from the British Library

Library of Congress Cataloguing in Publication Data
Little, Adrian, 1969–

The political thought of André Gorz / Adrian Little.
p. cm. – (Routledge studies in social & political thought)
Includes bibliographical references and index.
1. Gorz, André – Contributions in political science. I. Title.
II. Series.

JC261.G67L57 1996 96–7013
320.5'315'092–dc20 CIP

ISBN 978-0-415-13866-6 (hbk)
ISBN 978-0-415-86243-1 (pbk)

CONTENTS

To Sinead

ACKNOWLEDGEMENTS

Throughout the course of this project I have been lucky enough to receive abundant sympathetic criticism. I owe immense gratitude to Michael Kenny who spent a lot of time providing rigorous and illuminating analysis of early drafts. I have also benefited from the perceptive comments provided by Andrew Dobson. In my time at the Queen's University of Belfast I received welcome assistance from Vince Geoghegan and Bob Eccleshall. John Keane helped me to establish contact with André Gorz; Conrad Lodziak, who initially introduced me to Gorz's work, provided useful commentary on my early research.

I thank Caroline Wintersgill and James Whiting at Routledge for their assistance and the comments of two anonymous reviewers for Routledge provided much food for thought. The two reviews contrasted although both were supportive. The most interesting point of disagreement was my sympathetic attitude towards Gorz's work. One reviewer felt I was not critical enough of Gorz's theory, the other felt it was not suitable to criticise Gorz for the sake of being critical. I tend to concur with the latter perspective but I hope to show that one can be sympathetic towards one's subject and simultaneously make critical comments where they are thought to be necessary. In any case I value the effort of the reviewers and they raised several extremely relevant points. None of those acknowledged above can be held responsible for any errors that remain as the final product is of course my responsibility.

INTRODUCTION

This book is a critical evaluation of the thought of André Gorz which has been largely neglected in political theory in the UK. Most references to Gorz are based upon his most famous book, *Farewell to the Working Class* (1980), which has been open to misrepresentation from those who wish to classify Gorz as a theorist of work and class. It is important to redress the imbalance which has been created by the misinterpretation and categorisation of Gorz's theory by those who fail to understand the complex and original totality of his thought.

Gorz was born in Vienna in 1924, the son of a middle-aged Jewish businessman and a young Catholic typist. From his early years he remembers being the centre of his mother's attention. She attempted to imbue the young Gorz with the bourgeois values of financial success and Aryanism. Subsequently she changed the family name from Horst to Gorz to eliminate the identifying mark of Judaism, cajoled her husband into adopting Catholicism and named Gorz 'André' after an actor. Gorz believes that pressure from his mother hindered him from forming a stable identity which manifested itself when, as a youth, he flirted with Nazism in an attempt to find a mode of social insertion or self-identity.

In his late teens, Gorz discovered political philosophy and became engrossed with Sartre, Hegel and Marx. He was particularly engrossed by Sartrean existentialism and came to value the radical political philosophy that was expressed by the existentialist theorists in France. When he met Sartre and De Beauvoir in Lausanne in 1946 at the age of 22, they were impressed by his thorough understanding of Sartre's work. Subsequently Gorz moved to Paris and became a journalist, working mainly on *Les Temps Modernes* and *Le Nouvel Observateur.* Slowly he became increasingly prominent in post-war French socialist debates in the late 1950s and early 1960s. Moreover he became a close personal friend of Sartre who wrote the preface to *The Traitor*, Gorz's semi-autobiography, published when he was only 34 (Sartre 1989; Marcus 1992).

From this brief biographical account, it is possible to identify the reasons why individual autonomy and self-determination have become the dominant factors in Gorz's political theory. Given his alienation as a child, it is also clear why the existentialist doctrine, with its concentration on individual liberation, was attractive to the young Gorz. From this background he went on to develop a highly original perspective which, although critical of the work of Marx, can be located within the Marxian tradition.

The conventional view of Gorz is primarily based upon his conception of work and class conflict. Commentators such as Meiksins Wood have presented Gorz's theory as anti-Marxist, arguing that Gorz wishes away the need for class conflict and seeks reform rather than revolution (Meiksins Wood 1986: 15–18). Others, such as Hyman, contend that Gorz has supplanted the revolutionary proletariat with a new class, a new revolutionary subject – the neo-proletariat (Hyman 1983). One of the most critical approaches to Gorz has been taken by Sayers who believes that Gorz misconceives human nature by denying the human need to work. Furthermore Sayers argues that Gorz pays lip-service to liberal individualism by creating an ascesis of domestic labour (Sayers 1988, 1991).

Frankel is one of many commentators to analyse Gorz as a utopian theorist. Rather than taking an ideological approach to categorising Gorz's theory, Frankel attempts to assess Gorz within the context of other 'utopian' thinkers who hail from different ideological traditions (Frankel 1987). Others such as Giddens have chastised Gorz's utopianism by asserting the theoretical dangers that arise from utopian political theory. Unlike Frankel, Giddens is critical of the utopian approach to political theory employed by Gorz because it is, to his mind, unrealistic (Giddens 1987: 275–96). More sympathetic discussions of Gorz's utopianism have come from Geoghegan and Keane, who both recognise the important questions that utopian theory can pose to the 'realism' of more orthodox theory (Geoghegan 1987; Keane 1988).

Gorz is often interpreted as a 'green' thinker, primarily by commentators who have little sympathy with political ecology. Others such as Bookchin, Pepper, Dobson, and Eckersley reject the idea that Gorz is an ecological theorist (Bookchin 1980–1; Pepper 1984; Dobson 1990; Eckersley 1992). Bookchin believes that Gorz is an apologist for

Marxian orthodoxy and denounces Gorz's attempt to hijack ecology to bolster socialist theory. Eckersley adopts an ecocentric approach and rejects the claims that thinkers such as Gorz, who openly profess anthropocentric socialism, can be ecological theorists. Dobson is broadly more sympathetic to Gorz than Bookchin and Eckersley, but still recognises that Gorzian theory is not green. Most analysts of green politics deploy strict criteria for membership of the green canon. As such, it should not be surprising that few who analyse political ecology rigorously describe Gorz as a Green. Arguably the term 'post-industrial' is more useful in categorising Gorz's work (Kenny and Little 1995).

Despite the work of all the commentators mentioned above, the totality of Gorz's work has generally not been considered. On the contrary, most analysts tend to discuss Gorz within the criteria of their own subject matter or discipline. Consequently, these brief analyses tend to be, at best, partial because they do not recognise the coherence of Gorz's overall agenda. This book will attempt to evaluate Gorz's theory critically through an analysis of his work from the 1950s to the 1990s. In so doing we shall see how Gorz's work has matured and identify recurrent themes in his theory over the course of forty years.

Gorz has had many diverse and varied influences. His theoretical foundation is based on Sartre's existential philosophy. Despite his criticisms of Marx and Hegel, these two theorists have undoubtedly had a deep effect on Gorzian thought. Another important source for Gorz in the 1970s was Illich who has long championed small-scale society, educational reforms and the deprofessionalisation of many social tasks (Illich 1973). A more recent influence on Gorzian theory has been the second and third generation of critical theorists. Gorz has engaged with the complex theory of Habermas and the work of Offe on welfare and employment (Offe 1984). Before this Gorz's only dialogue with the Frankfurt School consisted of his friendship with Marcuse who debated with Gorz on many matters in the 1960s and always provided food for thought.

Viewed as a whole, Gorz's theory can be seen to be vibrant and original. Furthermore, it is also far-reaching in the range of issues it addresses. Gorz's integration of socialist and existentialist doctrines in a political programme has also been a notable achievement. This study will demonstrate how the attempts of commentators to categorise Gorz without reference to his intellectual foundations do his theory an extreme disservice. A critical evaluation of Gorz's radical critique shows his theory to be as sophisticated as it is original. The dynamism of Gorzian theory offers much to the development of a new, radical socialism which can challenge the power of capitalism and prioritise individual emancipation.

1

GORZ'S POLITICAL HERITAGE

Existentialism and communism

In the years immediately following the liberation of France at the end of the Second World War, the French Communist Party (PCF) was at its strongest. Indeed in the 1946 legislative elections the PCF won the single largest share of the vote with 28.6 per cent (Hazareesingh 1994: 312). Simultaneously the existentialist movement, with Jean-Paul Sartre as the figurehead, was becoming the strongest leftist intellectual grouping in France. By this time Gorz had moved to France and established contact with Sartre. Having first met Sartre in Lausanne in 1946, Gorz went on to become the political editor of Sartre's existentialist journal *Les Temps Modernes* (LTM) in 1961. Whilst Gorz published a variety of work in the late 1950s, his later work on LTM and *Le Nouvel Observateur* was to bring him greater notoriety.

MUTUAL ANIMOSITY: THE EXISTENTIALISTS AND THE PCF AFTER 1945

Gorz's personal stance on communism and the PCF in this period was extremely close to that of Sartre in as much as it varied between open hostility and pragmatic acquiescence. Between 1952 and 1956 Sartre could almost be regarded as a 'fellow traveller' (Caute 1973). Nevertheless the communists never quite overcame their suspicion of existentialist theorists and their relationship with Sartre was always a little uneasy. In any case the attempted fusion of Marxism and existentialism has always remained important in Gorzian theory as it did in Sartre's political works. That PCF intellectuals, such as Garaudy, treated existentialism contemptuously is a sign of their own materialist dogma rather than the failure of the existentialists to further the radical critique of capitalism (Garaudy 1970, 1971). The tendency of the PCF was to ostracise socialist thinkers, like Sartre and Gorz, who posed critical, ideological questions about Soviet policy. Ironically Garaudy was expelled from the PCF by conservative elements in 1970 (Wilde 1994: 87; Johnson 1981: 155).

In the early 1950s Gorz was part of a group including Sartre, De Beauvoir, Camus and Merleau-Ponty, amongst others, which developed an existential approach to Marxism, thereby confounding PCF proclamations under the then leader Maurice Thorez. Whilst not all of these central figures were to maintain the existentialisation of Marxism through the upheavals of post-war French communism, Gorz continued to see this as his task. It was, for Gorz, the ultimate objective; indeed, following the death of Sartre in 1980, he viewed his work as a continuation of Sartrean ideas (Gorz 1989b: 279). As Davies has observed, *Farewell to the Working Class* provides:

> a scintillating application of Sartrean themes – passivity, resentment, scarcity, autonomy, reciprocity, patriarchy and mental pre-logique to the specific socio-political conjuncture of the late seventies and the early eighties.
>
> (Davies 1988: 207)

The feature that has characterised Gorz's work since the 1950s is his constant stress on individual liberation as a prerequisite for socialist change. The prerogative for Gorz has been to restore individuality to its rightful place at the forefront of liberatory struggle – clearly an existentialist objective. Essentially this depends upon reclaiming individuality from the constraints of 'possessive individualism' which permeate liberal democratic regimes. Hence, whilst the neo-liberalism that has developed since the late 1960s and early 1970s has been portrayed as the champion of individual freedom, most of the radical Left has continued to privilege the collective. Furthermore the centre Left has come to engage with the question of individualism within the discourse of the New Right, that is, the freedom of individuals to consume, to be enterprising, to own property. In short, Gorz seeks to rescue the concept of individuality from the possessive individualism of neo-liberal theory.

It is apparent that Gorz's task is as difficult now as it was in the 1950s. Whilst he realises that the individual remains alienated, he has witnessed the colonisation of individuality by the Right. This is partially due to the failure of the radical Left to engage with the question of the individual in the post-war years. Gorz's belief is that the collective freedom which is championed by the radical Left cannot occur without individual liberation – a view he shared with Herbert Marcuse (Marcuse

1972b). This corresponds with the original aims of the existentialist movement as voiced by Sartre in the first issue of LTM before he had even met Gorz. There he stated that the aim of the journal was to 'participate in bringing forth certain changes in our society. . . . Without being materialist . . . we want to side with those who want to change both the social condition of a man and his conception of himself' (Hirsch 1982: 41). Thus the ultimate goal of socialist revolution for the founders of LTM was reliant upon the freedom of the individual. In effect, the existentialists were identifying individual autonomy as the primary factor for radical social change. This was to become the rallying call for the French students and workers twenty years later.

The late 1940s were a period of immense rivalry between the existentialists and the PCF. The PCF line was that the existentialists were anti-Soviet and thus, given the close personal relationship between Stalin and PCF leader Maurice Thorez, anti-communist (Johnson 1981: 43). This was a misconception on the part of the PCF because the objections of Sartre at this time were to the lack of discussion and self-criticism within the communist movement and not to the cause of communism itself. In short, the existentialists were criticising Stalinist dogma rather than posing rigorous ideological questions.

The communist suspicion of the existentialists probably reached its peak during Moscow's dispute with Tito in 1948 (Wilde 1994: 141). The Yugoslavs had been expelled from the Cominform, the international Communist organisation, on charges of authoritarianism. French intellectuals such as Pierre Herve accused Tito of being a fascist on the grounds that no party conference had taken place in Yugoslavia since the 1930s (Caute 1964: 178). This hypocrisy within the PCF and the communist movement as a whole was seized upon by Sartre who criticised the approach of Moscow. After all, Stalin was not beyond reproach for his bureaucratic centralism and lack of democratic accountability. Furthermore Sartre realised that incidents such as these could do substantial damage to the communist movement because it added fuel to the anti-communist lobby in Western Europe. Nevertheless, in the eyes of the PCF, Sartre was merely continuing to criticise their party/Stalin and was not, therefore, working in the interests of communism. Against this view, Sartre argued that the communist movement had to provide a united front in opposition to American neo-colonialism.

In the late 1940s and early 1950s it became apparent that the intellectual credibility of the PCF was being questioned because of its unconditional acceptance of Stalinist policy. Whilst some states within the Soviet bloc were prepared to question the Stalinist hierarchy, Thorez and the PCF remained fiercely loyal. Simultaneously Sartre was regarded as an enemy by the party because of his revisionism and his immense appeal to the disillusioned youth who felt alienated by traditional communist politics.

1952–6: FELLOW TRAVELLERS

Nevertheless, the situation during the Cold War was beginning to bring Sartre closer to the French communists. The reasons for this were twofold. Firstly, in 1951, Thorez, having suffered a stroke, went to the Soviet Union for treatment at the behest of Stalin. He was to remain in the USSR until Stalin's death in 1953 (Johnson 1981: 46). During the intervening period Jacques Duclos took hold of the reins of the party. His immediate goal was the amalgamation of all pro-peace and anti-imperialist groups that were developing. Hence the movement was opening its doors to more disparate support and when Sartre returned from the Vienna peace conference in 1952, he was willing to adopt a less critical approach to the party. The second reason for this new mood of rapprochement was the success of the PCF in articulating the now widespread anti-American fervour that was sweeping France. Whilst the PCF had, since the war, consistently warned about the danger of political subsidy from the Americans, the Right had welcomed the Marshall Plan. By the early 1950s though, the end of Marshall aid had produced a bitter reaction from de Gaulle. Thus the communists were handed the moral high ground on the issue of sweeping American influence (Johnson 1981: 42–3). The wave of 'Americo-phobia' also corresponded to Sartre's post-war warnings and so pushed the PCF and the existentialists closer together.

The Korean War set the seal on their uneasy alliance. The American aggression in Korea, albeit reacting to the North Koreans' initial strike, inflamed communist and existentialist passions to the extent that by 1952 the relationship between Sartre and the PCF was relatively harmonious. Nevertheless it was notable that the PCF intellectuals never really adopted the anti-imperialist discourse which was to characterise the rise of the New Left. This created a political problem for the PCF because most of the enemies of French imperialism in the post-war years in Africa and Asia had similar Marxist-Leninist leanings to the PCF. The silence of the intellectuals in the PCF in the face of French colonial exploits in Madagascar, Tunisia, Morocco, Algeria, Syria, Lebanon and Indo-China was abhorrent to independent intellectuals such as Sartre. It appeared though that by 1952 he was prepared to overlook this tacit justification of French colonialism in order to support the communist movement as a whole from the onslaught of criticism it was receiving from the Right. This criticism was to be silenced in 1952 by the growing anti-American feeling that allowed the communists to present themselves as morally correct.

There was universal unease on the Left at the brutal police suppression of the anti-American 'Ridgeway' riots in Paris on 28 May 1952 (Johnson 1981: 48). The conservative Pinay government (1952–3) had started to purge the communists in their own French version of McCarthyism. General Ridgeway, an American who was prominent in the Korean War, had been appointed as the new NATO commander in Paris and upon his arrival he was greeted by demonstrations orchestrated by the PCF against the American usage of biological warfare in Korea. The demonstrators were attacked by the police and several leading communists, including Jacques Duclos, were arrested on false charges. This led to a political backlash against the government's tactics that pulled the Left closer together. Indeed it is clear that the existentialists, including Gorz and Sartre, saw this repressive action by the government as the point at which the Left in general had to close ranks to preserve their mutual cause.

This was the period when the theorists of the PCF and the existentialists converged to the greatest degree. Nevertheless Sartre was more sympathetic to this alliance than other members of the existentialist movement such as Camus and Merleau-Ponty who believed that, in effect, this closing of ranks was an endorsement of Stalinism. This may have been an overestimation but Sartre was certainly beginning to understate some of the more idealistic elements of his existentialism. It also outlines the degree of expediency that Sartre was willing to exercise in his desire to unify the Left. Chiodi gives another explanation for Sartre's attempt to fuse existentialism and Marxism:

> What Sartre accepts from communism is its demands that limited 'bourgeois' humanism be replaced by a universal humanism, and that the only way of achieving this is by removing the means of production from the hands of a single class and placing them at the disposal of the entire collectivity. But he continues to hold that the political action this demands can only take place with, as its driving force, an ideology which recognises the existentialist anthropology as its proper foundation. If the demand for this is

> couched in terms inimical to Marxism, Sartre considers that its effects will be sterile, but if existentialism declares its support for Marxism at the politico-cultural level it will thereby gain a position within Marxism whence it can instigate a transformation of its ideological basis.
>
> (Chiodi 1976: 7)

Sartre clearly perceived Marxism as a potentially useful theory for the transmission of existentialist doctrines but he was aware that this required a rigorous restructuring of the Marxian method to remove economism and incorporate existential phenomenology. Thus, in maintaining that individual freedom was reliant upon the freedom of that individual's class, he was not really erring from the existentialist track. The two, as Gorz has long maintained, are interdependent. As Marcuse put it: 'no revolution without individual liberation, but also no individual liberation without the liberation of society' (Marcuse 1972b: 48).

A notable feature of this period was that it signified the end of a unified French existentialist movement, to the extent that it was ever really 'unified'. Sartre had been its figurehead and his disagreement with the other leaders, Camus in particular, was to lead the way for a wider unification of New Left interests in France after Sartre's split with the PCF in 1956. The period up to 1956 marked the emergence of a more reformist tendency in the communist movement as a whole. The Korean armistice minimised one source of contention and the accession of Malenkov and Khrushchev to power in the Soviet Union following Stalin's death, and the slightly more revisionist discourse which they adopted, increased hopes within the PCF that a new unity could develop with the moderate Left. In so doing they hoped that the PCF could end the Algerian crisis which had escalated in 1953.

However Guy Mollet, the leader of the socialist Section Française d'Internationale Ouvrière, rejected the offers of the PCF to create a new alliance. Despite this the communists were to support Mollet in the next election and he duly came to power (1956–7). His first step was to seek special powers from the assembly to suppress the unrest in Algeria. Reluctantly the PCF ensured the passage of these special powers by abstaining in the vote – a move that was to seriously undermine their credibility. Hence a new regime of terror was created in Algeria with the large-scale execution of many nationalist guerrillas (Hazareesingh 1994: 238). As a civil rights exercise it was abhorrent; as a socialist exercise it was disastrous. The Left was torn apart and in

1957 the government was overthrown. It was only at this time that the intellectuals within the PCF were able to voice support for Algerian independence fully. Nevertheless, by this time their credibility amongst independent intellectuals was minimal and the Left was decimated.

REOPENING OLD WOUNDS

Whilst the apparently inconsistent behaviour of Sartre had disrupted the unity of the existentialists, Gorz remained faithful to his mentor. Indeed, before his own publishing career began, Gorz appears as something of a Sartrean acolyte rather than a political theorist in his own right. Having been a 'fellow traveller' between 1952 and 1956, Sartre strongly criticised the Soviet repression of the Hungarian Revolution in October 1956. This in effect marked a complete return to his mutual hostility with the PCF of the late 1940s. Sartre severed his ties with the PCF and the animosity that preceded the Korean War was reinstated. That Gorz and Sartre followed the same intellectual path in these years was no coincidence. Nor is it merely an indicator of Gorz's admiration for Sartre, rather it signifies the close political proximity of the two. Even during his sojourn with the communists, Sartre never renounced his idealism or his individualism. Because of this it is clear why Gorz believes that his 'utopian' and individualist writing in the 1980s is a logical extension of Sartre's critique.

Prior to 1956 Sartre had understated his criticism of the Soviet system in order to maintain solidarity with the anti-American and peace movements that were growing in France. The Soviet invasion of Hungary, though, was considered a blatant abuse of the Soviet Union's military power and it led to Sartre's famous comment that the USSR had opened fire on an entire nation (Caute 1973: 350–7). This is perhaps the point at which a shift in the political agenda that created the French New Left occurred most clearly. Nevertheless the denunciation of the repression of the Hungarian Revolution by the existentialists need not have proved so controversial if the PCF had not seen fit to overlook the candid abuses of civil and individual liberty that were taking place in Hungary. In their attempt to maintain a good relationship with the Soviet leadership the PCF supported the invasion of Hungary – a stance that was irreconcilable with the beliefs of the existentialists. LTM perceived the Soviet intervention in Hungary as a return to Stalinism. Thus, following the revolution, a group of intellectuals, including Sartre and De Beauvoir, signed a letter protesting against the Soviet action. Whilst they proclaimed their belief in socialism, they disagreed with the violent suppression of Hungarian independence, insisting that socialism could not be achieved at bayonet point (Caute 1964: 227). The Kadar regime in Hungary, maintained by the Red Army, was infringing, the signatories argued, the liberty of socialist writers who were being imprisoned or sentenced to death. Kadar continued to persecute anti-Soviet socialists such as Heller, Feher and Markus until his removal from power in 1988 (Wilde 1994: 145–6).

The PCF support for the USSR over the Hungarian Revolution seriously damaged the party in France. It was apparent that the Left had torn itself apart. In the following years France was to witness the rise of the Right with the re-election of Charles De Gaulle as president in 1958. This period of right-wing presidential leadership was to continue until 1981. The division between the existentialist movement and the PCF was to expand long before the electoral decline of the French communists. The primary reason for this split was the reaction of the communists to the colonial exploits of the French government in Algeria. Whilst Sartre voiced extreme caution about the course of the war, the PCF had difficulty criticising it, given that they had agreed to the special powers granted to the Mollet administration that had led to the escalation in repressive violence. Not only had the PCF pandered to Soviet aggression in Hungary, but also they were failing to criticise French colonialism in North Africa. It appeared, to their existentialist critics, that the communists were bowing to public opinion rather than their own principles because the intellectuals of the party were still moving with the prevalent anti-Muslim sentiment in France. This discredited the party intellectuals leaving the new breed of socialists and Leftist independents, such as Gorz, in a stronger position to articulate the ideas of the young socialists.

Opposition to the Algerian War was widespread amongst leftist intellectuals, including Frantz Fanon, Claude Bourdet, and Albert Memmi who all joined Sartre in criticising French policy in Algeria. Influential thinkers such as Cornelius Castoriadis and the Trotskyite 'Socialism or barbarism' group were also critical. Whilst 'Socialism or barbarism' were far from intellectual partners of the LTM theorists, they were also to play an important part in the new dynamism of the French Left which was to precede the 1968 uprising. Indeed their idea of 'autogestion' (the concept of greater workers' control in the workplace and the development of this ethos in society as a whole) was to become an accepted part of French New Left theory, the primary doctrine of trade unions including the influential Confédération Française Démocratique du Travail (CFDT: French Democratic Confederation of Labour), and an influential principle in Gorz's *Strategy for Labour* (Gorz 1967).

The main activists in the movement which led to the 1968 Paris uprising were to find their intellectual basis in a disparate group of New Left thinkers who had found the deterministic dogma of the PCF too much of a political burden. Sartre had attempted to bring a new culture of self-criticism into the PCF and failed. Nevertheless he still viewed it as an important organ for liberatory change. It had, however, left the way open for a new generation of theorists to articulate concerns on the Left over problems in the Third World which were intrinsically linked to the colonialism issue. The PCF treatment of French colonialism left them in a weak position as far as this debate was concerned. Hence Sartre and Gorz became important political theorists for the socialists who had to find a new direction after the failure of the PCF and the moderate Left to challenge De Gaulle's hegemony. Along with activists such as Daniel Cohn-Bendit and radicals like Regis Debray, they were to become the central intellectual figures in the revolt of students and workers in 1968. It is evident that after 1960 Gorz's influence in the political arena increased substantially.

A NEW DIRECTION FOR THE FRENCH LEFT

Whilst Gorz and Sartre always maintained the necessity of the revolutionary mass body (though not necessarily a political party), it had become apparent that the PCF was fragmenting rather than unifying the interests of the Left. Gorz realised that the actual achievement of socialist change would rely upon a body encapsulating widespread socialist support. In the mould created by Marx and Lenin, Gorz, like many theorists of the Left, advocated the decentralisation of the revolutionary body after the achievement of the socialist goal. By 1960, however, it had become obvious to Gorz that the growth of unrest in French society was not being articulated by the PCF – a body that was now bereft of both credibility and groundswell support. For this reason Gorz called for a transformation of the traditional forms of socialist organisation. He was to write in 1969 that, at the beginning of the 1960s, his task was one of

> showing that capitalist development, though it attempted to shape the conscious needs of the working class, gave birth to new needs and new exigencies which are potentially revolutionary. And that these new exigencies are slow in producing a new

> radicalism because they do not recognise themselves in traditional methods and objectives of the trade union and political struggle.
> (cited in Howard and Klare 1971: 390)

Gorz was beginning to look for new motors of revolutionary change and new organisations for articulating socialist aspirations. It was obvious that the PCF in its present guise could not be the party of change. Furthermore the trade union movement also appeared to be regressive. Writing in 1965, Gorz articulated the changing face of work in French society in a form that was heralded as post-Fordism in the 1980s, although Gorz is by no means a post-Fordist thinker (Gorz 1975: 127). Gorz believed in 1965, as much as in the 1990s, that trade unions had failed to change as the nature of work changed. Thus they had not realised that the technical division of labour would ensure that full employment was impossible. Instead of creating a new discourse concerning the quality of work, trade unions continued to prioritise full employment – essentially a quantitative goal. This being the case it was all the more unlikely that the unions could represent the new militancy of the working class. Whilst Gorz perceived that French workers were becoming uneasy with the possibility of unemployment and the changing face of work and the policies of the De Gaulle administration, he could not see how this uneasiness could be articulated by the unions which were entrenched within the confines of traditional trade union politics (Gorz 1967). Thus it appeared that the conventional mediators of socialist unrest were redundant in the situation that confronted France in the mid-1960s. This new situation necessitated a new strategy. If the traditional organisations of socialist politics were not prepared to employ a new strategy, a new body was required to articulate radical socialist concerns.

Meanwhile, for Gorz, a new means of transmitting liberatory impetus was becoming apparent – the student movement. Gorz believed, though, that the students had to cooperate with workers if a united socialist front was to come about. Given the differing social base for these separate movements, this alliance was going to be difficult to forge and even more difficult to maintain. Whilst this proved to be the case in 1968, it was nonetheless apparent to Gorz, at the time, that the intellectual Left should assist the formation of such a union. Gorz demonstrated that, in seeking to embrace a wider revolutionary base than the labour movement, he was moving away from traditional Marxist-Leninist discourse:

> the struggle of the student unions for emancipation and valorisation of the student labour power is equivalent, in the

> educational and cultural fields, of the workers' struggle in the field of industry. But all the evidence suggests that this struggle can become and remain truly socialist, and avoid the pitfalls of reformism, only if it is extended and sustained by a strong working-class revolutionary movement. Left to itself student trade unionism, however socialist its thinking and objectives, cannot transcend the limits of corporatism, but must inevitably relapse into it if its aims are not taken up by the working-class organisation and inserted from the outset into an overall social struggle, safeguarding the student world against its own idiosyncrasies and myths.
>
> (Gorz 1975: 119–20)

Nevertheless it appears that the alliance of New Left interests that did come about was more accidental than strategic. This may also be a partial explanation for its failure. The forces that were to become known as the New Left were created out of a perceived necessity rather than a conscious strategy on the Left despite the efforts of Gorz and Sartre to promote such a strategy. The fact that these groups were so disparate is perhaps an indicator that the uprising of May 1968 was doomed to failure. Despite Gorz's recognition that a new strategy was required, it is apparent that a new strategic force never emerged. The New Left fervour of the 1960s was as much distinguished by its disunity as its unity. The socialist intelligentsia recognised the necessity for a new third way between orthodox communism and social democracy but never succeeded in creating a force capable of bringing together the disparate interests involved.

Whilst Gorz was continuing to advocate the need for a revolutionary party, it was apparent that no such party was emerging. Whilst the independent Left recognised this necessity, they came no closer to actually achieving unity. Nevertheless it is apparent that, amongst the socialist intelligentsia, Sartre and Gorz had a substantial influence on the activists of 1968. Cornelius Castoriadis, whose advocacy of workers' control in the workplace was a focus of New Left interest in France, denied the influence of Sartre on the students. This view has been scorned by Gorz:

> You, Castoriadis, do not find in Sartre 'one single sentence' (you emphasise these words) that 'in any measure' prefigures the American 'movement' and student movements in Europe – in short May '68. You must therefore not have been in the United States or you would have experienced the decisive influence of

> what you disdainfully term Sartre's 'Third-Worldism' on the American 'movement'; you must not have been alongside students in Berlin and Paris for whom Vietnam, Che, and the anti-imperialist struggle were cardinal references: you must not have been among the students who in May '68 carried Sartre triumphantly on their shoulders into the great, overflowing amphitheatre of the Sorbonne.
>
> (Gorz 1977b: 109)

Whilst this reads like an emotional fanfare to the efforts of Gorz's mentor, it nonetheless contains a fundamental truth about the nature of the independent New Left theorists in France. Gorz criticises Castoriadis for seeking to gain a copyright on knowledge. As no co-ordinated socialist grouping arose in the 1960s, different writers sought to score intellectual points over one another to magnify the extent of their own influence. Whilst Gorz did not overemphasise his own role, he was fiercely defensive of Sartre's influence and, in this sense, he got involved in a certain amount of fairly unimportant mudslinging. Thus Gorz chastised Castoriadis by stating that 'the sound of the guillotine that punctuates your assertions and your arrogant desire to be the only one that is right are intolerable' (Gorz 1977b: 109). Basically Castoriadis' aim was to criticise Sartre's approach to the communist movement and his selective consent to its tactics. That Sartre vacillated on his critical approach to the PCF and the Communist Party of the Soviet Union (CPSU) is true as observed above. Furthermore the fact that his inconsistent reaction to Soviet policy caused consternation amongst other existentialists is not contested. Yet the essential point is that Sartre and Gorz believed in the early 1950s in the necessity of a unified socialist party and, at that time, the PCF, despite its defects, was the only organisation that could possibly perform the role of the mass party. However the fact of Sartre's volte-face over the PCF did leave him and his followers open to criticism.

Following the Hungarian Revolution, Sartre and Gorz came to advocate a unity of New Left, anti-imperialist, Third-Worldist interests in the 1960s. Whilst they were prepared to take on board the 'Socialism or Barbarism' idea of 'autogestion', it appears that Castoriadis was unwilling to engage with their success in influencing the student uprising. The political theory that informed the uprising of May 1968 was by no means unified but this cannot have been aided by the reluctance of the communists and many of the independent socialist intelligentsia to engage in a meaningful discourse with the trade unionists and students.

This, at least, is what Sartre and Gorz consistently attempted to do albeit unsuccessfully. Ironically it appears that the post-Marxist political aims of Castoriadis in the early 1960s were to prove influential on Gorz's work. Indeed Boggs groups both Gorz and Castoriadis within a larger stratum of leftist thinkers including Luxemburg, Lukács, Gramsci, Sartre and the Frankfurt School who 'shared . . . a deep view of social transformation incorporating a fuller understanding of mass consciousness and collective subjectivity than was possible within orthodox Marxism' (Boggs 1995: 185). What this suggests is that the New Left in France were too concerned with their differences (real or otherwise) to unify on their areas of common concern. Hence, despite the similarities in their perspective, Gorz and Castoriadis failed to agree on a common foundation for the French New Left.

Gorz's ideas on the unity of worker and student interests is perhaps best demonstrated by his communication to the Gramsci Institute conference in 1965 (Gorz 1975: 109–31). There he attemped to set out the main grounds for common concern and he paved the way for the prominent role he was going to play in the growth of revolutionary fervour that culminated in May 1968. Having become political editor of LTM in 1961, Gorz was to provide the editorial backbone of the journal in the late 1960s and early 1970s. During the 1960s, Sartre began to develop what became known as his Third-Worldism. He concentrated on neo-colonial and imperialist matters which centred on the power that the United States was exercising in the Far East and Central and South America. Sartre criticised the French governments for colluding with the Americans and even called France itself an American colony. Whilst Sartre became engrossed with these issues, Gorz was able to undertake the important task of the critique of Gaullism. He did this through the framework of his analysis of 'neo-capitalism' which he outlined in *Strategy for Labour* (1967).

Sartre and Gorz recognised the link between the critique of neo-capitalism and imperialism as they witnessed the increasing number of workers recruited to France to share in the new material wealth and to counteract the employment surplus. The editorial stance of LTM in the mid-1960s was, then, characterised by the analysis of imperialism and neo-capitalism which manifested itself in an overt anti-Americanism. Davies points out that 'its [LTM] support for Castro and Ho Chi Minh are rapidly subsumed in an all-embracing anti-Americanism which itself is rendered consistent with the review's anti-Stalinism, anti-Gaullism and anti-structuralism' (Davies 1988: 176).

Thus, in the analysis of international socialist movements in the

1960s, although LTM may have sympathised with Castro and Guevara, its policy was moving towards a broader rejection of American foreign policy and American influence in Paris. Although Sartre and Regis Debray concentrated on international politics, Gorz wrote in an LTM editorial that the United States was manipulating the Sino-Soviet disjunction in its actions in Vietnam and that the role of socialists was to assist the freedom movements in Indo-China and in the Americas (Debray 1968; Gorz 1965b). Again it was evident to the loose New Left coalition that the destruction of American power required support for all anti-American, socialist groupings. Rather than concentrating on the ideological differences in worldwide liberation movements, it was more important to support them on the basis of their anti-Americanism. Although LTM did not set out to create an explicit editorial policy due to the multitude of individuals who contributed to it, it is apparent that the diminution of the American power base and the destruction of its colonial influence was the dominant motivation behind LTM editorials.

The French empire had been considerably undermined by this stage. It was becoming ever more apparent that France was counteracting its decline by engaging in neo-colonialist activity for the USA. The spotlight had therefore lifted from Algeria and was now firmly concentrated on Indo-China. Whilst LTM criticised American policy in Vietnam consistently (Gorz 1965b), this was to be surpassed in prominence by the student/worker uprising in Paris and the Soviet invasion of former Czechoslovakia. Gorz was primarily concerned by this stage with home affairs but, as Davies has observed, the colonial issue had created new problems in France:

> Because of a labour shortage caused by economic expansion under De Gaulle, and because of the return of part of the workforce to Italy and to Algeria and the existence of higher wages in West Germany, France imports high numbers of non-French unskilled workers. Exported by colony or neo-colony, where colonialism has undermined the agricultural systems and created unemployment, these workers arrive in France to be greeted by exploitation and racialist harassment.
>
> (Davies 1988: 183)

This situation concerned Gorz because he saw that although the French state was reaping the benefits of having workers who had not been raised in France, they were weakening the power basis of the traditional working-class and workers' movements. This was because, on the whole, these immigrant workers were non-unionised and were prepared to work for less material reward than the French worker. The capitalist power base benefited from this influx of foreign workers in three ways. Firstly, the system desperately needed more workers; secondly, the basis of the trade unions was undermined; and thirdly, as Davies notes, the immigrant workers caused 'a number of French workers to be drawn into the petit bourgeoisie and to embody the racialist pretexts to which it typically has recourse' (Davies 1988: 183). Gorz realised that a new underprivileged group was being created in these new immigrant workers who suffered even more than the working class due to racism from the working class as well as the petit bourgeoisie (Allen and Smith 1974: 40–1; Gorz 1970c). This sort of disenfranchised minority was to become of prime importance to him in the 1970s as he searched for a new unifying power on the Left. On the whole though, at this stage, Gorz usually left the question of immigration to other contributors to LTM as he did with women's rights, for instance, which was dealt with by Simone De Beauvoir and various occasional women contributors to the journal. Gorz concentrated on the critique of neo-capitalism and the education question. Despite this, the issues of race and gender were going to set the agenda for the next generation of the French New Left. In accordance with thinkers such as Marcuse and Touraine, Gorz has consistently maintained that emancipation will be feminist or it will not occur at all (Gorz 1987b: 85–6). However this is an area that Gorz could have centred on in the 1960s – in the end it remained an implicit issue before he exposed his position on female emancipation in the 1980s.

On the basic level Gorz's involvement in the May movement occurred because much of the readership of LTM was to be found in the higher education sector. The Third-Worldism of LTM was of crucial interest to the French New Left but nevertheless it was Gorz's concentration on home affairs and neo-capitalism that struck a familiar note with students and workers alike. Coming from an existential perspective, Gorz was able to articulate the failure of the neo-capitalist system in France to satisfy basic ontological needs, hence his criticism of consumerism as the manifestation of the creation of artificial wants. Gorz was heralding an emancipatory denominator, that is, the inability of the system to satisfy basic and existential needs and, therefore, the right of individuals to withdraw from the system. Whilst this was a fairly orthodox Marxist belief, it must be remembered that Gorz was speaking in the terms of the early Marx in a period when the determinism of French structuralist Marxists such as Althusser was dominant. The structuralists deliberately avoided engaging with the theoretical problems thrown up in the early Marx describing these as immature writings. Given the Stalinism of the PCF and the ubiquity of structuralist dogma, Gorz was providing a new existentialist/humanist socialism that coincided with the experienced dissatisfaction of needs that students and workers in France felt at that time. Furthermore Gorz was identifying the problem in an accessible manner which was less theoretically dense and more politically focused than other Marxist intellectuals of the age such as Althusser (Althusser 1971). The opposition of Gorz and Sartre to PCF intellectuals also struck a chord with the disillusioned student body – indeed both were coming to regard the Italian Communist Party (PCI) as a much more radical and progressive organisation than the PCF.

By this stage Gorz had come to the forefront within LTM. At this point his relationship with Sartre achieved its greatest reciprocity because Gorz was developing and concretising Sartre's critique. By 1969 though, Sartre had become engrossed with Maoism, a perspective which contradicted the stance of LTM which continued to champion the radical and libertarian ideas emanating from the Italian communists (Letter from Gorz to the author 8 January 1992). Although Sartre was writing less for LTM, his existentialist perspective was being extended and developed by Gorz.

THE MEANING OF 1968

By the time of the student/worker uprising in 1968 Gorz believed that the party political system held no real potential for the development of emancipatory socialism. His hostility to both capitalism and Stalinism meant that the party political arena was a void as far as Gorz's theory was concerned. Whilst the PCF maintained their Stalinism and the socialist parties played the part of moderates within the dominant Gaullist discourse, it was obvious that neither group looked like sustaining emancipatory policies. Nevertheless Gorz was still, in the late 1960s, promoting the necessity of the revolutionary party. He was to place his hope for this leadership on the dual organisations of the trade unions and student movements. He shared with the students, in particular, horror at the events taking place in the Vietnam War. The development of emancipatory potential in the student movement was, according to Daniel and Gabriel Cohn-Bendit, intrinsically linked with the war:

> This process has been greatly accelerated by the war in Vietnam, which struck many students and intellectuals as utterly scandalous,

> not only because it represents an attempt by the Americans to dictate to the rest of the world, but also because the 'socialist' bureaucracies are prepared to stand by and let it happen.
>
> (Cohn-Bendit and Cohn-Bendit 1968: 32)

This rejection of traditional methods of radical socialist action (i.e. by the Communist Party) was substantiated by the differing opinions taken by the PCF and LTM over the Soviet invasion of Czechoslovakia in 1968. Whilst the PCF failed to denounce Soviet actions, Gorz proclaimed the temporary victory of the Czechs in overcoming Stalinist dogmatism. The fact that the Czech people were subsequently suppressed by the Soviet army merely added substance to Gorz's argument for the Marxist intelligentsia to engage in the creation of a hegemonic project involving the disadvantaged sectors of society. It was obvious to Gorz that the Soviet Union was no longer in a position to provide this impetus, given that he believed that the invasion of Czechoslovakia had shown 'a complete indifference for the cause of socialism and of revolution in the world' (Davies 1988: 190). Furthermore, when the French students did provoke the mobilisation of the working class, they faced opposition not only from the trade unions but also from the PCF, which denounced the May uprising to prove to the socialists that it could be a reliable and stable partner in a coalition government. Nevertheless the efforts of the students forced the trade unionists to try to commandeer the unrest of May 1968. As the Cohn-Bendits have emphasised, the impact of the student uprising was so great that

> the trade unions and parties of the Left were forced, willy nilly, to call a general strike for 13th May 1968, in an attempt to take the political sting out of the student movement. But, having demonstrated their solidarity with the working class throughout the day, the students did not disperse quietly – that very night they took the Sorbonne. Students were suddenly freed from their intellectual imprisonment, and communication, discussion, explanation, were, all at once, easy and meaningful.
>
> (Cohn-Bendit and Cohn-Bendit 1968: 64)

Gorz explained the failure of the May movement by voicing the widespread belief on the independent Left that the PCF and the trade unions were to blame for not capitalising on the disorder to enhance their revolutionary base (Gorz 1970a; Posner 1970; Reader 1987; Sartre 1974). The ideal situation for the Left to increase its sphere of influence had come and gone without any real support from traditional socialist groups. Indeed, as the Cohn-Bendits have noted, the communists, the student union, and the Socialist Party attempted and succeeded in dissuading the 22nd March Movement from taking the Ministries of Finance and Justice at the height of the uprising on 25 May. The Cohn-Bendits chastised these traditional socialist groups because

> These 'revolutionaries' were quite incapable of grasping the potential of a movement that had left them far behind and was still gaining momentum. As for us, we failed to realise how easy it would have been to sweep all these nobodies away.
>
> (Cohn-Bendit and Cohn-Bendit 1968: 70)

Whilst the establishment of French neo-capitalism had certainly been dealt a blow, no genuine addition to the cause of liberatory socialism came about. It took thirteen years for France to elect a socialist president after May 1968, and even then François Mitterrand developed policies which bore no resemblance to the liberatory socialism that inspired the students and workers. Even after the May events though, Sartre and Gorz still believed that a body was required to coordinate the activities of spontaneous revolutionary groups. Evidently the May movement had shown little sign of maintaining a multifaceted organisation after the initial strike. Without the support of the party and the major unions to organise the revolutionary groups who were inspired by the student unrest, the emancipatory impetus was always doomed to be uncoordinated. These groups could not correspond as a mass movement without external organisation to direct the unrest in a specific direction. Nevertheless Sartre realised that even if the PCF had supported and coordinated the May unrest, they would probably have attempted to absorb the revolutionaries into their own framework.

The ultimate failure of the May movement also led Gorz to call for the destruction of the university (1970b). Gorz was sceptical of the university because he felt it was primarily a breeding ground for the reproduction of 'elites' and by 1970 he was renouncing the university as the source of emancipatory potential. As Davies notes:

> Gorz asserts the double dysfunctionality of higher education. On the one hand, says Gorz, free access means that academic success is no longer a guarantee of upward social mobility; the university is no longer able to perform the function of selection necessary to the hierarchical division of labour and it is therefore an embarrassment to capitalism. On the other hand, it is incapable of providing an alternative general education which would destroy

> the existing division of labour. In the context of class struggle, it is of no real use to either side.
>
> (Davies 1988: 194)

For this reason Gorz believed it was better to abolish the present university system which was important in reproducing the dominant culture. To place too much emphasis on this piece, which was written at a time of immense disappointment for those involved with the May movement, would not do justice to Gorz's wish to counter social isolation by opening up any arena for political dialogue. Nevertheless there is a link between 'Détruire l'université' (Gorz 1970b)and Gorz's later work. In his own words:

> the university is not to be abolished as a place where knowledge is acquired and exchanged and produced, but as *an institution* to reproduce the nation's elite and dominant culture. Since the reproduction of elites cannot be its function *if* its access is to be open to all, it needs to have a different purpose – in short: the full and free development of individuals, regardless of its functionality to the State, to business and to the social structure – and needs to be rebuilt on a new basis by destroying the old one.
>
> (Letter to the author 8 January 1992, original emphasis)

The value of this article is primarily in marking out the point where Gorz began to diverge from the other editors of LTM, although he was to remain there until 1983. The declining interest of Sartre was also critical in the decreasing influence that LTM had throughout the 1970s. Whilst 'Détruire l'université' may not be the most representative or sophisticated piece of Gorz's work, it indicates the point where he began to look for a new liberatory vehicle and a new body to engage in an emancipatory socialism that was not tainted with vanguardism. The groups that were to become Gorz's new subjects in the struggle to overcome neo-capitalism were to be the new social movements. Indeed Gorz's scepticism about revolutionary potential developing in the university corresponded to the beliefs of many of the student activists of 1968 for they felt that their universities were mere cogs in the capitalist machine. In the words of the Cohn-Bendits:

> cultural inequality is no accident, but part and parcel of the oppressive structure of both capitalist and communist societies and in fact ensures their survival. This is precisely what the revolutionary students were trying to say when they decried the universities and schools as 'factories of privilege': the present

> educational structure ensures that the majority of working class children are barred not only from the bourgeois society we are trying to overthrow, but also from the intellectual means of seeing it through.
>
> (Cohn-Bendit and Cohn-Bendit 1968: 14)

Sartre and Gorz were to realise after 1968 that the revolutionary potential outlined by the intellectuals was capable of being appropriated by the dominant sectors of society. Thus, as Davies has noted, the dominant classes were able to appropriate knowledge and use it for their own purposes. The cultivation of the dominant elite in universities was a prime example of capitalists influencing a potentially emancipatory group (students) to further their cause.

Gorz maintained his prominent role in LTM until the mid-1970s when he became influenced by the growing environmental problem and the revolutionary potential of political ecology. Nominally he was to remain a member of the LTM editorial group until 1983 but after the mid-1970s his contribution was minimal. His work became more prominent in the realm of political theory and he no longer used the widespread output of LTM as a vehicle for his thought. In any case, since the demise of Sartre and Gorz's abdication of responsibility, the influence of LTM had waned considerably. Although Sartre was the lifeblood of the journal, it is more than apparent that Gorz was equally influential in maintaining LTM through the late 1960s and early 1970s. Indeed it was under the guidance of Gorz that the journal became a predominantly 'political' journal rather than a literary and arts journal (Davies 1988: 218–21).

The failure of the May movement in general and the PCF in particular to engage with what Gorz saw as the primary problems in the struggle to overcome neo-capitalism undoubtedly led him to seek a new source of socialist organisation. What remained from the pre-revolutionary era was his belief that a mass party was still required to unite smaller revolutionary groups. For Gorz, the struggle for autonomy, which was epitomised by the ecology movement, was to become the new guiding force for human emancipation. What he witnessed in 1968 was the failure of traditional socialist organisations (and intellectuals) to come to terms with a socialism driven by a new, vibrant spontaneity that built its fusion around the lack of fulfilment of existential needs in neo-capitalist society. In Gorz's words:

> What is at issue is not . . . to condemn the explosive, libertarian and imaginative nature of the May Movement. What is at issue

> is the incapacity of the political and trade union machines to guide the audacity and imagination which the movement had released towards actions which could not subsequently have been nullified, and towards goals which, once attained, would have effected irreversible changes in the social system and set in motion the process of dislocation.
>
> (Gorz 1975: 37)

GORZ AFTER 1968

Whilst 1968 did not effect irreversible changes in the French social system, it did create a new dimension in Gorzian theory. He had witnessed the failure of a revolution based around orthodox Marxist ideals, even though the PCF had failed to recognise this. Gorz's work in the 1970s and 1980s would subsequently adopt a much more revisionist stance and the discourse he adopted had much less resonance with Marxism-Leninism. Gorz's influence on socialist politics prior to 1960 was minimal but, throughout the 1960s, he outlined a dynamic existential socialism which was influential on the 1968 uprising in Paris and is even more relevant to the radical critique of capitalism in the 1990s. In the words of Boggs:

> Gorz in the 1960s emphasized the need to break with the dominant authoritarian and economistic models of socialism, arguing that it was necessary to go beyond the false choice between insurrectionary and old-fashioned reformism. The complexities of modern society would demand a much more sophisticated understanding of socialist objectives *and* the methods for achieving them: ends and means were inseparably connected.
>
> (Boggs 1995: 99)

The events of 1968 assured Gorz that the search for the Third Road in socialist politics had developed into a crisis for the Left. Even though the PCF had had little influence on the initial impetus of the 1968 revolution, the events did demonstrate that leftist uprisings faced extreme difficulties in overturning the prevalent capitalist order. Throughout the 1970s communist parties in Western Europe and leftist intellectuals in general searched for a new road to socialism which was not intrinsically part of an international Leninist movement. This development came to be known as eurocommunism which, according to Dunleavy and O'Leary, was linked to the earlier revisionism of Kautsky who 'considered that through parliamentary victories the working class was capable of conquering the rest of the state' (Dunleavy and O'Leary 1987: 242).

At no stage was Gorz part of the eurocommunist 'movement' but it is interesting to note that the Italian communists had a bigger influence on Gorz than the intellectuals in the French Communist Party. The PCI were much more committed to eurocommunism and democratisation than the PCF which had problems throwing off the cloak of Leninism and accepting other anti-capitalist movements such as feminism and peace groups. This was typified by the way the PCF justified the invasion of Afghanistan by the Soviet Union in 1980 and their support for the suppression of Solidarity in Poland in 1981 (Hazareesingh 1994: 308). Furthermore the PCF was none too enthusiastic about European integration – a process that Gorz felt was positive (Boggs 1995: 97–138). Despite Gorz's scepticism of eurocommunism in the PCF, some commentators have linked the development of 'post-Marxism' (in which they include Gorz's theory) to the growth of eurocommunism in the 1970s (George and Wilding 1994: 123–4). As I shall show in the next chapter, Gorz began the development of 'post-Marxism' (if that is what one wants to call it) in the mid-1960s – it did not take the failure of 1968 to persuade him that Leninism was no longer an adequate strategy to challenge neo-capitalism. Meanwhile

> the communists failed to adapt to these changes in the core political values of the Left, and thus appeared to be swimming against the current of history. Their predicament (and lack of intellectual flexibility) was only too well underscored by their feeble response to the collapse of Soviet-style Communism in the late 1980s and early 1990s.
>
> (Hazareesingh 1994: 306)

Faced with the inability of French communists to embrace democratic reform, it should not be surprising that Gorz recoiled against them. His political activism decreased and he took to writing anti-productivist, post-industrial socialist articles under the influence of the burgeoning green movement of which he became a prominent figure in France and Germany, in particular. He became increasingly disillusioned with the inability of French communists to sacrifice sacred cows and develop a new perspective. Boggs notes that

> At a time when the manufacturing sectors were beginning to decline, the PCF clung to a heroic vision of the proletariat standing face-to-face with capital that was more appropriate to an

> earlier capitalist period. Immersed in working-class culture, the party upheld traditional virtues linked to religion, family, hard work, and clean living. This social location in French politics explains why the PCF could so energetically support traditional growth oriented programs (including nuclear power) while self-consciously distancing itself from new movement themes.
>
> (Boggs 1995: 126)

Gorz's disillusion with the Communist and Socialist parties in France was complete when the two parties formed a government pledged to radical policies under President François Mitterrand in 1981. The government was committed to a programme of speedy economic growth (Wilde 1994: 44) – a view which did not endear it to those who had discovered political ecology. However, it was an uneasy alliance that stumbled through until 1984, when it split as the Socialist Party (PS) lurched rightwards (as did many social democratic parties in Western Europe during the 1980s) and the PCF, having left the government, took comfort in the ideological safety but political inertia of Leninism (Hazareesingh 1994: 242; Boggs 1995: 127).

The resultant void on the Left in France was not filled by a political party and it was left to individuals like Gorz and Alain Lipietz to articulate post-industrial or post-Fordist ideas to a variety of organisations including trade unionists, new social movements and groups associated with the European Community. Gorz concentrated especially on the trade unions who were not tied to the PS in the way that the labour movement underpins socialist parties in Germany and the UK (Hazareesingh 1994: 246). However Gorz's ideas found little sympathy on the French Left which missed the point by either maintaining workerist policies of economic growth (the PS) or cocooning itself in ideological dogma (the PCF). This leaves us with three central questions which the rest of the book must answer:

How exactly did Gorz's ideas develop in the turbulent years between *Strategy for Labour* and the eventual 'success' of a leftist government in France?

Why were Gorz's ideas largely ignored until the 1980s?

And, most importantly, what is it that has made Gorz's work so pertinent now?

2

WORKERS' CONTROL AND SELF-MANAGEMENT

A radical strategy for labour?

Gorz initially drew political attention to the meaning of work in neo-capitalist societies with the publication of *Strategy for Labour* in 1964. In this book he set out to concretise and contextualise Marx's theory of alienation through an experiential interpretation of the technical division of labour. At this stage Gorz advocated the development of workers' control, workers' self-management and finally self-governing socialism – clearly a 'workerist' agenda. The text adopts a comparatively orthodox Marxist stance when placed alongside later Gorzian work such as *Farewell to the Working Class* (1980). Nevertheless, *Strategy for Labour* was revisionist for its time because it was written when Marxism-Leninism was still dominant in French socialist circles. The book engaged with other socialist political theories of the 1960s and 1970s that were prepared to question the assumptions of Marxist-Leninist discourse (Braverman 1974; E. P. Thompson 1967; Horvat *et al.* 1975; Baran and Sweezy 1968; Mallet 1975; Mann 1973).

MARXISM AND THE NEO-CAPITALIST DIVISION OF LABOUR

Gorz felt that it was essential for the development of self-governing socialism to analyse the ways in which the nature of work had changed since Marx's time and to understand the alienation that had been created by the technical division of labour in the second half of the twentieth century. Only through such an analysis could socialists attempt to create a mass party capable of fusing disparate revolutionary groups. Most Marxists in the early 1960s were reluctant to abandon class conflict as the motor of social change, and in this climate Gorz still concentrated on the factory as the site of socialist change despite his underlying view that it was virtually impossible for traditional class conflict to herald any fundamental, radical change. Arthur Hirsch has summarised Gorz's perspective on the crisis of not only neo-capitalism but also the poverty of socialist theory:

> To overcome the capitalist division of labour, to create the conditions for the decentralisation of power and autonomy, to implement self-management, to overcome alienation, it would be necessary to reject an industrial technology based on the domination of the individual and nature and to create in its place a 'post-industrial' technology based on cooperation between individuals and cooperation with nature.
>
> (Hirsch 1982: 227)

Gorz's clearest, historical analysis of the labour process is to be found in *Critique of Economic Reason* (1989a) in which he gave his strongest theoretical argument for the abolition of work-based capitalism. He pressed for changes in trade union practices to counter the increasingly pervasive power of technical reason in the changing methods of capitalism. This is a theme which he initially elucidated in *Strategy for Labour*, although in the 1960s he still believed that the polyvalent worker was capable of providing a vanguard for socialist change. The advent of post-Taylorist working conditions, with emphasis on greater self-management in the workplace, led Gorz to retract this belief in his later work. In the 1960s, though, Gorz was attempting to understand the alteration in class definitions caused by the new division of labour and technology whilst still viewing the industrial working class as the key force for historical change (Hirsch 1982: 238).

In *Strategy for Labour*, Gorz started from the traditional Marxian standpoint of alienated labour, explaining how workers must not be permitted to realise their creative essence if capitalism was to remain efficient. In order to achieve this, Gorz suggested that companies try to gain exclusive power over workers' capabilities by employing them from an early age to gain qualifications useful only in that industry. Whilst a higher technical knowledge was required by the worker in modernised industry, as opposed to traditional manual labour, the control of the worker over the means of production was actually decreasing. No longer could the worker gain any control over what was produced and, furthermore, the technical knowledge required to understand the new means of production meant that the function of modern technology was available only to elites of expert workers. The traditional manual labourer was reliant not only upon alien technology but also upon a new hierarchy of experts who possessed technical knowledge.

Gorz felt that this elite, empowered by their knowledge of the productive process, could become a new vanguard for the rest of the working class – another notion that he would retract in the 1980s. He failed to recognise, at this stage, that because these workers had technical knowledge and skills, they were divided from the rest of the working class because they were unable to experience the same needs and motivations as non-technical workers. Hence experts were divided from other workers due to their knowledge of the technical process. They functioned as experts only and never as sovereign workers or as members of the proletariat.

At this early stage though, Gorz, along with Marcuse, noted that the ethos of new forms of technical employment was spreading to all areas of civil society – a view that would be taken up by Habermas and Keane at a later date (Keane 1988; Habermas 1987: 356). In other words, technical reason was completing the final erosion of the realm of autonomy. In 1964 Gorz speculated that self-management as the precursor of self-governing socialism was the only means to halt the advance of neo-capitalist technical reason. This is a sign that Gorz, perhaps naively, underestimated the residual capability of capitalist reproduction. However he was correct in his diagnosis of the problem at hand:

> At the confines of civil society which is formally free, industry maintains a despotic and authoritarian society, under a hierarchy and discipline of military character, which demands of its workers both unconditional obedience and active participation in their own oppression. Whenever the chance arises, this militarised society tends to expand beyond the limits of the company, invading every sphere of civil life, and claiming for itself the right to represent the realities of capitalist society itself.
>
> (Gorz 1965a: 318)

The way to counter this situation, Gorz believed, was to struggle for self-management and autonomy within the workplace. He reasoned that most industrial unrest was being caused by the abolition of the worker's autonomous character. Although the primary forms of worker unrest, such as wage claims, were ostensibly struggles to earn more financial reward for services rendered, Gorz argued that they signified the struggle of workers to try to gain compensatory financial reward for the mutilation of their creative human faculties by the technical division of labour. Therefore the workers did not necessarily favour more money over an increase in autonomous time but rather found that, through modern trade union practices, the only way to fight the employer was to press for higher wages. Gorz argued that wage claims neither increased worker autonomy nor undermined the basis of alienation. Essentially neo-capitalist society was structured so that individuals were forced to sell themselves as workers to maintain their own existence. This being the case it was not unusual that workers sold this negation of their self-determination at as high a price as possible.

The essence of Gorz's somewhat orthodox Marxian argument was that wage claims and disputes masked a more widespread undercurrent of discontent amongst workers. Moreover, Gorz noted that the international division of labour and the consequent centralisation of the decision-making process further undermined genuine worker autonomy. Yet there is little insight at this stage that the march of socialism may have to take place outside of the domain of work. In short, the seeds of emancipatory potential that Gorz outlined were still sewn on the factory floor. Hirsch has suggested that, for Gorz:

> Popular power must be exercised by the workers themselves and not subordinated to management or the government. In this sense it is an autonomous power. Decentralisation and workers' autonomy, then, were essential to Gorz's concept of self-management.
>
> (Hirsch 1982: 224)

It is apparent that in the 1960s Gorz maintained that popular power could develop only through greater control of the point of production by the workers, yet trade unions were palpably failing to carry this objective out. It was, in essence, through control of the factories that neo-capitalism was able to subordinate individuals and society and preclude liberatory mobilisation. Gorz reasoned that the process of wage claims had reinforced the power of the employers to make decisions about production without having to consult workers who were preoccupied with pay matters to the detriment of their creative sovereignty. Thus management could reorganise their quantitative and qualitative decisions to incorporate wage claims without any significant loss in profit and without worker consultation. Gorz argued that this was creating a 'lobotomised proletariat' who sought only to escape from the productive process. Gorz, like Marcuse, believed this escape was found primarily in the passive indulgence of the culture industry – a system of leisure and entertainment specially tailored to meet the needs of the alienated individual, or rather to solidify the existence of capitalism in ensuring that the individual remained subordinated and inactive outside the workplace. For Gorz, the daily diet of lobotomised entertainment had to be countered by seeking to gain more worker autonomy in the factories. This would consequently lead to a more critical attitude from workers to the inertia of the culture industry. The thrust of this argument derived from the Marxist notion of base and superstructure. Certainly Gorz's aim of worker autonomy was laudable, but democratisation of the workplace would not necessarily lead to an ideological restructuring of culture and civil society. The early Gorz employed the language of economistic workerism rather than that of individual liberation which characterised the work of Marcuse, for instance, writing at the same time (Marcuse 1986, 1972a).

Gorz's ideas in the 1960s and 1970s struck a chord with humanist Marxists in the USA, particularly those involved with the *Telos* journal in St Louis. The most significant leftist publication in the US in this period was Harry Braverman's *Labor and Monopoly Capital* (1974). Whilst Braverman and other prominent American Marxists such as Baran and Sweezy adopted a more orthodox line than Gorz, there are some interesting comparisons to be made. Braverman was hostile to the notion that a new working class was developing which would become a new revolutionary vanguard – indeed he argued that despite new technical work practices the proletariat remained a class-in-itself (McLellan 1979: 329). Gorz, on the other hand, noted a fragmentation of the working class which split the worker movement to the core. His role was, as it always has been, to identify the means through which the proletariat could become a class-for-itself. Given his workerist perspective in the 1960s, his only genuine hope (wrongly) was that technical workers would become a vanguard for a united proletariat.

As it happens both appear to have been errant in their assessment of the technical division of labour and neo-capitalism. Braverman's belief that the breakdown of the industrial system had not changed the identity and make-up of the exploited may well have been true but it did not remain the industrial proletariat that Marx envisaged because it did not have the potential to become the historical agent of revolutionary change. Merely identifying who the exploited are is not the same as explaining how they will overcome their exploitation – ironically this is a criticism that later Marxists have directed at Gorz (Meiksins Wood 1986). Gorz, on the other hand, placed an ill-conceived and over-optimistic faith in the technical working class to subvert their superior position to other workers in the spirit of socialist camaraderie and lead the proletariat as a new vanguard. Both theories misconstrued the situation. Whilst Braverman hankered after a bygone Marxian ideal which argued that because an exploited class exists (albeit a divided one), then Marx's view of the nature of class conflict was still applicable, Gorz equally overlooked divisions amongst the working class and the obstacles to it becoming a class-for-itself. Although Gorz would retract this view in the 1970s, he clearly placed far too much faith in workerist politics in the 1960s. An even more optimistic assessment of the revolutionary perspective of the 'new working class' came from Mallet who argued that events such as May 1968 showed that new technical workers were no longer content with disputes over pay:

> Precisely because its elementary demands are largely satisfied, the new working class is led to ask itself other questions whose solutions cannot be found in the sphere of consumption. Its objective situation places it in the position of seeing the deficiencies in modern capitalist organisation.
>
> (Mallet 1983: 81)

It is fairly simple with the benefit of hindsight to question this perspective as activity in the sphere of consumption has unquestionably risen since Mallet's time. However it would appear that Mallet was correct to argue that consumption cannot provide solutions to individual needs – the result, though, has been that people have withdrawn even further into the domain of private consumption. The ultimate problem with Mallet's view, as with Braverman and the early Gorz, is that identifying members of the working class is not the same as figuring out how they can carry out their role in Marxist theory as the historical agent of social change. Writing in 1973, Mann offered a more realistic assessment of the 'new working class':

> it is doubtful whether the conflict between 'new workers' and their employers can be elevated to the status of a major 'contradiction' . . . even in France, the new workers' sense of *opposition* and *identity* is relatively weak despite apparent concern with a restructuring of the total society. This is precisely the opposite revolutionary failing of the traditional working class, strong on identity and opposition, weak on totality and alternatives.
>
> (Mann 1983: 92, original emphasis)

WORKERS' CONTROL AND SELF-MANAGEMENT

It is important nonetheless to understand the form of worker autonomy that Gorz advocated. It was to begin with workers' control and to develop into self-management. These concepts were particularly influential amongst socialists from the former Yugoslavia such as Supek who outlined the difference between them:

> Workers' control must be distinguished from workers' self-management, for workers' control involves class antagonism toward employers and the existence of antagonistic class power relations, while workers' self-management represents the surmounting and disappearance of class antagonistic relations and the creation of a new work community of producers, and this means that, in addition to the workers, all other 'working people' . . . also manage the enterprise.
>
> (Supek 1975: 11)

It is apparent that the early Gorz demonstrated a stronger faith in the possibility of the alienated worker overthrowing the exploitative conditions of the realm of necessity than was the case in his more mature work. Whilst the factory remains the site of potential conflict in the work of the later Gorz, it is supplemented by the recognition that mass unemployment has undermined the workplace as the axis of socialist conflict. This is in stark comparison to his analysis in the early 1960s when, in times of relatively full employment, he believed that the workplace was where

> the workers can reject oppressive work-relations, subject them through conscious action to organised workers' control, determine the conditions of labour through their persistent will to attain independence, and thus maintain and assert their class consciousness. It is there that they can strive towards the human emancipation of the worker as their supreme goal.
>
> (Gorz 1965a: 320)

Gorz's optimistic assessment of workers' control was not borne about by the model established under 'market socialism' in the former Yugoslavia. Whilst Gorz was not trying to present Yugoslavia as a perfect prototype for enterprises in the West, it is helpful to look at the analysis of Yugoslavian market socialism provided by Benson (1974). He points to several problems that arise regarding class structure which include the limited number of workers involved in the running of the enterprise, the power that is still held by management over workers' councils, the day-to-day decisions that take place below the level of the council, the different roles played by manual and non-manual workers and the increase in industrial action (Benson 1974: 257–73). In a sense it appears that the old conflicts of interest in the workplace remain in the Yugoslavian experience – a point which can lead to the idea that work itself should be minimised and relegated as the nub of human activity to be supplanted by more autonomous endeavours. Whilst Benson defends self-management against the view that, in Yugoslavia at least, it was a system of authoritarian political control, he does make the valid point that 'self-management theory does not acknowledge the principle of class conflict and treats all disputes as soluble through the formal channels . . . while the management can initiate disciplinary action against the workers, there is no device by which workers can effectively move against managements' (Benson 1974: 268). Although this would not be Gorz's model of self-governing socialism, it makes the point that it is difficult to subvert the hierarchical nature of industry and to place it under a new socialist logic. Gorz's perspective adheres to that of Pateman who was much more upbeat about the possibility of furthering participatory democracy through a system of workers' self-management (Pateman 1970: 100–2).

Whilst it seems apparent that the notion of self-management has problematic implications for the relations between different types of workers, it has been popularised in more recent times by Dahl and Gould (Dahl 1985; Gould 1988; Pierson 1995: 161–88). Both Dahl and Gould press the claims of self-management as a right which enhances democracy by engendering more participation in decision making – a foundation for the establishment of a new market socialism (Pierson 1995: 164–5). Pierson notes pertinently that the politics of time is a problem with self-management because participation is inevitably time-consuming and the consequences could lead to a minority of unrepresentative individuals choosing to exercise their right to participate (as was the case in Yugoslavia: Pierson 1995; Benson 1974).

To my mind though, the most important point is that these contemporary advocates of self-management appear to be more concerned with maintaining the role of markets than developing socialism. It seems odd to promote the cause of workers' self-management when most countries in Western Europe have a large residual pool of unemployed people and an even larger (and growing) group of individuals whose work is primarily on a short-term contractual basis. Where Gorz can be taken to task for his workerism in the 1960s, it seems inexplicable to return to these ideas in an era which has much fewer potential participating workers. In other words, is it not more pertinent to ask why individuals have to work long (often unsocial) hours delivering pizzas or packing bags at supermarkets rather than basing our vision of socialism on these workers spending even more time at work participating in decisions in which their vote may be relatively worthless? In societies which are incapable of spreading employment equitably, what value does self-management have for people who cannot or do not want to work?

Of course the debates over workers' councils and self-management go back beyond the 1960s – in some ways Gorz's views can be traced back to council communism, although Gorz does not indicate the influence of thinkers like Pannekoek (McLellan 1979: 170–4). Like Gorz in the 1960s, Pannekoek railed against the minimalist effects of trade unions and political parties in liberating the proletariat at the start of the twentieth century (Boggs 1995: 51–3). Pannekoek, following Luxemburg, criticised both the parliamentary influence exalted by Kautsky and the Marxist-Leninist revolution in Russia:

> He concluded that in Russia 'Marxism' (or Leninism) became the modernizing ideology of a radical intelligentsia bent on mobilizing a small proletariat behind essentially state-capitalist objectives. The predictable result was a new system of production directed by a state bureaucracy and rationalized by a centralized planning apparatus.
>
> (Boggs 1995: 53)

The similarities with Gorz are obvious but the council communists soon became obscured within trade unions or communist parties and this development concurs with Gorz's view in the 1960s that an overall body was needed to coordinate the activities of small self-managing enterprises – a position which had earlier been promoted by Gramsci (McLellan 1979: 178). The council movement quickly imploded bound by the workerist agenda which it had promoted against the prevalent statist objectives of European communist parties. Boggs notes that 'Ironically, the productivism and localist impotence of the council movement arose from the same mechanical separation of politics and economics that was a major flaw in social democracy, with the order of emphasis now reversed' (Boggs 1995: 55).

It should be apparent that, from Pannekoek through Gorz to contemporary market socialists, the notion of self-management and the supposed extension of a more participatory democracy has always been burdened with workerist ideas which actually do very little to liberate individual workers from the governing economic rationality that underpins work in capitalist societies. Certainly the expansion of democratic procedures is a worthy aim but is it one that should be pursued within the paradigm of work?

An interesting examination of the Dutch experience of worker participation which demonstrates the downfalls of workerism, particularly with regard to autonomy, has been provided by Leisink and Beukema (1993). By examining the model of industrial citizenship employed in Dutch legislation, they argue that the perceived aims of participation and worker autonomy remain mostly unfulfilled. The first point is that the smaller the company is, the less works councils exist and the less influence workers have in decision making. Moreover women are disproportionately under-represented in works councils because they are over-represented in part-time, contracted, and flexible working jobs which have less influence in the enterprise (Leisink and Beukema 1993: 164–5). The other major trend that they note is that there is little communication between works council members and the rest of the employees and trade unions – a point which correlates with Pierson and Benson in their analyses of self-management. Leisink and Beukema conclude that

> it is not very likely that peripheral workers will benefit from an introduction of work redesign by the management. Combining these considerations we may assume that there is a real danger of those workers who are relatively best off, using the participation opportunities which they have to promote their own interests. Such a kind of workers' participation would clearly not be a full realization of the principle of autonomy.
>
> (Leisink and Beukema 1993: 170)

TECHNOLOGY AND THE ROLE OF TRADE UNIONS

It is important to note that Gorz, in this early phase, confounded critics who portray him as anti-Marxist (Meiksins Wood 1986), just as his later work would negate those who previously classified him as a classical Marxist. Gorz has defended his perspective by claiming that '*Strategy* wants to be considered as Marxist; for the quite simple reason that it addresses a public of left-socialists and labour unionists who would accept new approaches only if they bear a Marxist legitimacy' (Letter to the author 25 March 1993). This is not a wholly persuasive argument as Gorz has never appeared to be reluctant about voicing his radical opinions – indeed his renown is, to some extent, based on a reputation as a vigorous polemicist. It appears that over the space of thirty years Gorz has seen fit to adopt a more revisionist stance in response to the declining role of the traditional proletariat in the industrial process.

It is not easy to present *Strategy for Labour* as a complete break with orthodox Marxism because in the 1960s many felt, as Supek notes, that the concept of workers' self-management was a logical extension of the Marxian tradition:

> There is a widespread opinion that workers' self-management is a theory elaborated especially by Proudhon and the anarcho-syndicalists and that it cannot be connected with the Marxian conception of socialism. This conception is advocated in particular by the proponents of so-called statist socialism. . . . However those acquainted with the works of Marx and Engels know that workers' self-management is the logical consequence of Marx's critique of bourgeois democracy, at the centre of which is the organisation of rule in the form of the state, as well as of Marx's theory of the alienation of labour.
>
> (Supek 1975: 4)

Nevertheless, in the 1960s, Gorz came to believe that emancipatory potential within the workplace was underdeveloped by the trade union movement and Marxist sympathisers. Furthermore, the idea that the struggle over pay and conditions in the factory connected to the demands for workers' control or power was a problem. Gorz realised that trade unions must attempt to gain greater control over the productive process to restrict the arbitrary judgement of the employers. The radicalisation of the trade union movement is a persistent theme in Gorz's work from the 1960s to the 1990s and his argument has usually been that unions were actually extending the control and decision-making power of the employers (Gorz 1989a: 219–42). The employer had, in most cases, some space for financial manoeuvre and the relative appeasement of workers through pay bargains could only help to maintain the authority and power of management. Gorz recognised that trade union concentration on the price of labour left 'the employer free to exploit the labour force in whatever way and in whatever conditions are convenient to him' (Gorz 1965a: 324). As such, he realised the ineffectiveness of wage claims for long-term worker well-being and the problems of corporatism that would dog the Left in the 1970s.

Essentially, Gorz was attempting to highlight the centrality of the power of employers and to demonstrate how they were using technical development to increase their authority over their disenfranchised employees. Hence they were able to use and develop technology that undermined the creative essence of the workers and simultaneously accelerated employers' control. A similar perspective has been outlined by Marglin:

> A due regard for the role of economic power and the institutional constraints on the use of power are as important to understanding socialist economic development as to understanding the development of earlier economic systems. Under socialism (at least in its Soviet strain), no less than under feudalism and capitalism, the primary determinant of basic choices with respect to the organisation of production has not been technology – exogenous and inexorable – but the exercise of power – endogenous and resistible.
>
> (Marglin 1976: 46–7)

This theme of power and its misuses has been a consistent and vital strand of Gorzian theory from *Strategy for Labour* onwards. He has consistently advocated the minimalisation of employment as it remains of central importance in manipulating the financial, temporal and spatial resources and power of individuals. Even when Gorz was still shackled by the Marxist-Leninist discourse, this point set him apart from the dominant Marxist orthodoxy in France emanating from the PCF. The battle for power within the workplace constituted the central theme in his early writings on the nature of work. Thus Gorz reasoned that the struggle for permanent worker power was a prerequisite of political power. This traditional Marxian standpoint was not a falsehood in itself, on the contrary it was vitally important, but it had to be accompanied by the recognition that worker power would not lead automatically to individual freedom in the realm of autonomy or social life in general. In the 1960s Gorz appeared to be underestimating the disjunction between the realm of necessity (or the heteronomous sphere) and the realm of autonomy, which he would distinguish more clearly in his later work (Kenny and Little 1995: 280; Gorz 1989a). Nevertheless he did signal this theoretical development in *The Division of Labour* in 1976 when he felt able to articulate his theories in what could be termed post-Marxist language:

> the working class must learn to use these weapons by immediately linking the struggle against factory despotism and idiotic jobs with the struggle against every form of domination and exploitation, and with the struggle against the 'rationality' of capitalist production itself.
>
> (Gorz 1976: 60)

It is clear that Gorz's analysis of capitalist power was closely linked to the technology that it employed. There were early signs in *Strategy for Labour* of the direction his work would take when he reasoned that

'Technical progress must coincide with human progress'(Gorz 1965a: 326). Gorz's argument, in accordance with Marcuse, was that the form of technology employed by capitalists was specifically designed to assist the division of labour, increase alienation, create a dysfunctional civil society and threaten the creativity of workers (Marcuse 1978). Power was further concentrated in the hands of employers and workers' self-management was precluded. In Hirsch's words:

> technology is not a neutral tool to be used regardless of the type of society one seeks. The type of technology a society chooses will largely influence the quality of social relations in the production process and in society at large. On this point Gorz wholly agrees with Marx.
>
> (Hirsch 1982: 225)

Gorz did not criticise technology itself but rather the ownership of technical resources by capitalists and the power that this conferred upon employers. Again this is a consistent theme in Gorz's thought, for he has pointed out repeatedly that the project of reducing work is made possible by the extension of new technology to minimise the time individuals must spend in the realm of heteronomy – a point also raised by Aronson in his critique of Sartre (Aronson 1977: 216). Hirsch has emphasised the similarity between Gorz and Marx on this point, suggesting that 'what he [Marx] objected to was not industrial technology itself, but the private appropriation of the socially produced wealth it made possible' (Hirsch 1982: 226). Whilst Gorz would denounce the productivism inherent in Marx's writings during the 1970s, there were similarities between their ideas on technology before the former developed a green dimension to his thought. As is often the case with *Strategy for Labour* though, the idea that an alternative to the productivist strategy would be necessary is discernible. Geoghegan has observed that

> His commitment to this type of strategy rested on a broader belief that workers must develop an alternative to the present to become revolutionary. No reliance can be placed on some kind of unconscious collision between forces and relations of production.
>
> (Geoghegan 1987: 124)

In analysing the centrality of work in early Gorzian theory it must be acknowledged that the dominant feature of capitalist reproduction in the 1960s remained alienated labour. Increasingly though, the practice of colonising human time through labour was being complemented by the rationalisation of new technology and its extension into the realm of mass culture. As the instruments of technical reason impinged on the private sphere, the realm outside the workplace was generally no longer a space where individuals were creative or politically active. New forms of passive entertainment were being engineered which helped to direct alienated individuals further into the private sphere (Lodziak 1986). When Gorz reasoned that trade union activity must liberate workers at the point where they were alienated, the factory, he was underestimating the power of other factors that were ensuring the colonisation of time and space outside the realm of necessity. Again it was Marcuse who proved to be more foresighted in this period:

> Today . . . private space has been invaded and whittled down by technological reality. Mass production and mass distribution claim the *entire* individual, and industrial psychology has long since ceased to be confined to the factory.
>
> (Marcuse 1986: 10, original emphasis)

This contrasts with Gorz's more workerist perspective. Hirsch points out that

> Gorz advocated workers' control at the point of production as its [the mass party] basis. Self-management by the workers in their factory councils was the only way for the working class to maintain control of the factory, the party, and society at large.
>
> (Hirsch 1982: 223)

Clearly Gorz believed that the struggle for the liberation of society would be fought and won in the industrial field. Hence he reasoned that workers' control of the factory would enable workers to generate autonomy in all facets of life. Again it is clear that he was yet to make the clear distinction between activities carried out in the heteronomous and autonomous spheres, a theme that would animate his later work.

A REFORMIST AGENDA?

Whilst Gorz was to shift his ideas, commentators such as Stephens have continued to champion the emancipatory potential of workerism into the 1980s:

> the struggle for workers' control is particularly important because workers' control gives people personal experience in exercising democratic control over the economic order. Furthermore, since it expands the power base of the working class, it not only

> entails immediate benefits but, unlike economist gains, it also strengthens the bargaining position of the movement in the next confrontation with the opposition.
>
> (Stephens 1979: 82)

As Pierson has noted, there is a certain similarity between Stephens' ideas and those of Kautsky and the Austro-Marxist perspective (Pierson 1991: 30). Likewise Gorz's incremental road to socialism in the 1960s can be linked to this tendency, although he did defend the revolutionary party. The fragmentation of the working class that followed the technical division of labour and the consequent mass unemployment that it generated in the 1970s and 1980s led Gorz to move away from these ideas in his later work, whilst many of the Left, including Stephens, have continued to champion this reformist approach. Part of Gorz's theoretical shift was caused by his analysis of the strategy of employers in deploying new technology in *The Division of Labour* (1976a). Employers realised that, in the increased competition that followed the economic downturn of the 1970s, it was not in their interest to promote an adversarial relationship towards workers. With the decline of blue collar mass production and the need for more skilled workers, there came a more cooperative attitude to relations between technical employees and their employers. Previous adversarial policy had given trade unions the power to exercise an exclusive influence over the political practice of their employees. Advanced technology enabled employers to start developing the worker as a genuine agent of capital – a technical expert worker who was the very antithesis of the traditional, industrial working class.

When Gorz observed that 'modern industry's dominant tendency is no longer the maximum exploitation of the workers by every means possible, the carrot and stick method. . . . The dominant tendency . . . is to "integrate" the workers into the system' (Gorz 1965a: 329), he was recognising the ability of the capitalist to set a new agenda for an elite of technical workers whilst their trade unions floundered in a strategy from a bygone age. For instance, Gorz suggested that trade unions 'instead of fighting against new machines and the new work patterns they impose . . . should fight about the type of machines, the way they are installed, the new work patterns to expect, the classifications to be established, before the reorganisation takes place' (Gorz 1965a: 321). Thus he believed that trade unions had to try to play a greater part in the decision-making process so that any change in management policy would be immediately apparent to the workforce. This could only happen through workers' self-management. For Gorz, this would be a stepping stone to the greater democratic accountability of employers and eventually a means to the end of creating self-governing socialism. Similarly Supek has observed that

> it is a mistake to equate workers' self-management, as the highest form of the participation of workers and employees in managing the enterprise, with self-governing socialism, which is a longer process of social transformation in the direction of achieving direct democracy as well as the full control of the producers over national income or labour and, at the same time, full control of consumers over the production of consumer goods that truly correspond to real 'human needs'.
>
> (Supek 1975: 8)

Whilst this corresponds with the Gorzian approach, Gorz did stress the centrality of workers' self-management as a main part of the long-term reformist political strategy of replacing neo-capitalism with liberatory socialism. Lebfevre, another prominent figure on the Left in France, adopted a similar attitude towards the promotion of workers' self-management (Lefebvre 1975: 19). Whilst aware of the risk of integrating trade unions within the capitalist nexus, Gorz went on to explain how steady, but limited, structural reform would lead to workers' self-management. Stephens has noted how Gorz differentiated between 'structural' and 'reformist' reforms (Stephens 1979: 82). Thus Gorz recognised the failure of reformism to achieve any fundamental alteration to the capitalist system despite reforms concerning wages, conditions and the welfare state. All of these were incorporated into the capitalist system without a breakdown in the rationality it promotes and the hierarchical structural authority that it imposes on individuals. Gorz advocated trade union activity based upon structural reforms that would bring the capitalist system to a state of crisis through an increase in revolutionary consciousness among individual workers. This heightened revolutionary consciousness would develop through what Gorz termed 'partial victories'. He suggested that each 'partial victory' that workers gained in blocking unpalatable management decisions was another step along the road to workers' control:

> After each partial victory, each reclassification, reorganisation, investment or dismissal which the trade union prevents or imposes, the workers' power is reasserted; the workers' consciousness is heightened; and the employers' freedom and the sovereignty of capital are whittled away.
>
> (Gorz 1965a: 331)

Clearly, despite employing a Marxist-Leninist discourse, Gorz disagreed with Marx on the nature of social change – a view that would be more forcefully presented in *Farewell to the Working Class* (Gorz 1987b). He believed that 'partial victories' for the workers, expressed through unions committed to structural reform, could steadily build strata of democracy in the workplace that would undermine, and eventually supersede, the dominant capitalist order. Thus Geoghegan has stated that 'the logic of the resulting strategy is that low-level and particularist demands concerning work conditions, etc. can develop into ever higher and more radical objectives: for worker control of management, for the suppression of capitalism, and so forth' (Geoghegan 1987: 125). Moreover Erik Olin Wright has expressed the view that 'the problem of effecting structural reforms of the capitalist state itself in order to undermine the atomizing effects of the state is . . . problematic. But if the class capacities of the working class are to develop, such reforms are of critical importance' (Wright 1978: 244–5).

As Gorz witnessed the effects of the technical division of labour in the 1970s, he would retract these positive ideas for social change due to the fragmentation of the industrial working class. The technical division of labour was integrating expert workers into the capitalist project, giving them access to privileged information and skills, and alienating them from other manual workers. Rather than creating an educated and polyvalent working class, the technical division of labour was dismantling the proletariat as the major agent of emancipatory action. Gorz realised, at this point, that liberatory activity must not be restricted to the location where domination and repression took on their most physically coercive form and seek to raise the struggle for autonomy in the public sphere, outside the workplace. This did not mean that the struggle should be abandoned within the factory. The point was to bring the fight for freedom from the workplace into the realm of everyday activity.

Gorz would continue to champion the abolition of the division of labour and employment itself, but he realised that work was not the only means by which capitalism ensured legitimacy and reproduction. Whilst Gorz's concept of 'partial victories' can be criticised with the value of hindsight, he never departed from his revolutionary project as he felt that structural reforms would generate a legitimation crisis for the capitalist state (Stephens 1979: 83).

There are some indications at this stage that Gorz realised the importance of cultural and ideological issues in the continued reproduction of capitalism. In echoing the traditional Marxist perspective on alienated labour, he suggested that the struggle to overcome exploitative work processes must be based on an understanding of why this exploitation takes place. Gorz's main target in this account of exploitative work practices was 'consumer affluence' which again hints at a developing environmentalist perspective:

> to fight against exploitation in the name of consumer demands, without questioning the actual purpose of exploitation (i.e. accumulation) and the type and order of consumption offered by advanced capitalist society, is simply to immobilise the working class in a position of deference to the basic choices, values and ideas of that society.
>
> (Gorz 1965a: 336)

In short, he argued that the continued exploitation of workers was closely bound up with the creation of false needs and priorities by capitalist society which were manifesting themselves in the accumulation ethic of 'consumer society'. When trade unions concentrated on pay claims as the means to fight the employer, they were playing their part in the long-term capitalist project. Whilst quantitative goals were undoubtedly important, at the centre of these claims was precisely the need to consume more, which substantiated the wasteful production of non-necessary consumer goods. In effect, the policy of the employer was being vindicated, the policy of productivism and excessive consumption was being incorporated into trade union activity. Gorz suggested that 'as long as such economic demands are purely quantitative rather than qualitative, they fail to make any real impact on the system and hardly even contribute to the strengthening and heightening of class consciousness' (Gorz 1965a: 336). On this point it is worth quoting the words of Mann which echo Gorz's perspective:

> As trade unions are organised toward the attainment of economic bargaining gains, they tend in practice to lose sight of control issues, whether those concern the immediate work situation or wider-ranging questions of industrial structure. With the increasing trend toward productivity bargaining, job control is viewed by trade unions as something which can be exchanged periodically for economic rewards; typically workers will gain some shop-floor control informally, and indeed surreptitiously, and then sign it away in union–management negotiations.
>
> (Mann 1973: 22)

Clearly trade unions were not doing enough to subvert the logic of economic rationality which is the foundation of the work-based society and Gorz came to realise that, while unions remained workerist, there would be no challenge to the technical division of labour.

BREAKING WITH WORKERISM

In the 1970s and 1980s Gorz recognised that quantitative employment policies and the search for full employment could no longer be part of the liberatory socialist programme. Following his encounter with political ecology in the 1970s, he realised that full employment was intrinsically linked with over-production, consumption and wastefulness. These phenomena could not be tolerated in any emancipatory society and, as Gorz argued, socialism had to take on board many ecological imperatives. The technical division of labour was simultaneously eroding workers' self-determination and producing greater and more damaging capitalist technology. Gorz argued that work must be viewed as a qualitative form of human activity. In essence, socialists should aim not only to rehumanise employment but also to minimise it and prioritise ecological compatibility. Gorz realised that the technical division of labour within neo-capitalism was ensuring the continuance of mass unemployment. Unless trade unions began to adopt a more qualitative programme, they would remain isolated from the needs of individual workers. Socialist politics had to emphasise the creative essence of the individual instead of pandering to the quantitative imperatives of productivism. In the words of Hirsch:

> Gorz concluded that such increased international division of labour and centralisation of control above the plant level in the headquarters of the multi-national corporation had effectively undermined the possibility of workers' autonomy at the point of production. On the basis of this technological change Gorz concluded that workers' councils could not develop into independent centres of workers' autonomy and workers' power.
>
> (Hirsch 1982: 239–40)

Gorz would still attempt to engineer greater autonomy within the workplace for workers, a goal that led him to call for the reduction in working hours as a prerequisite of social change. Whilst he recognised that the battle must take place on the industrial level, he also realised that the struggle against management power must incorporate an attack on the technical reason of modern capitalism outside the factory. On what he called the 'urban level', he stated that pressure must be applied to 'the oligopolies' grip on the cultural, social and economic aspects of urban life: public transport, land and property, local government, the amenities of leisure, etc.' (Gorz 1965a: 339). Again the direction of future Gorzian analysis was laid out as he foresaw the increasing control that capitalism was gaining throughout society. The elimination of traditional employment by the technical division of labour led Gorz to concentrate on the means of social control and reproduction outside the workplace. The impact of technical reason appeared to be creating a dehumanised society where individuals, without the opportunity to exercise their essential creativity in the workplace, also found space outside the heteronomous sphere governed by the dictates of capital. Not only were the means of leisure and welfare owned by the dominant capitalist class but they were also used to promote the logic of growth and consumption which enabled capitalists to maintain authoritarian control and hierarchy. It was no surprise, therefore, that

> Economic, cultural and social development is not directed as a priority towards man's development and the fulfilment of his social needs, but first and foremost towards the production of those objects which can be sold for maximum profit, no matter what their usefulness or lack of it. Creative work is stunted by considerations of financial profitability or social stability. At the same time millions of working hours are squandered, in the process of neo-capitalist competition, on often minor but always expensive modifications to consumer goods, whose aim is hardly to enhance the product's aesthetic or use-value.
>
> (Gorz 1965a: 344)

Clearly Gorz believed that mass production, and the promotion of the ethos of mass consumption, was, ultimately, the central factor in the reproduction of neo-capitalism. He realised that the ethos of mass production was driving individuals to try and seek solace in privatistic lifestyles in the search for some form of autonomy and self-determination. By extending control outside the workplace, capitalism was maintaining subservience to its logic through complete colonisation of the time and space of the individual, thereby ensuring little possibility of emancipatory mobilisation. Gorz realised that it was not necessary to 'civilise social relationships' if the individual could be 'civilised' and socialised through passive leisure and consumption routines. Dehumanisation in the workplace was being complemented by colonisation of the realm of individual autonomy in the maintenance of social control and reproduction.

Gorz was one of the first thinkers on the Left to understand that

Keynesian economics had to be jettisoned. The much higher levels of unemployment that were to follow in the 1970s and 1980s and Gorz's discovery of the radical programmes of new social movements concretised this view. Put in context, his theoretical shift corresponded with a more general move away from workerism in socialist debates (Cohn-Bendit and Cohn-Bendit 1968; Grahl and Piccone 1973; Marcuse 1986, 1972b; Touraine 1974).

However the conclusions of *Strategy for Labour* show the orthodox Marxist stance to which the young Gorz adhered. In advocating a series of partial worker victories as the path to socialism he was not only retaining work as the central paradigm of social reproduction, but also suggesting that each victory would heighten the level of worker consciousness. He concluded that 'all this clearly presupposes a leadership with an overall perspective, capable of devising a concrete "global alternative" to capitalism, in the light of which each reform that is won will derive its meaning. The advance towards socialism will be made in this way or, not at all' (Gorz 1965a: 352). Geoghegan has noted that

> The feeling one gets on reading these sixties pieces is of new material imprisoned in old categories. Although rejecting Bolshevik vanguardism, Gorz still reveals the heritage of Marxist-Leninist vocabulary and concepts. The working class may have changed its composition but it is still the revolutionary subject, the ultimate repository of hope. The institution of the party as *the* party also reveals this link with the past. These categories are however clearly bursting at the seams.
>
> (Geoghegan 1987: 127)

Geoghegan is correct to emphasise how Gorz's work in the 1960s still operated within the dominant paradigm of Marxian orthodoxy. Gorz, though, argues unconvincingly that this manipulation of Marxian discourse was purely pragmatic: 'It's mainly a question of language: you have to speak the same language as those you want to be understood by' (Letter to the author 25 March 1993). It seems clear that Gorz is not prepared to accept the view that his work in the 1960s was as orthodox as it comes across. Perhaps these origins do not suit a theorist variously described as a traitor, a heretic or an iconoclast. However *Strategy for Labour* did provide indications of Gorz's future rejection of the stifling restrictions of this traditional approach and the creation of an original socialist theory that was both vibrant and critical. In Geoghegan's words:

Throughout, Gorz's central concern, the production of the future in the present, still shines through the opaque coating of residual Marxism-Leninism.

(Geoghegan 1987: 129)

3

POLITICAL ECOLOGY AND SOCIALISM

A new vanguard?

With the publication in 1975 of *Ecologie et politique (Ecology as Politics)*, Gorz became one of the first theorists to attempt to reconcile political ecology and socialism (Gorz 1987a). Since then many socialists have tried to incorporate environmental goals into their political programmes (Bahro 1982; Pepper 1993; Ryle 1988; Williams n.d.). Simultaneously, non-socialist theorists have attempted to revitalise and modernise their political ideologies with elements of environmentalism as it has become more popular (Hay 1988). Most political ecologists have rejected the efforts of theorists from other ideological traditions to commandeer the green political message, preferring instead to emphasise the ideological autonomy of political ecology and, by implication, some kind of green ownership of certain ideas (Porritt and Winner 1988). It is important to clarify the factors that constitute ecologism and to differentiate between political ecology and environmentalism, or dark green and light green politics, although clear barriers between these ideas may be superficial (Kenny 1994: 239). Dobson, though, has stated that 'it is principally the limits to growth thesis, and the conclusions drawn from it, that divides light-green from dark-green politics' (Dobson 1990: 73). Wissenburg centres on the difference between ecocentrism and anthropocentrism as the major factor which defines the boundary between shallow and deep ecology, perhaps ignoring the fact that there appear to be differing degrees of anthropocentrism amongst deep ecologists (Wissenburg 1993: 5). Kenny may be closest to the mark when he suggests that 'it is worth remaining openminded about this ideology and regarding sceptically attempts to erect boundaries around "core" principles' (Kenny 1994: 223).

LOCATING GORZ WITHIN THE GREEN CANON

Within Dobson's framework, Gorz's position in the green political tradition is ambiguous. Gorz accepted the theoretical message behind the *Limits to Growth* report (Meadows *et al.* 1972) but is hardly a dark green theorist – his work abounds with too many references to the emancipatory potential of alternative technology and is more obviously located within the socialist tradition. Having said that, Gorz's commitment to limits to growth is much less stringent in the 1990s than when he first encountered ecologism (Gorz 1994: 102–15). Is Gorz, then, merely an environmentalist? According to Dobson:

> the principal difference between the two is that ecologism argues that care for the environment (a fundamental characteristic of the ideology in its own right, of course) presupposes radical changes in our relationship with it, and thus our mode of social and political life. Environmentalism, on the other hand, would argue for a 'managerial' approach to environmental problems, secure in the belief that they can be solved without fundamental changes in present values or patterns or production and consumption.
>
> (Dobson 1990: 13)

If it is apparent that Gorz is not an ecologist, a point on which most political ecologists would agree, then it is equally clear that he advocated the kind of structural change that far exceeds the demands of environmentalism. Thus, in accordance with Eckersley, it is possible to classify Gorz as an eco-socialist, although even this label is problematic as he courts ecology mainly for the reason that it is anti-capitalist and encompasses radical potential and is therefore, to his mind, of use to socialists (Eckersley 1992: 127–9; Kenny 1994: 241–2). Gorz was as critical as deep ecologists of the 'managerial' approach employed by environmentalists to tackle ecological problems. The Gorzian task was to promote a reconciliation between socialism and ecology against 'capitalist environmentalists', rather than to develop an overtly ecological or green programme.

Another eco-socialist whose work parallels many of Gorz's ideas is Rudolf Bahro. Bahro began his life in former East Germany where he developed a Marxian critique of authoritarianism in state socialist societies (Bahro 1982, 1984, 1986; Geoghegan 1987). As a result he was imprisoned and on his release moved to former West Germany. He began to engage increasingly with political ecology and socialist debates on green politics in the late 1970s, including the work of Gorz. Bahro joined the German Green Party (Die Grünen), articulating a fundamentalist revolutionary ecology, but by 1985 he had left the party. Bahro had become disillusioned with the attempts of the German Greens to achieve parliamentary power and political respectability (Hulsberg 1988). By toning down their ecological idealism for political power, the German Greens had, according to Bahro, turned their back on the ethos of political ecology. Whilst Bahro's fundamentalism is in sharp contrast to Gorz's pragmatism on the ecology question, it is useful to distinguish the effects that green politics managed to generate amongst socialist thinkers. Nevertheless it is pertinent to note that both Bahro and Gorz believed that there was common ground on which red and green thinkers could build a revolutionary theory.

Despite the theoretical endeavour of thinkers such as Bahro, the political fusion of socialism and ecology has proved troublesome with no definitive version of 'eco-socialism' emerging. Furthermore Gorz has undoubtedly been deeply influential on the green movement in Europe, without a noticeable lessening of the political gap between red and green. For instance, Gorz's writings have clearly influenced the Green Party in Ireland when they state that 'Full employment for all adult human beings would be a social and ecological nightmare' (Green Party of Ireland 1989). The necessity of an alliance between socialism and ecologism is vital in Gorz's thought, although other ideologies from anarchism to fascism have also sought to incorporate green politics into their programmes (Bookchin 1980, 1982, 1986; Hardin 1968). Most thinkers on the Left who feed off ecology, such as Weston and Ryle, do so because green political thought is seen to be radical. Thus much eco-socialist literature has sought to display the inherent contradictions between ecologism and capitalism (Weston 1986; Ryle 1988). Nevertheless it is apparent that state socialism as in the former Soviet Union, with its reliance on productivist industrialism, was wholly incompatible with ecology. Despite this, Gorz believes that ecological exigencies can be incorporated into the radical socialist critique. In itself this should not be problematic for Greens – elements of political theories are often transferred across (sometimes artificial) ideological boundaries without losing their original reference point. The important point is that green ideas can be hijacked by thinkers from other ideological traditions which are then presented as being green when they are a far cry from political ecology.

In any case many criticisms of Gorz's ecology have emanated from within the green movement, especially concerning his plan to adapt technology for liberatory ends. Most ecologists have adopted a much more adversarial approach to technology which, they believe, is representative of the industrialism which they seek to undermine. However on closer inspection Gorz has much in common with, for example, the German Greens in their renowned 1983 programme:

> It would be a mistake to infer from all that rhetoric that greens are unqualified Luddites, though. Sensitive though they are to all the ways in which modern technology has made life worse, they are also alive to the possibility that it might also make life better. In particular, they welcome the fact that, 'with the use of modern technologies, productivity has in many cases reached a level which would . . . make it possible to reduce the working week while maintaining full pay'.
>
> (Goodin 1992: 189)

Thus, by the criteria of the more ecocentric analysts of green politics, Gorz is certainly not an ecologist but it is possible to locate him in a wider green canon without sacrificing his originality to mainstream environmentalism (Eckersley 1992). Yet Gorz's anthropocentrism is clear when he states that 'Nature is not "friendly to mankind" and the issue is not to be friendly to it but to produce a culture respectful of the complexity and diversity of the ecosphere' (Letter to the author 25 March 1993). Even anthropocentric thinkers have recognised that Gorz's advocacy of a technological road to ecological sufficiency does not correspond to ecologism. Dobson has argued that 'Gorz's recommendations of autoproduction and reduced work-time are not . . . Green recommendations' (Dobson 1990: 165). However this is not a totally negative comment as Dobson does not believe that anthropocentrism is realistically avoidable, indeed he states that weak anthropocentrism is an inevitable consequence of the human condition which should be encouraged within the green movement. Thus, in reply to Porritt's criticism of anthropocentrism, he suggests that

> This [anthropocentrism] will not do damage to the ecologists' case; in fact it enables them unashamedly to put the human onto the ecological agenda – an agenda from which, for reasons associated with its aims, the centrality of the human being has all but been erased.
>
> (Dobson 1990: 64)

Dobson's view provides ample justification for assessing the value of Gorz's work in the light of green political thought. He is not just a socialist on the eco-bandwagon. Rather the major difficulty with

Ecology as Politics is that it is, at times, inconsistent compared to Gorz's other works. Although it is probably Gorz's most 'utopian' book, he advocated too many authoritarian measures in his green programme to correspond with his wider emancipatory plan (Frankel 1987; Geoghegan 1987; Keane 1988). A fusion between centralist and libertarian measures runs throughout the book, a feature that is arguably a natural by-product of green political theory (Ophuls 1977). Regardless, *Ecology as Politics* contains several recommendations which appear to be extremely relevant, particularly in Western Europe, which are extended more thoroughly on a global scale in his later work and expressed in a more sophisticated manner (Gorz 1985: 92–100; 1993, 1994).

It is important to evaluate the ideological importance of ecology in Gorz's socialism, and subsequently to identify whether the political programme which Gorz identified can be called Green. Whilst Bookchin has criticised Gorz rather hysterically and inaccurately for attempting to manipulate ecology to promote his 'Marxism', it is clear that his solution to ecological exigency was anti-productivist and it is therefore difficult to categorize it as Marxist (Bookchin 1980–1: 188). Hirsch, contradicting Bookchin, believes that Gorz

> based his analysis of the ecology crisis on marxist premises. But is his conclusion marxist? Evidently not. For in denying that the solution to the crisis of capitalism lies in economic growth, is he not implying an 'inversion' of the productivist logic of marxism also? If that is the case, then marxism is Gorz's springboard from which he leaps 'beyond' into the unknown.
>
> (Hirsch 1982: 238)

The problems in trying to classify Gorz in a category within the green tradition is exacerbated by a third view which is the antithesis of Bookchin's perspective and also contradicts Frankel and Geoghegan. Writing from an 'eco-Marxist' standpoint, Pepper correctly states that 'Gorz's is a "post-industrial utopian" vision of future work and social organisation which is also "post-Marxist": rejecting Marx's emphasis on collective, social production'. However he continues by making an ill-informed assault on Gorz claiming that he is an elitist (an obvious misreading of the later Gorz) and, in words that ecocentric thinkers and eco-anarchists like Bookchin would deplore, Pepper makes the startling assertion that Gorz's work 'is also a very green (and anarchist) vision' (Pepper 1993: 123). Obviously Pepper is unaware of Gorz's constant assertion that the state must play a prominent role in a post-industrial future.

Whilst all of these views do little to clarify Gorz's standing in green politics, they do stand to make three points very clear: firstly, Gorz has obviously been palpably misread and misrepresented by at least two of the commentators above (Bookchin and Pepper, to my mind); secondly, that green political thought is as riddled with divisions as any other ideological tradition; and thirdly, and most importantly from my perspective, Gorz's work has been somewhat shabbily treated by some green commentators who are preoccupied with the process of pigeon-holing and ideological categorisation at the expense of proper critical evaluation.

GORZ'S GREEN CRITIQUE OF CAPITALISM

Gorz's starting point in *Ecology as Politics* was that environmentalism was being commandeered by the dominant groups in Western society. He recognised that the governments of most developed nations, irrespective of their form of government, increasingly displayed a modest commitment to tackle the problems of the environment. Gorz suggested that this was hypocritical because the pollution that the industrialised nations were trying to counteract had been created by their own productivist, short-term industrial policies. Gorz observed that this environmentalist discourse was primarily concerned with minimalising pollution within the dominant industrial framework. Instead of aiming to reform industrial practices around ecological exigencies, industralised nations were attempting to support their technological structures by incorporating an ostensible environmentalism. These environmental policies, which were advocated by the governments of most industralised nations, tended to concentrate on conservation of the local and national environment rather than the restructuring of industrial technology. Simultaneously, in a process Gorz called 'boundless imperialism', the dictates of multinational capital ensured that much manufacturing industry and consequently the worst pollution was devolved to the Third World (Gorz 1987a: 114–30).

Whilst industrial capitalists had little interest in green issues, they proved capable of manipulating them when political imperatives made environmentalism necessary. To this extent Gorz reasoned that 'when factual evidence and popular pressure can no longer be denied, the establishment suddenly gives away – what was unthinkable yesterday becomes taken for granted today, and fundamentally nothing changes' (Gorz 1987a: 3). Like Bahro and other 'eco-socialists', Gorz realised that capitalists were capable of hijacking environmental problems for the promotion of their political programmes. Capitalism has proved that it can incorporate 'an environmental conscience' which is insufficient to counteract the ecological crisis that industrialism has created (Dobson 1990: 9). Gorz sought to show that an environmental concern had to be coupled with a desire for structural change if society was to avoid a systematic crisis. For this reason he believed that the ecology movement had to recognise some of the causes advocated by liberatory socialist theory. Thus he stated that 'it is . . . time to end the pretence that ecology is, by itself, sufficient: the ecological movement is not an end in itself, but a stage in a larger struggle' (Gorz 1987a: 3). Clearly remarks like these are going to irritate political ecologists and other green thinkers but they do represent the views of many socialists who have encountered green political thought. Essentially 'eco-socialism' is a doctrine where socialists select elements of green thought to substantiate their challenge to the capitalist system. This is not a highly original thesis but it is one that should be kept in mind by those who seek to portray green political thought as an extension of orthodox Marxism (Pepper 1993). Although Bahro promoted a fundamentalist ecologism, he agreed with Gorz's point that political ecology and socialism could enjoy a mutually beneficial relationship:

> It would be mistaken to assume that red and green confront one another. For there are reds or leftists who have understood the priority of the ecological challenge and thus become at the same time genuine Greens. And there are people from all other lines of the political spectrum through to quite far on the right who have equally understood the priority of the ecological challenge.
>
> (Bahro 1982: 59)

Gorz instigated this idea in *Ecology as Politics*, and suggested that the reproduction of capitalism would ensue, unless popular consciousness could be concretised around an emancipatory programme built upon the foundations of political ecology and socialism. Thus he believed that capitalism would be able to withstand the ecological crisis unless the green movement was prepared to coalesce with liberatory socialism. Murray Bookchin, still intent on protecting social ecology from Marxism, has stringently rejected Gorz's claim that there is a link between liberatory socialism and political ecology:

> To distinguish ecology from environmentalism and to explore the social thrust of ecological thinking as distinguished from the merely technical strategies of environmental thinking would

> actually compel Gorz to confront the serious challenges a radical social ecology raises to his own mode of thinking – notably, socialist 'thinking'. For the real conflict that faces the Left so far as society and the natural world are concerned *is not between a specious form of bourgeois 'ecology' and socialist politics, but between a libertarian form of social ecology and an economistic, technologically orientated form of socialism – in short, Marxism.* This is not what Gorz intends to do. Ecology is effectively reduced to environmentalism all the more to spuriously fuse Marxist thinking with the ecological issues of our time.
>
> (Bookchin 1980–1: 179, original emphasis)

Whilst Bookchin is justified in claiming that Gorz did not differentiate between ecology and environmentalism clearly enough, he fails to recognise the explicit rejection of Marx's economism and productivism in Gorz's *Ecology as Politics*. Gorz's intention was to demonstrate that advanced capitalism could incorporate an environmental face and that it would, in all probability, have to introduce limited reform of its systems of production due to environmental pressures. Nevertheless Gorz recognised that this did not amount to ecologism. In the more conservative spheres of environmentalism, Gorz argued, the aim of the movement was merely to limit the polluting effects of industrialism. Gorz went beyond this conservative environmentalism by suggesting that capitalism with an environmental face was no more palatable than traditional capitalism. The implication was that the traditional industrial and productivist ethics of capitalism would still remain and the development of an environmental façade would obscure the increasing ability of capitalism to maintain and reproduce its methods of domination.

Like Gorz, Bahro has also suggested that there must be a unification of red and green to counteract this conservative environmentalism:

> Socialists and Greens . . . have long had a certain standpoint in common, which has now become decisive for world history. This common standpoint is a radical critique of capitalist industrialism. Many Greens may initially think not of capitalist industrialism but of the consequences of the industrial system in general. But in this respect they are misled. This is easy for them to see if they look back in history and ask when the basic attitudes they proceed from first came into being.
>
> (Bahro 1982: 24)

Bahro was careful not to equate socialism with Marxism or state socialism – a trap into which many ecologists fell. Porritt, for instance, has reserved equal criticism for theorists of capitalism and communism because both ideologies supported industrialism (Porritt 1986). Certainly capitalism and Marxism promote productivist industrialism but Gorz's socialism is consistently anti-growth and anti-productivist. The refusal of some Greens to see anything in socialism or communism beyond orthodox Marxism and state socialist societies does not assist the cause of ecology, which, Gorz argued, has much to learn from liberatory socialism. Dobson too has recognised that Porritt's treatment of industrialism as identical in both capitalism and communism is too simplistic because it suggests that there has been some convergence between the interests of labour and capital – an idea that is clearly anathema to most socialists (Dobson 1990: 179). Martell points out that the inexorable logic of industrialism is not regularly challenged in disciplines such as sociology which makes the transition from industrial to post-industrial society problematic (Martell 1994: 16–24). The question remains as to how the socialist goal of human liberation can be complemented by the green concern for the liberation of nature. For Gorz, technology should play a central part in this search for dual emancipation, although the type of technology employed must be closely monitored:

> Even more than their labour-power, the technical apparatuses of capital expropriate individuals' lived relationships and their senses. It is only eco-socialist modernization, not the ecological restructuring of industrial society, that can offer solutions, in this respect, which are neither technocratic nor authoritarian.
>
> (Gorz 1994: 42)

TECHNOLOGY AND LIBERATION

Gorz's thesis, which corresponds with Marcuse's analysis of the effects of technology, contends that a society governed by the ethos of technological productivism is intrinsically hierarchical. This is so because the uses to which technology is presently put ensure that authoritarian control is accentuated. Marcuse reinforces this view by claiming that 'technology . . . cannot be isolated from the use to which it is put; the technological society is a system of domination which operates already in the concept and construction of techniques' (Marcuse 1986: xvi). Gorz has argued that this does not mean that technology itself inherently generates hierarchy but that industrialised societies manipulate technology to further authoritarian social control. For instance, as Giddens has noted, late capitalist societies constantly use technology to create more efficient means of surveillance (Giddens 1985: 302–10). Whilst the influence of critical theorists such as Marcuse on later green thinking is apparent, it also seems clear that some 'green' thinkers such as Gorz offer a road out of the theoretical cul-de-sac in which some critical theorists have found themselves regarding the ubiquity of technical rationality (Dobson 1993: 207–8; Eckersley 1992: 97–117).

Gorz adopted an anthropocentric approach to the solution of the problems created by the instrumental reason of the industrialised societies. Thus he was able to envisage the unproblematic usage of technology for emancipatory ends, whilst many ecocentric theorists have difficulty with the integration of technology into their programmes. Dobson, in his narrow definition of political ecology, goes so far as to suggest that Gorz, and others such as Alvin Toffler, cannot be located in the green tradition because their visions for the future are largely technology-based (Dobson 1990: 98). However, as Goodin notes, most green political programmes such as that of Die Grünen in 1983, have promoted some kind of alternative or intermediate technology which does not form a hegemonic hold over the everyday life of individuals: 'It puts people more in control of their own lives. It permits people to live and work in more human-sized communities. It is more in tune with both human purposes and the natural order' (Goodin 1992: 192).

One of the most important writers on alternative technology, David Dickson, has remarked that 'we see technology reflecting and reinforcing social relationships' (Dickson 1974: 87). In this spirit, Gorz asserted that the encouragement of compatibility and conviviality in social relationships could be assisted only by alternative, convivial technology. It would be pertinent to stress, though, that this technology may 'reflect' and 'reinforce' social relationships but it does not itself constitute them. Similarly Wiesenthal notes that, although there are very good reasons for developing alternative technology, not every problem has a technological solution (Wiesenthal 1993: 124–35). Indeed it is a standard green view that most of the global environmental problems cannot be altered by technology alone but by changes in the way we live (in the West in particular) to decrease excessive consumption and wasteful lifestyles (Martell 1994: 74).

Pepper is more technocentric (although he denies this) when he reasons that 'as societies, we collectively employ different technologies to change nature, with clear political results' (Pepper 1993: 113). Obviously the technology we use will have an impact on the way we live but Pepper appears to imply that political change will come about *through* the use of non-capitalist technology rather than using it as a catalyst for political change, especially outside of the workplace. Technology can liberate the possibilities available as an alternative to capitalism but it cannot, by itself, realise those possibilities. The sum of these arguments is that there is no clear structural link between technology and social relationships as in the Marxian notion of base and superstructure. Rather the bond between the two is much more fluid and less functional. This perspective allows space for those such as Carter who suggest that convivial technology sits more comfortably with green direct democracy than modern hard technology (Carter 1993: 39–62). Taken at face value we should note that the adoption of convivial technology may assist green aims without actually bringing about 'green direct democracy'. So the most positive aspect of convivial technology may be that it 'asserts values other than "economic efficiency", and can also help establish ethical, participatory, communicative and aesthetic criteria' (Ferris 1993: 20).

This is a notion that has escaped much green theory and, consequently, many ecologists have sought historically regressive answers to the environmental problems that capitalist technologism has created. Gorz rejected the suggestion that the eradication of hard technology would abolish hierarchical social relationships and replace them with conviviality. One of the most noticeable arguments in *Ecology as Politics* comes in Gorz's attack upon this assumption in his development of an ecological and liberatory alternative (Gorz 1987a: 42–50). Gorz observed that technological innovation, aimed at accentuating hierarchical social relationships, adversely affected humanity and the environment. Hence the solution to this problem in industrialised societies was to tackle the ownership and control of technological resources. This corresponds with the thesis of Dickson who also lamented the effects of technology on hierarchical social relationships: 'The technology of Western society . . . has come to embody the exploitation of both man and the natural environment which have characterised the political system within which it has been developed.' He concluded that 'the desire to maintain hierarchical relationships has led to the adoption of production techniques that appear to require them' (Dickson 1974: 43, 87). Hence Dickson and Gorz agreed that the challenge to technological hierarchy in industrialised societies had to ensure the integration of ecological imperatives within the overall socialist objective. This line traces a third path between those environmentalists who see alternative technology as the ultimate panacea for our ills and eco-Marxists such as Pepper who stress that it is not the type of technology but the ownership and organisation of technology which oppresses people (Pepper 1993: 238–9).

The original thrust of *Ecology as Politics* was that the green movement had to seek not only survival but also a fundamental change in the practices of the capitalist world economy. Gorz illuminated the process by which capitalist societies managed to incorporate environmental goals into their productivist strategies. He argued that the capitalist system initially attempted to find new markets for growth in areas of ecological concern. For example, Western capitalist interests have realised that there are markets to be found in the sale of previously 'free' resources such as air and water. The need for clean, pure water for human life is undeniable but the availability of it is hindered by the polluting effects of industrialism. Whilst it is the mode of capitalist production that is affecting the quality of water, capitalists are able to market pure bottled water as an alternative. In this way modern capitalists can face up to the ecological exigencies which are directly related to their industrial practices and still manage to expand their sphere of growth and profit. Furthermore this bottled water must either be purified or else it must be taken from a pure environment. Both of these forms of producing pure water still entail some degree of industrial activity (Dobson 1990: 86–8). This example substantiates Gorz's arguments that capitalists are capable of expanding growth and profit by commandeering environmental imperatives. Similarly Geoghegan has observed that

> capitalism's apparently limitless ability to co-opt previously subversive ideas is borne out by the experience of the ecology movement. Capitalism initially huffed and puffed at the ecologists, correctly sensing that ecology was expensive, but then stole their clothes when it became clear that further expansion required care for the environment. Since the increased costs are passed on to others, capitalist ecology eventually leads to economic stagnation and crisis. This will not act as a springboard to revolution but merely cause social regression combined with an increase in private and public monopolies.
>
> (Geoghegan 1987: 127)

It should be noted that this economic stagnation was not immediately apparent and that environmental developments have enabled new diversified sources of profit for capitalists. However Gorz (and most political ecologists) believe that this process is finite due to natural limits. Nevertheless the green movement, in its environmentalist strands at least, has underestimated the degree to which capitalist industrialism has ingrained hierarchy and ecological incompatibility into its structures. Consequently environmentalists have not adequately prioritised the necessity of the abolition of global capitalism for the development of an ecological society. As a global entity, capitalism has been capable of redirecting resources to different parts of the world to manipulate relatively unpolluted areas – a point that was highlighted in the Earth Summit in Rio in June 1992. This policy has pacified some conservative Western environmentalists who tend to be bought off by apparent remedies to environmental problems in their own countries. Frequently, the problems of the global environment are addressed by conservative Greens from an extremely occidental and sometimes nationalistic perspective. Indeed much conservative environmentalism abounds with nationalistic fervour concerned with the preservation of national areas of natural beauty rather than the global ecosystem. Meanwhile, those in the Third World are increasingly reliant upon the most industrial methods of production of global capitalism whilst the material benefit of their labour is spread around the developed nations (Gorz 1987a: 91–7). As soon as companies in developed areas, such as the Rhine valley which Gorz cites, realise that to maintain production they must clear the air they have polluted, then they have the choice of an expensive filtering system or relocating to an undeveloped (and thus relatively unpolluted) environment.

In *Ecology as Politics*, Gorz was primarily interested in analysing the reproduction of an environment in the Western nations, in which capitalists could maintain their mode of production and their margin of profit. He observed that the maintenance of production, albeit with more environmentally sensitive methods, would lead to increased capital costs for capitalists in the industrialised societies which would lead to either a decline in profits or higher prices for goods (Gorz 1987a: 6). Both of these outcomes have been witnessed in Western Europe since Gorz made this prophecy in 1974 but, importantly, the system has proved resilient enough to shrug off these side effects of environmental degradation. Again the step between crises in capitalism and the creation of a new society has appeared insurmountable. This point is clarified by Wall who points out that 'a Green future is *technically* feasible. The question then is whether it is politically achievable' (Wall 1990: 58).

As ever Gorz's analysis is centred on how to achieve the future society and how to popularise the views that have emanated from Greens and post-industrial socialists. The first step in this process is to debunk the myths that have been generated by Western governments and industrialists to justify their policies. For Gorz, the greatest of these myths surrounds the notion of economic growth.

THE MYTHS OF ECONOMIC GROWTH

The ability of capitalism to withstand environmental pressures has not led to a new ecological world economy, but has secured the means by which capitalists have increased profits under the auspices of a more humane, environmental rhetoric, despite the efforts of environmental pressure groups to point out hypocrisy. The long-term aims of ecological movements, and especially green political parties, do not tally with the dominant political structure in liberal democracies (especially in the UK) as several writers have noted (Wall 1990: 59–77). It would seem that only a complete reconstruction of contemporary institutions would enable ecological goals to be properly enacted – a project that may be best advanced by more discourse between political ecologists and sympathetic socialists.

Nevertheless ecologists and green activists have been reluctant about the adoption of their aims by the traditional political parties because of the limited attraction of the limits to growth thesis to other ideological traditions. It is important to note that Gorz's somewhat uncritical acceptance of limits to growth has been tempered in his later work when he has actually attempted to outline the economics of reduced working hours (Gorz 1994: 102–8). Goodin believes that the doom-laden anti-growth comments of the green movement have left the mainstream political debate free to be colonised by pro-growth ideologues (Goodin 1992: 99). More importantly, and this is not just due to the presentational failure of their ideas by Greens that Goodin implies, the notion of shackling growth has not actually entered the political agenda. The untruths that are abundant about economic growth in the West have been a focus for the later Gorz (1989a, 1994). Likewise Dobson has outlined green criticisms of some of the myths associated with the capitalist ideology of growth:

> The traditional idea that rates of unemployment can be brought down only by increased growth is challenged at two levels; first, that further growth and subsequent investment in the same direction (i.e. labour-saving technology) can result only in more

> unemployment not less; and second, that the rates of necessary growth projected by traditional political interests are unsustainable anyway.
>
> (Dobson 1990: 86)

It is clear that the advocates of industrial growth have consistently promised that individuals will, in the future, achieve greater material security. Often this philosophy is assumed rather than theoretically justified. Unfortunately, once the majority of individuals succeed in reaching a predetermined level in the social hierarchy through the consumption of a luxury good, that good ceases to be a luxury. Gorz argues that the desire to ascend the social scale (a myth designed by the ideologists of growth to encourage consumption) could be satisfied only by the consumption of further luxuries (Gorz 1987a: 70–7). This ideology of consumerism in capitalist societies clearly runs counter to the qualitative emphasis regarding the use of resources in green political thought (Dobson 1990: 90).

The logic of consumption in industrial capitalism created not only a crisis in consumer needs but, more importantly, a corresponding crisis in ontological and existential needs. These problems were not surprising to red and green thinkers who criticised the advent of 'consumer society'. Again the removal of the structures of 'consumer society' was a common objective for liberatory socialists and political ecologists. This objective relied on an inversion of the capitalist logic of growth and accumulation that encouraged excessive production and consumption. The work of Bookchin is prominent in this area of ecological debate:

> Capitalism not only validates precapitalist notions of the domination of nature by man; it turns the plunder of nature into society's law of life. To quibble with this kind of system about its values, to try to frighten it with visions about the consequences of growth is to quarrel with its very metabolism. One might more easily persuade a green plant to desist from photosynthesis than to ask the bourgeois economy to desist from capital accumulation.
>
> (Bookchin 1980: 66)

Critics of ecological plans for limited growth have suggested that any attempt to reverse the modern trend for high growth would result in a decline in the living standards of society. Gorz has demonstrated that this idea is false because the logic that reasons that less consumption leads to greater inequality relies on the supposition that resources cannot be more equitably distributed (Gorz 1994). In fact the promotion of negative growth relies on a more equitable distribution of fewer resources, in a much less wasteful fashion. Predictably those who purveyed the ideology of growth had most to lose from any redistribution of resources. Gorz contended that 'lack of realism consists in imagining that economic growth can still bring about increased human welfare, and indeed that it is still physically possible' (Gorz 1987a: 14). This perspective fits comfortably with Gorz's existentialist background as the notion of scarcity permeates persistently in the latter as well as in green political thought. It is the notion of scarcity that provides inspiration for all followers of the 'Limits to Growth' perspective (Dobson 1990: 80).

Having discussed the ideology of the economists of growth, Gorz drew on the work of Ivan Illich in an attempt to promote the creation of alternative technology suitable to small-scale society (Gorz 1987a: 55–64; Illich 1973). Gorz contended that political economy and small-scale production were incompatible because political economy became an effective discipline only when the means of production became externalised from the conscious will of the individuals involved in the process of production. Thus, in the small-scale communities that Gorz celebrated, production tended to be directed towards the manufacture of socially necessary goods, that is, goods that were identifiable human needs. In these communities, as opposed to all industrialised and productivist societies, goods produced according to necessary human prerogatives tended to be consumed by the individuals involved in their production or at least by members of the same community. Here Gorz reiterated the core of Marx's critique of bourgeois political economy. Gorz accepted that individuals had to unite to appropriate the means of their subordination (primarily capitalist forms of work) or else remain within the constraints of a system which imposed its rationality of growth and profit upon the very life-organisation of the community. This, as Hulsberg observed, also corresponded to the ecological imperative:

> There is universal agreement within the Greens that in their critique of the capitalist production system, the main demand has to be not for work but for a different kind of work: the suppression, not amelioration, of the despotic form of labour organisation in the capitalist factory or large office.
>
> (Hulsberg 1988: 183)

Dobson has countered Hulsberg's point by stating that the logic of work is inherent within green political thought:

> Greens will . . . be very sceptical of the workless future because they think work is a good thing to do. In this respect they insert themselves in a tradition that has it that work is a noble occupation; that it uplifts the spirit and helps create and reproduce ties with one's community.
>
> (Dobson 1990: 109)

It is obvious that, on the whole, Greens do not differentiate between creative work and capitalist employment as specifically as Gorz does. Nevertheless Gorz believed that ecology could inform socialism about the inefficiency which resulted from the rationale of industrial economics. Thus, political ecology had the potential to become an effective doctrine if it attacked the basis of modern economic thought and ensured that new, oppositional politics returned to the public sphere. Others such as Pepper maintain that older categories regarding work and employment remain pertinent to the defeat of capitalism (Pepper 1993: 123). Gorz believed that ecology could give socialism a new vitality that could help to overcome social isolationism (privatism) and enable individuals to participate in the political process. Clearly the rise of political ecology and 'green' issues has led to some degree of individual repoliticisation. Nevertheless Gorz was aware that the eco-centricity of political ecology and the anthropocentricity of Marxist theory would probably preclude any concrete alliance between red and green politics which he deemed vital – a point with which Bahro concurred:

> they [the greens] want to overthrow all conditions in which people are debased and humiliated. But this was precisely the categorical imperative of the young Marx. General emancipation will never come about if we destroy the earth itself. And this destruction can only be prevented if we mobilise people on the basis of their most fundamental emancipatory impulses.
>
> (Bahro 1982: 18)

Bahro draws an important link between this type of ecological thought and that of the early Marx which shows that not all 'eco-socialist' or 'eco-Marxist' thought shares the same basic ideological tenets. This idea corresponds with that of Eckersley who identifies a difference between humanist eco-socialists such as Gorz and Enzensberger and more orthodox eco-Marxists such as Howard Parsons who reiterate the Marxist 'technical fix' to the problems of capitalism (Eckersley 1992: 82–95; Enzensberger 1988: 253–95; Parsons 1978). In the humanist 'eco-socialist' tradition, Gorz suggested that the global community had to limit the industrial production which polluted the biosphere and needlessly wasted finite, natural resources. The alternative scenario was a world of technofascism where the limits on production would be centrally imposed by 'ecological engineers' working on behalf of centralised institutions and relying upon capitalist technology (Gorz 1987a: 78–91). Again Gorz appeared to be aware, in typically iconoclastic style, that ecology could be manipulated in an authoritarian, despotic manner by ideologues of the Right:

> Environmentalists use ecology as the lever to push forward a radical critique of our civilisation and our society. But ecological arguments can also be used to justify the application of biological engineering to human systems.
>
> (Gorz 1987a: 17)

Equally Gorz still advocated the use of science and technology to liberate humanity. He suggested that, whilst he believed that nature was not sacred, he was apprehensive about the development of new forms of domination taking the place of natural processes. Science and technology were not inherently deficient; the problem concerned the way technology and science were manipulated in industrialised societies. This corresponds with the analysis of Goodin who has observed that 'the issue, then, is not how to do away with modern technologies altogether but is rather one of how to choose in a discriminating way between them' (Goodin 1992: 189).

Thus Gorz contended that 'the struggle for different technologies is essential to the struggle for a different society' (Gorz 1987a: 19). By this he meant that the development of certain technologies influenced the institutions of society; nuclear technology, for instance, encouraged centralised and hierarchical relations in society – a view substantiated by Thompson (Gorz 1987a: 99–113; E.P. Thompson 1980). Whilst Dobson agrees with this analysis, he recognises that the production of solar energy technology is a potential area for future growth, profit and pollution for capitalists. He has argued that the basis of an ecological energy policy has to be located in a contraction of human consumption: 'Reduced energy use, for the Green movement, involves reduced production, and reduced production involves reduced consumption' (Dobson 1990: 104). The point is clear – technology can be of use to political ecologists but it cannot dictate the lifestyles people live; the necessary alteration in lifestyle must be a conscious and rational decision.

Presently, it is not in the capitalist interest to encourage the use of solar energy because there is still considerable profit to be made from traditional, finite sources of energy, but, as traditional forms of energy become more scarce and environmentalism more prominent, it is possible that capitalists could realise a profit-making alternative in solar energy. Hirsch has outlined the potential of alternative energy sources whilst being aware that these could be misused by capitalist owners:

> Renewable energy sources such as solar, tidal, or wind power use decentralised technologies on a human scale, subject to control by all. Until someone figures out how to meter the sun or bottle the wind, such energy sources are free. They cannot be sold and they cannot yield profits. (Though the equipment needed to convert such sources into usable energy can be monopolised to yield profits.) These renewable energy technologies are potentially democratic and anti-capitalist, whereas nuclear technology has a decidedly authoritarian and capital-intensive bias.
>
> (Hirsch 1982: 237)

One of the most important features of the alternative technology Gorz celebrated was that the tools of production would be small scale and convivial – a term Illich coined to define socially accessible technology. Gorz suggested that technological tools had to be available to and controlled by a local community. Furthermore, joint control had to be exercised over localised technology by producers and consumers. Gorz realised that the implementation of dual control of technical resources against the imperatives of capitalist regimes was a formidable task. To this extent he observed that the transformation of society without a transformation of technology was improbable. However, as Tokar has noted, the manufacture of electronics that is involved in Gorz's 'information technology' would also pollute and, consequently, would not fit comfortably with the ethos of political ecology (Tokar 1987). This view is reinforced by Martell who characterises Gorz as a high-tech post-industrial utopian:

> environmentally friendly technological developments may themselves not be as clean as they are thought to be. Some enthusiasts [Gorz] for the post-industrial or information society look optimistically at the environmental implications of a shift from heavy manufacturing industry to service and information industries based on computerization and information technology.

> However, many of the processes that go into the manufacture of computer technology are actually very dirty chemically.
>
> (Martell 1994: 74)

Again it is evident that Gorz's ideas, though informed by ecology, are not green in the ecocentric sense of the word. Gorz preferred to prioritise the importance of decentralisation in socialism if it was to avoid the pitfalls of 'technofascism'. Here Gorz's distinction between liberatory socialism and Marxism is evident. Geoghegan notes this distinction when he states that 'Like Bahro, Gorz finds Marxism deficient with respect to ecology. It shares the growth perspective of its capitalist opponents. As such its future perspective is, in this respect, its weakest aspect' (Geoghegan 1987: 128). Despite his critique of Marxism, Gorz is equally sure that a reconciliation between nature and humanity was impossible within the framework of capitalism, because ecologism, even in its anthropocentric form, was fundamentally incompatible with capitalism. Once again Gorz's diversion from classical Marxism on the politics of nature is apparent as even Marx saw potential in the system of capitalist industrialism – a point clarified by Grundmann:

> Marx welcomed the growth of productive forces and, what is more, praised even capitalism for developing the productive forces in a hitherto unknown way. Thus . . . industrialism for him was part of the historical tendency of the productive forces to develop – an indispensable condition for the advent of a communist society.
>
> (Grundmann 1991: 4)

Gorz's critique of 'capitalist environmentalism' also highlighted how the pursuit of increased growth and constant profit led to an increasing degradation of finite resources. As long as it proved profitable, industrial capitalism increasingly substituted human labour with capital. No sooner had capitalist technology created a machine that increased the margins of profitability, than the machine was replaced by a more efficient and productive machine. Gorz illustrated how the principle of durability was excluded from the equation of capitalist technological expansion. As machines, and the technology required for their production, became more sophisticated and less labour intensive, capitalist owners tended to direct their capital resources towards greater technological refinement and away from variable capital (labour). Efficiency and profitability were the guiding factors behind employers' policy on capital. Thus Gorz observed how the system of advanced capitalism reproduced greater capital intensity and rendered human labour increasingly unnecessary. He therefore believed, in accordance with most 'eco-socialist' thought, that this increasing level of growth could not expand infinitely and that it would eventually reach its limit. Although Gorz had apparently diverged from Marxian orthodoxy on the question of ecology, his language and framework of analysis at this time still demonstrate his Marxist heritage. In the words of Hirsch:

> Gorz still viewed marxism as irreplaceable as an 'instrument of analysis'. In fact, he gave a convincing interpretation of the economic origins of the ecology crisis using such traditional marxist economic concepts as crisis of overaccumulation, increasing organic composition of capital, declining rate of profit, and a crisis of reproduction of the means of production.
>
> (Hirsch 1982: 237)

Gorz argued that, in capitalist societies, methods such as limiting the durability of products could be used to increase turnover, demand and profit. The consequent increase in production that this turnover engendered was intended to maintain areas of industrial profit for capitalists. This production was unnecessary for both the world community and the environment but was essentially designed to bolster the level of profitability for capitalist employers. This situation, Gorz suggested, was an essential feature of capitalism involving the deliberate limitation of the durability of products and indeed the creation of goods with in-built obsolescence to engender increased turnover and to perpetuate the myth of the value of economic growth (Gorz 1987a: 24).

Gorz argued that the promotion of ecological exigencies required an inversion of capitalist logic so that less would be consumed to protect global resources. Whilst Gorz envisaged the disintegration of capitalism due to the limits on its growth, capitalism has proved capable of re-directing its resources to less capital-intensive sectors such as the tertiary sector, a flaw in Gorz's argument which he remedied in his later work (Gorz 1989a). Nevertheless, in the 1970s, he made the important observation that goods for consumption in advanced capitalist societies still had to be manufactured. Therefore it was problematic to refer to this society as 'consumer society' because a core industrial base remained in place which at the time was deemed necessary. Yet again the foundations of Gorz's ecological critique of Marxism were evident as he urged socialists to abandon productivist economics. He believed the implementation of the socialist agenda required a radical critique of the classical Marxist portrayal of social change – a critique that he later presented in *Farewell to the Working Class* (Gorz 1987b).

THE POVERTY OF AFFLUENCE

At this stage, though, Gorz focused on the critique of the 'poverty of affluence' which was the phrase he used to describe the failure of Western consumerism. His advocacy of sufficiency, durability and ecological compatibility in productive techniques enabled him to deploy his critique against state socialist as well as capitalist societies. He attempted to show how a rich life entailed a concentration on producing less, whereas a life of affluence or over-production and over-accumulation was, in effect, a life of wastefulness (Gorz 1987a: 28). The central thesis of Gorz's argument was that individuals were not socially insecure through a lack of material goods but through the nature of the goods produced and the methods of their production:

> The *persistence* of poverty in advanced industrial societies cannot be ascribed to the same factors as the *existence* of poverty in the so-called underdeveloped countries. Whereas the latter can, in the final analysis be attributed to physical shortages, which can be overcome by the development (under specific conditions) of the forces of production, the persistence of poverty in rich countries must be attributed to a social system which produces poverty at the same time it produces wealth.
>
> (Gorz 1987a: 28, original emphasis)

Clearly Gorz believed that poverty was a situation which, beyond the bounds of human necessity, was relative to the existence of affluence. Destitution occurred when there were insufficient resources to ensure material security for the members of a society, whereas poverty occurred when the resources of a community were inequitably distributed. Gorz also outlined the manner in which this poverty was produced. One cause was the monopolisation of resources in the hands of the affluent – a consistently recurring theme in Gorz's theory. This monopolisation not only accentuated the scarcity which modern society encountered but also ensured the material and ideological subordination of one class to another. Gorz realised that the scarcity of natural resources reproduced poverty and that capitalism accentuated this poverty by implementing 'artificial scarcities' through the destruction of these resources. Thus, for Gorz, socialist theory must prioritise a theory of needs. Ryle has commented on the imperative to reconstruct the theory of human needs for both socialism and political ecology:

> Greens and eco-socialists have accordingly not only to raise the question of needs in itself, as a political question, but to develop political/economic frameworks within which the transformation of needs can be advocated or made real. . . . We have to emphasize the contradictory nature of our present satisfactions, and the frustrations (often of non-material needs) that these entail. And we have to make the satisfaction of an agreed set of basic needs an economic priority.
>
> (Ryle 1988: 71)

Ryle indicates a central focus of green political thought, namely that there needs to be a radical re-evaluation of consumerist values in Western society. Greens relentlessly argue for the creation of a post-materialist lifestyle, although, as Smart notes, the reversal of patterns of consumerism is a difficult process to instigate (Smart 1992: 94). Moreover, Greens find it difficult to persuade people that they should restrain themselves to the extent that they limit human reproduction (Martell 1994: 48–9). Although Gorz was concerned about population levels, he focused on the reproduction of poverty which he felt was accelerated by consumerism and the creation of luxury goods, of which the use value was not readily apparent. Simultaneously the access to these luxury goods was reliant on the ability to pay for them. Hence a status value was conferred upon luxury goods which, when they became more accessible to the majority, was transferred onto a new luxury product. The privilege of consuming goods which were not necessary but which required restricted access was that they were limited to the affluent, that is, they created and reproduced poverty. Gorz was extending the focus of ecological theory on consumerism by highlighting the human and social effects as well as the negative environmental implications. Hulsberg realised that Gorz was one of the few socialists to attempt the development of ecology in this way. In general though, Hulsberg argued that political ecology was misunderstood within socialist debate because socialists, with the exception of writers like Gorz and Bahro, failed to recognise the importance and ubiquity of the ecological message (Hulsberg 1988: 2). Marxist and Neo-Marxist discussions of needs have often been slow to take up the imperatives of scarcity and natural limits, but, more recently, there have been more sophisticated attempts to address environmental issues, although these do not really go anywhere near far enough to satisfy political ecologists (Doyal and Gough 1991).

These green criticisms of anthropocentric views of needs (i.e. theories of *human* need) are also applicable to all of Gorz's work. However Gorz's analysis of poverty was valuable in an ecological context as it challenged the manipulation of resources which produced social inequality, instead of viewing the imbalance of human resources as an issue external to the green agenda. Along with the production of socially necessary and non-polluting goods, he realised that inequality in power had to be abolished if there was to be an effective challenge to technological capitalist structures. This realism constituted a valuable addition to the ecological critique of capitalism. It was also a critique which vindicated the promotion of an ideological alliance between political ecology and socialism. In short, according to Gorz, the material inequality which the Greens and socialists sought to eradicate could be eliminated only by the abolition of social inequality:

> equality in consumption can only be the result of, and not a means to, the achievement of social equality. The latter depends upon the abolition of hierarchical order. If a hierarchy of powers and functions persists, it will soon reestablish both material and symbolic inequalities (as has occurred in authoritarian socialist societies). If it is abolished, material inequalities will lose their social significance.
>
> (Gorz 1987a: 32)

Alec Nove has noted how, beneath the clothing of ecological idealism, there lurks a residual realism that informed the political programme that Gorz advocated for radical change. Nove states that

> Gorz is no fanatic, he well realises that economies of scale exist too and cannot, for certain productive activities, be ignored save at prohibitive cost. He therefore accepts that some branches must continue to produce on a large scale: electricity generation, say, heavy chemicals, steel, oil, to name a few. His idea is that workers should take turns to work in such industries as these, and devote to them as few hours as modern technology makes possible, so as to fulfil themselves in small-scale activities.
>
> (Nove 1983: 199–200)

Nove's comments display the enduring link between Gorz's radical critique of capitalism and industrial productivism and his programme for socialist change, although Nove gives the somewhat misguided impression that Gorz justifies numerous heavy industries. However his comments do help to clarify the Marxian origins from which Gorz began his engagement with ecological theory. He took on board much classical Marxist thinking in his attempt to formulate a critique of capitalism. Nevertheless Gorz's dismissal of productivism has led to much criticism from orthodox Marxists to complement the disapproval of Gorzian 'eco-socialism' by ecocentric commentators (Eckersley 1992). The antipathy from Marxists towards Gorz's fusion of socialism and ecology is misguided insofar as he has maintained labour (or, more accurately the manipulation of temporal resources) as the central paradigm of social reproduction. Nevertheless Gorz criticised orthodox Marxists for failing to realise that material welfare was a valid objective as long as it was accompanied by a rejection of the hierarchical stratification in society. He argued that Marxists had become victims of the value system created by commodity relations. This led Marxists to adopt a one-dimensional approach to the abolition of social stratification. Whilst he is rather simplistic in directing this criticism at all Marxists, Gorz was correct to point out that Marxist-Leninist discourse was slow to engage with the element of self-criticism which green theory had encouraged in the work of Gorz and other thinkers on the Left such as Bahro. Bahro also observed the inability of the Marxian orthodoxy to come to terms with the problems highlighted by the prominence of green political thought:

> Marxists have so far rarely considered that humanity has not only to transform its relations of production, but must also fundamentally transform the entire character of its mode of production, i.e. the productive forces, the so-called technostructure.
>
> (Bahro 1982: 27)

In the light of Bahro's point it is useful to summarise how Gorz has used green ideas to promote a radical alternative to advanced capitalism. Gorz illustrated his recommendations for the foundation of a radical, eco-socialist critique of capitalism in the conclusion to his section on 'Ecology and Freedom' (Gorz 1987a: 40–2). Firstly, he recognised that over-production and wastefulness have rendered a change in the capitalist mode of production inevitable. He reasoned that the crisis of capitalism could be halted only by a fundamental break from the ideology of growth towards a new ethos which was guided by the premise of less growth and socially useful production.

Gorz also concluded that the link between 'more' and 'better', which was prioritised by productivist ideologies, no longer existed. To counteract this he advocated social production and less consumption – anathema to the ideology of growth in elements of both right and left-wing theory. Gorz suggested that it was an ecological necessity that production and consumption were minimalised, although he was less than clear about how to carry this process out – a residual feature of Gorz's work until recently. Wiesenthal, on the other hand, has been much more forthcoming about the possibilities of ecological consumption (Wiesenthal 1993: 155–71). Gorz's view in the relatively early phase of eco-socialist debate in the 1970s, however, was that the problem had to be identified before a solution could be outlined. He stated that poverty in the industrialised nations was created by the types of goods produced and the technology used to produce them. He suggested that this situation could be altered only by social production, that is, production which was not exploitative and which did not confer luxury status upon the goods consumed. A prerequisite of abolishing poverty, Gorz argued, was the realisation that socially necessary labour time was much smaller than appeared the case in industrialised capitalist society. It followed logically that the production of only socially necessary goods would reduce the overall amount of time individuals in a society had to spend at work. This theme, for which Gorz has achieved the greatest renown, was primarily concerned with the achievement of equality in social recognition through the equitable distribution of work to all those capable of working.

Gorz's socialism undoubtedly gained much from the integration of political ecology into his radical critique. In effect, close examination of his work suggests that he has understood the importance of integrating the red and green traditions which is explained by Ryle:

> a 'refounded' socialism must . . . take up the challenge of ecology and green movements. Both the negative, constraining limits of ecological responsibility and the positive, utopian critical thinking which that responsibility provokes are essential aspects of any serious political reawakening.
>
> (Ryle 1988: 100)

Gorz used ecology, following the disappointment of the failure of the 1968 revolution in Paris, to inject fresh dynamism into his socialist programme. He accepted the challenges that ecology posed to the methods and beliefs of Marxism. Gorz believed that the minimalisation of socially necessary labour time could open up new spheres of autonomous action within the community. Thus he observed that the lifestyle endured within the present system could be eliminated and a new, diversified, spontaneous lifestyle could take its place. Whether the ecology movement could eliminate the elements of centralism that preclude the spontaneity that Gorz advocated is highly questionable. Nevertheless the rejection of the ideology of growth validated the place of ecology in posing fundamental questions about socialist theory and, vitally, Gorz realised that socialists must not permit the appropriation of ecological goals to be undertaken by the ideologues of capitalism.

As such, *Ecology as Politics* should be regarded as a contribution to Gorz's enduring critique of capitalism rather than as a prophecy for change. In this respect, Gorz's appropriation of ecological thought in the 1970s constituted a natural progression in his work in his quest for a revitalised socialist critique of capitalism. In the words of Hirsch:

> both the new left and the radical ecological perspective are anti-technocratic, and both stress decentralisation, autonomy, and self-management as desirable social values. Thus it is not surprising that many of the former activists of May 1968 found in the ecology movement an expression of the aspirations of the May revolt.
>
> (Hirsch 1982: 229)

The development of green political thought in the 1970s was a major challenge to the oppositional hegemony of the Left and few engaged with it as much as Gorz. However the next project in Gorz's work was to demonstrate why the Marxist Left had to abandon their orthodoxy when it came to achieving social change. It was this task which was to provide the inspiration for Gorz's next and most controversial book, *Farewell to the Working Class*.

4

REFORMULATING MARXISM

Class conflict and the state

Before 1980 Gorz's work was not particularly well known outside of France but with the publication of *Farewell to the Working Class*, he was to become a central figure in the debates on the Left in Europe and in the USA (Gorz 1987b). The book sparked much debate because, although it is evident that Gorz remained within the Marxian tradition, he had reserved considerable criticism for Marxist orthodoxy, particularly in the area of class struggle. Gorz believes that the lessons from Marx are fundamental to emancipatory politics but he rejects Marx's belief in the collective appropriation of the means of production by the industrial working class. In this light *Farewell to the Working Class* can be viewed as one of the seminal expressions of post-Marxist theory.

The starting point of the book was to show that traditional forms of Marxian class analysis had become redundant in the context of advanced capitalist society. Gorz set out to explore the possibility of developing a new mode of class theory which necessitated socialist consciousness but rejected Leninist vanguardism (Boggs 1995: 46). Gorz's prioritisation of the goals of individuality and individual autonomy over the notion of proletarian revolution, though, left him open to the charges of rejecting collectivism and class struggle. Commentators such as Meiksins Wood have questioned Gorz's place in the Marxian legacy because he underplays the role of workerism in class struggle and emancipatory politics. A close reading of *Farewell* negates this criticism and shows that Gorz is more concerned with a radical critique of Marx than a rejection of class conflict.

Other commentators, such as Hyman, have criticised Gorz for seeking to supplant the revolutionary proletariat with a 'new middle class' or a 'new working class' capable of commandeering the means of production (Hyman 1983). This was a mistaken analysis of Gorz's perspective which coupled his work with that of 'new working class' theorist, Mallet, for instance (Mallet 1975). Whilst Mallet was rather positive about the revolutionary potential of the new working class, Gorz was much more sceptical about a purely workerist road to socialism – indeed he criticised Mallet in a manner somewhat similar to Mann and Mandel (Gorz 1976a: 182; Mandel 1982; Mann 1973). As Berger and Kostede have observed, Gorz's point in *Farewell* was not to 'replace workers with other groups, such as students, the "new" working class, or the new middle classes. No social group remains entrusted with an exclusive and privileged revolutionary role' (Berger and Kostede 1982: 230).

REJECTING THE HISTORICAL MISSION OF THE INDUSTRIAL PROLETARIAT

Gorz asserted that the traditional class boundaries, which characterised Marx's conception of class struggle, had become blurred and that clear differentials between classes were no longer easy to distinguish. Consequently it was difficult to devolve the power of social emancipation to any one specific social class. Nevertheless Gorz did not dwell on the analysis of class boundaries in *Farewell*, despite this being a fairly common approach to the discussion of class politics in modern socialist debates which attempt to revitalise Marxist class analysis (Meiksins 1986; Wright 1985).

Gorz was more concerned with forging a critique of why the majority of the Left was continuing to champion the productive ethos of full employment in an era when the possibility of such a situation had long since disappeared and was, to Gorz's mind, no longer desirable in any case. Because Left institutions such as the trade unions addressed those in employment, a large underclass was left unrepresented due to their unemployment or underemployment. Gorz's main concern was to elucidate the plight of the substantial number of individuals who found their potential unfulfilled by the technical division of labour. He criticised Marxists who clung to the workerist belief that impoverishment amongst low-level employees would breed revolution because that perspective failed to recognise that there was a large sector of society already at a more impoverished level than those in full-time employment. Furthermore he realised that a rupture between the working class and the impoverished underclass had occurred which undermined the central tenets of Marxist class analysis. The 'working class', portrayed as the lower sector of society, was no longer working nor was it a coherent class. For Gorz, socialist politics had to renounce workerism to engage with the problems of the most poverty stricken sector of society. This group was no longer the lifeblood of the economic system; in essence technological developments had ensured that it was no longer necessary to capitalist industry not even in Marx's idea of a reserve army because the poverty trap ensured that the long-term unemployed were unlikely to regain stable full-time employment (Keane 1988: 81).

Given this situation, Gorz argued that the Marxist class analysis which regarded the proletariat as the motor of history and the harbinger of revolutionary change was outdated because the employed were no longer the most exploited sector of society. The industrial proletariat had been surpassed as the potentially revolutionary class by a fusion of the unemployed, part-time workers, non-unionised workers, and temporary workers into what Gorz called the 'neo-proletariat', that is, 'a non-class of non-workers'. Contrary to the reception these ideas received, this group was not put forward as a new motor of history but as exactly the opposite. This was a 'non-class' because its members had little comprehension of their potential or knowledge of other individuals in their situation. Whilst Marxist-Leninist theory intimated that revolutionary consciousness (as opposed to class consciousness) amongst workers was not essential due to the vanguard leadership, Gorz posited the idea that the only class of individuals capable of concretising their revolutionary potential was a group who were aware of their ability to change society – it was not enough for the proletariat to be a class-in-itself, it had to have revolutionary consciousness and a desired objective (Kitschelt 1994: 12–15). Gorz's neo-proletariat is aware neither of its potential nor its ability because it is a disunited group; this is one of the factors which renders it a non-class. In this sense *Farewell to the Working Class* is, in the words of Meiksins Wood, a 'counsel of despair' (Meiksins Wood 1986: 15). Nevertheless this does not mean that the neo-proletariat is devoid of emancipatory potential. Keane maintains that 'this non-class of non-workers is likely to succeed the old and decaying industrial working-class movement as the most powerful opponent of the capitalist system' (Keane 1988: 82), albeit with very little power.

Gorz perceives the role of radical critique to be the identification of emancipatory potential. Thus he observed that liberatory social change was reliant on a new class consciousness, which is not defined within the parameters of nineteenth-century capitalism, but one that is contemporaneous with the forms of class disidentification in advanced capitalist society. This task cannot be achieved by the neo-proletariat, in its present form, precisely because it is devoid of class consciousness.

As Meiksins Wood suggests:

> Gorz offers no revolutionary agent to replace the working class. It turns out that the 'non-class of non-workers', this new revolutionary lumpen-proletariat which apparently 'prefigures' a new society, holds that promise only in principle, notionally, perhaps metaphysically; it has, by his own testimony, no strategic social power and no possibility of action.
>
> (Meiksins Wood 1986: 77)

Meiksins Wood moves from this foundation to suggest that Gorz rejects class struggle as the motor of emancipatory change. Yet, in fact, Gorz is aware of the need for class struggle but believes that this cannot be concretised through the outmoded categories of orthodox Marxism that Meiksins Wood defends. She is correct to point out that Gorz does not identify a genuine revolutionary agent but he did identify a *potentially* emancipatory group at least. Ultimately Meiksins Wood relies on hypothetical conjecture that, in the absence of a revolutionary agent, restates the case of the industrial proletariat simply because it exists – *ouvrierisme* at its radical worst, even though the industrial working class exists in much smaller numbers than when Marx placed his faith in it. Again the distinction between Gorz and others such as Mallet and Cooley is significant at this point. Where Mallet saw technical workers as a new vanguard for all of the disenfranchised and Cooley believed technologisation would unite technical workers with other manual workers, Gorz believed technical developments created a greater split in the working class which precluded such a development (Gorz 1976b: 59–71; P. Thompson 1984b: 74–5). Gorz did not perceive his task to be the creation of a blueprint for a new revolutionary vehicle, he merely sought to elucidate the contemporary situation by analysing traditional Marxist class theory. The Gorzian perspective requires that, rather than using orthodox Marxian class analysis as the gauge of emancipatory change, a new vehicle for liberation must be sought to adapt to the specific conditions of advanced capitalism. He recognised that class antagonism did not necessarily affect the social reproduction of capitalism. In essence, capitalism was not wholly reliant on popular legitimation as writers such as Habermas (1976a) suggested:

> over the past twenty years, the link between the development of productive forces and the growth of class antagonism has been broken. This does not mean that the internal contradictions of capitalism are not considerable. They have never been more

> spectacular. Capitalism has never been less able to solve the problems it has generated. Yet this inability has not been fatal. Instead capitalism has acquired a barely examined and often poorly understood capacity to manage the non-resolution of its problems.
>
> (Gorz 1987b: 14)

The failure to comprehend fully the crisis of capitalism in classical Marxist theory is, for Gorz, based on the maintenance of the canon that the forces of production bring into being a material foundation for socialist change. In short, he rejected the notion that capitalism gave rise to social conditions for the creation of a collective class with the ability to commandeer the forces of production. Gorz believed that orthodox Marxists failed to recognise that the instrumental reason of capitalism was functional only for the reproduction of the logic of capital. This point can also be directed towards others on the Left who outlined crisis tendencies in advanced capitalism without recognising the resilience of capitalist reproduction (Habermas 1976a; O'Connor 1973, 1984). Gorz called into question the belief that capitalist organisation lent itself comfortably to collective appropriation by a unitary proletariat. The instrumental logic of work was directed towards the maintenance of capitalist reason instead of the transcendence of socialist rationality. It is from this starting point that Gorz sets out to highlight the problems of orthodox Marxism and attempts to formulate an understanding of contemporary class conflict that goes beyond traditional Marxism. In the words of Berger and Kostede:

> Gorz . . . focuses on the power which the proletariat is prevented from exercising by the capitalist organisation of factory work. It is not a question of the proletariat no longer existing, but of surrendering a conviction: that the proletariat is the exclusive agency of historical change.
>
> (Berger and Kostede 1982: 230)

Gorz prefers to emphasise the primacy of individual class consciousness for liberation, against Marx and particularly Hegel, whose theory suggested that 'history has a meaning which is independent of the consciousness of individuals and realises itself, whatever they may think, in their actions' (Gorz 1987b: 18). This orthodoxy has constituted and hampered many radical movements seeking the abolition of capitalism (Gorz 1987b: 20).

In essence, Gorz's critique lambasted the prophetic element of classical Marxism which glorifies the industrial proletariat as a revolutionary body and aims to predict how it will commandeer the tools of capitalist production. Gorz turns Marx on his head by suggesting that, because the proletariat is a class called into being by capitalism and is governed by the logic of capitalist reason, it is inherently non-revolutionary. Herein lies the foundation of Gorzian class analysis – the examination of the revolutionary potential of the proletariat and the most impoverished sector of society against the determinism of Marx. Furthermore he attempted to illuminate the political problem created by the belief that the proletariat is, by definition, revolutionary. Gorz's theory is not concerned with the creation of an idealistic utopia, rather it is based upon the analysis of contemporary social problems and the exploration of avenues for change. Certainly Gorz proposes ideas that he believes are desirable in future society, but to disregard his theories as bourgeois pipe-dreams, as Meiksins Wood does, lends little support to the cause of radical critique (Meiksins Wood 1986: 17).

TECHNOLOGY AND CLASS DISIDENTIFICATION

By the early 1980s Gorz had renounced some of the more classical Marxist ideas which he expounded in the 1960s, particularly in *Strategy for Labour* (Gorz 1967). Building on Marx's notion of the polyvalent worker, Gorz had believed that the development of technology would lead to the creation of a society of skilled technical workers with an in-depth knowledge of the productive process and, therefore, the ability to understand and commandeer those tools for socialist ends. In *Farewell to the Working Class*, Gorz rejects these ideas:

> Automation and computerisation have eliminated most skills and possibilities for initiative and are in the process of replacing what remains of the skilled labour force (whether blue or white collar) by a new type of unskilled worker. The age of the skilled workers, with their power in the factory and their anarcho-syndicalist projects, has now to be seen as an interlude which taylorism, 'scientific work organisation', and, finally, computers and robots will have brought to a close.
>
> (Gorz 1987b: 28)

Gorz recognises that the technical division of labour has been the latest step in the erosion of worker autonomy and the reproduction of an alienated and powerless workforce. Rather than heralding a new era of optimism for the advent of the polyvalent skilled worker, technology has maintained and increased the heteronomous regulation that characterises the logic of capitalism. It has also further limited the possibility of a proletarian revolution, given that the minimalisation of class consciousness has been a useful by-product of the prime motivating factors behind the technical division of labour, i.e. profit and growth. For Gorz, this means that

> The collective power of a class able to produce the world and its history has not been transformed into a subject conscious of itself in each of its individual members. . . . In a word the collective worker remains external to the living workers. Capitalist development has endowed the collective worker with a structure that makes it impossible for real, flesh-and-blood workers either to recognise themselves in it or to internalise it as their own reality and potential power.
>
> (Gorz 1987b: 29)

Gorz is asserting that the mechanisation and technologisation of contemporary work practices constitute the individual worker as a servant of the machine, a common observation in Marxist discourse on the technical division of labour. Whilst able to understand the workings of the machine itself, many individual workers are powerless to challenge the overall strategy of technocapitalism partly because the decision-making process is conducted on a larger stage than the factory itself. Nevertheless theorists such as Meiksins do not believe that deskilling has such a fundamental effect on class conflict, a view which challenges Gorz who believes that the technical division of labour has profound effects on the nature of class conflict. Meiksins claims that 'Skill . . . is not the same as class. If anything, de-skilling is more usefully understood as a symptom of class: that is, de-skilling – or what Marx referred to as "real subordination of labour to capital" – can only occur once a worker has become a wage-labourer' (Meiksins 1986: 106). Gorz argues that, in such a situation, it is unlikely that the individual worker, performing tasks devoid of skill due to the technical division of labour, will achieve liberation within the workplace. Rather than deskilling ensuring the development of revolutionary class consciousness, it will lead only to increased experience of uselessness and resentment for the disenfranchised worker.

Gorz observes that many contemporary individual workers are minute parts of massive, transnational, interdependent organisations which are inaccessible to the individual worker. Hence, radical class consciousness is unlikely to develop in a situation where alienated individual workers are involved in a technological work process which externalises the collective worker. For Gorz, the hierarchical, technical organisation which externalises individual proletarians from their collective being is an inherent part of contemporary capitalist domination. This privatistic, anti-social deprivation does not lead to the workplace becoming an area for emancipatory change, as Meiksins argues. Rather it leads to the conclusion that the abolition of work is the only means to abolish hierarchical class differentials. The situation is the same for workers performing menial, contracted work – they too have negligible power in companies which have no obligations towards them and in which contracted workers are not real members.

Gorz contends that this has fundamental implications for the Left, which must accept that

> the means of production and a considerable part of what is actually produced do not lend themselves to real and concrete collective appropriation by real proletarians. Then the problem will be that of changing the means and structure of production in such a way as to make them collectively appropriatable. That, however, is neither an easy nor an immediately achievable task.
> (Gorz 1987b: 32)

AUTONOMY AND EXISTENTIAL NEEDS

Gorz's solution is that emancipatory change can come about only through an increase in worker autonomy and a recognition of the political power of the disenfranchised workers. From the basis of Gorz's critique of 'the myth of collective appropriation', it is apparent that such a development in individual autonomy is a long way off. As a class called into being by capitalism, the proletariat is largely engaged in a search for autonomous existence or self-determination *within the capitalist system.* The struggle for independence is itself, for Gorz, a barrier to class identification. Nevertheless this does not mean that autonomy for the individual should not be a primary goal for the Left. In essence, Gorz believes that class consciousness and autonomy are interdependent and contemporary Marxists who assert the primacy of the collective and preclude debate on individuality are forced to create a mythical, revolutionary and transcendent proletariat which subverts ideas about individual autonomy which inspired the early Marx: 'The political imperatives of the class struggle have thus prevented the labour movement from examining the desire for autonomy as a specifically existential demand' (Gorz 1987b: 36).

In a manner akin to Marcuse, Gorz emphasises the importance of existential needs for socialist theory. The subordination of these needs (aesthetic, cultural, emotional, etc.) to the political necessity for socialism will inevitably lead to the repression of those needs within socialist society as witnessed in the economistic regimes that developed the former Soviet Union and Eastern Europe. Hence the struggle for socialism must be coupled with the subjective recognition of the need for existential autonomy. Gorz did not wish to deny the political reality of class struggle but to express the necessity of the autonomous proletarian as the liberatory agent through individual realisation of political exigency. Socialism, which flattens individuality in its orthodox discourse, will never be able to promote an alternative to capitalism which promotes existential autonomy. Essentially, for Gorz, socialism must unite class consciousness and individual autonomy or it will suppress proletarians existentially in a similar manner to capitalism.

Against this view, Hyman argues that 'it is right to insist that the abolition of capitalism must be a cultural as much as a material revolution; but Gorz here seemingly proposes that socialism will be established by spiritual conversion alone' (Hyman 1983: 292). If Gorz was presenting his ideas as a strategy for socialist change, then Hyman's comments would be justified. However he misunderstands Gorz's objective which is the identification of errors and misconceptions on the Left. Again the criticisms of *Farewell* tend to emanate from those who regard it as a prophecy for a socialist future. Hyman obscures Gorz's point because he fails to recognise that emancipatory change will come about *only* if there exists in society a widespread desire to satisfy existential needs that have been suppressed by capitalism. Gorz argues that the necessity of promoting autonomy is demonstrated by the resentment and impotence that is generated by contemporary capitalism:

> work now exists outside the worker, reified to the extent of becoming an inorganic process. Workers are there and fall in with the work that is done. They do not do it themselves. The indeterminate nature of work entails an attitude of indifference. All that matters is the wage packet at the end of the week or month.
>
> (Gorz 1987b: 38)

Therefore, opposition within the workplace tends to take the form of resentment against employers (and sometimes unions which are engaged in corporatist arrangements), rather than an autonomous, proletarian decision to negate the productivist goals of capitalism.

Instead of reacting against the failure of capitalism to meet existential needs, workers tend to comply with the identity conferred on individual proletarians by the system. Gorz does not suggest that the proletariat becomes imbued with capitalist values but rather that the system of waged labour renders the proletariat powerless to act upon autonomously developed beliefs and ideas. Subsequently, it is unlikely that those who are fortunate enough to be part of the 'tenured aristocracy of full-time workers' will generate the potential for emancipatory change. After all, this could jeopardise their position as part of the employed elite. In Gorz's somewhat dramatic words:

> It is difficult to see how things could be otherwise in a society in which the development of productive forces has ensured that every activity is socialised and thereby fragmented, rationalised, technicised and articulated with other activities through the mediation of the state apparatus. No consumption, production, communication, transportation, illness, health care, death, learning or exchange occurs without the intervention of centralised administrations or professional agencies. The centralisation of capital has destroyed the social fabric at its roots by destroying every possibility of autonomous production, consumption and exchange, whether for individuals, groups or communities.
>
> (Gorz 1987b: 41)

THE DUALISATION OF SOCIETY: REDUCING THE SPHERE OF HETERONOMY

The main consequence of this grim scenario is that centralisation breeds a sense of powerlessness within the heteronomous sphere which also translates into a pervasive element of private existence (Habermas 1976a). The desire for social transformation is compressed by an all-encompassing necessity to engage with the centralised state to satisfy the day-to-day requirements of existence. It is from this position that the widespread desire for self-determination is bred, whilst state bureaucracy simultaneously incapacitates any ability to act on autonomous thought. The state assumes a role where it monopolises the fabric of human existence, yet this places it in a position where much more is demanded of it than it can satisfy. A similar point has been made by Frankel:

> It is quite common for both Marxists and non-Marxists to argue that the distinction between state and society is now inapplicable

> because of either the general bureaucratization of life, or the rejection of historicist divisions between private and public. . . . I would argue that it is vital to retain a clear distinction between state and civil society and between public and private sectors, despite the massive interrelation and interdependence of the latter. Only by recognising these different spheres and the different logic of their functions can we get a real sense of the level and nature of specific forms of class struggle.
>
> (Frankel 1982: 261)

Consequently Frankel advocates a 'dualisation' of society that recognises the inherent contradictions of activities performed in the private sphere and those performed in the public sphere. However, as Phillips notes, it is not sufficient to democratise and open up the private sphere, if the domain of the state remains depoliticised (Phillips 1991: 119). It is also vital that some areas of human activity such as domestic work are not ignored in the democratisation process (Kymlicka 1990: 253–7). In a similar vein, John Keane, who has been at the forefront of the analysis of democracy within socialist theory, suggests that the only way to generate socialist democracy is to delineate clearly between the state and civil society and to make the former much more accountable to the latter (Keane 1988:3). However as several thinkers have noted any attempt to further the cause of democratic socialism must recognise the many complex links between the state and civil society (Boggs 1995: 21; Laclau and Mouffe 1985). However it should be noted that the latter perspective does not actually preclude the possibility of seeking to differentiate between two separate domains.

This is a useful framework in locating Gorz as he believes that the state is a powerful tool in the domination of the population and in the transmission of the requirements of capital to communities and individuals in the subordinate domain of civil society. Within this scenario, worker autonomy has no place. To counteract this situation, Gorz believes a negation of proletarian 'class-being' has to occur so that individuals realise that their existential autonomy is shackled by their existence as proletarians. Because the proletariat is a class called into being by capitalism, it must reject that class definition to achieve class struggle based on the prioritisation of existential needs. Gorz concludes that

> Although the possibility of such an act of negation exists ontologically in Marx (as also in Sartre), it does not necessarily exist in cultural terms. Workers' capacity to recognise the difference

> between their objective position as cogs in the productive machine and their latent potential as an association of sovereign producers is not inherent in the proletarian condition.
>
> (Gorz 1987b: 44)

This pessimistic perspective recognises that workers must renounce their role as servants of capital, whilst their class-being denies the possibility of such a renunciation. Again this assertion has been subject to misinterpretation by commentators such as Meiksins Wood who states that, in Gorzian theory, 'the experience of exploitation, of antagonistic relations of production, and of the struggles surrounding them . . . play little part in the formation of working-class consciousness' (Meiksins Wood 1986: 17). This demonstrates a fundamental misconception of Gorz's thesis. Of course he recognises that proletarian consciousness is formed by exploitation, but he observes that this could lead individuals to reject class struggle through 'the antagonistic relations of production' and search instead for fulfilment through the realm of autonomy and the abolition of work. Essentially Gorz argues that the formation of proletarian existence may allow individuals to comprehend that their condition in the heteronomous sphere does not correspond with their existential needs. Nevertheless heteronomous necessity may prove to counteract any attempts individuals make to negate their existence as proletarians. In short, individuals may be extremely aware of their exploitation without having the resources or opportunities to challenge those who exploit them.

In any case, it is likely, as Gorz suggests, that the technologisation of skilled labour has led to the negation of workers' belief in their sovereign creativity. Therefore the proletariat no longer perceives itself as the creative producer but rather as another cog in the productive machine. This abolition of worker creativity is the continuation of the process that has characterised every stage of capitalist development and has reached its most pervasive era in technocapitalism (Kellner 1989: 180). At no previous level of capitalist development has the creative sovereignty of the proletariat been so undermined. The longer capitalism has reproduced itself, the more powerless and deskilled the proletariat has become. Furthermore Gorz observes that power within the factory has been nullified by the integration and internationalisation of contemporary capitalism:

> the sites of production are no longer the sites of decision making and economic power. The social process of production has become opaque, and this opacity has come to affect the work

> process in every technical unit. The final destination and even the very nature of what is produced remains unknown. Apart from management, nobody knows exactly what the things being produced are for – and in any event nobody gives a toss.
>
> (Gorz 1987b: 48)

Skilled workers have accordingly been robbed of their (relatively) autonomous position in the early development of capitalism and placed in a position where the only power they possess is a limited ability to contribute their views to managerial initiatives. To a large extent this ability is decided and defined by the managerial hierarchy – not a pluralistic amalgam of employees as gurus of post-Fordism might have us believe. Gorz argues that workers'

> margin of autonomy amounts to challenging the organisation and speed of the required operations, the number and length of breaks, the size of work groups and the length of the working day. These have become the variables upon which workers' demands are now centred. This is not to say that they are the most important variables in the eyes of the workers; they are merely the only ones that allow some room for the expression of autonomous initiatives by work groups, the only ones that make it possible to assert some power.
>
> (Gorz 1987b: 50)

Therefore, whilst Gorz is critical of contemporary trade unionism for following the above goals, his opposition arises not because these goals are invalid but because they do not constitute the most important aims of the proletariat. These problems occur because of the relative powerlessness of trade unions in the face of transnational global capitalism. Moreover technocapitalist organisation and bureaucracy renders national unions fairly impotent. For Gorz, the power structure of the modern state means that power is functional to the technocratic system rather than being held by an individual or group. In such circumstances it is difficult to identify where oppositional activity should be directed given that managers are functional administrators of the system rather than the actual holders of power. Again this substantiates Gorz's advocacy of the abolition of work because there is no inherent worker power base *within* the workplace from which to activate the class struggle necessary for emancipation. This is due to the fact that, in order to preserve their working status, workers tend to be committed to the world of paid work and consequently they become a 'replica of capital' (Keane 1988: 80).

Hyman attempts to refute Gorz's arguments by suggesting that just as capitalism has necessitated deskilling, it has also facilitated re-skilling: 'the dynamics of capitalist production relations, with their complex patterns of division of labour and hierarchies of control, have always involved elaborate trajectories of skill, deskilling, and at times, re-skilling' (Hyman 1983: 286). Hyman assumes that re-skilling can lead to a rejuvenation of workers' power which would justify traditional forms of class struggle. Whilst re-skilling can lead to a relatively greater degree of worker autonomy within the workplace (as witnessed by the deployment of post-Fordist productive methods), the final product and the means of production overall are still controlled by employers. The ultimate power of individuals – autonomy and self-determination – still remains subordinated even if a limited process of re-skilling occurs amongst workers. Gorz argues that only a new politics of time, which incorporates the abolition of work, can prioritise the self-determination of individuals outside the workplace.

This point is equally applicable to Giddens who argues that re-skilling often occurs after deskilling and that this process can lead to greater *individual and collective empowerment* (Giddens 1991: 138–9). Whilst it is true that workers have had to learn new skills as new technology has been introduced to the workplace, this does not necessarily constitute a change in the structural relationships between workers and their peers and employers. Indeed Giddens astutely introduces a disclaimer in stating that '*provided the resources of time and other requisites are available*, the individual has the possibility of a partial or more full-blown reskilling' (Giddens 1991: 139, emphasis added). Quite so, but we must recognise that the structure of work mitigates against individuals having access to meaningful 'time and other requisites'. It is precisely this situation which encourages Gorz to argue for individual development outside of the domain of work.

Hyman's criticism of Gorz is primarily based around the deskilling debate in which Braverman has been a much more influential figure (Braverman 1974). In Gorz's theory though, the deskilling debate is only one of several factors he employs to substantiate his critique of capitalism and Marxist class analysis. For Gorz, the erosion of worker autonomy is inherently linked to the transnational nature of capital which ensures that individual workers (whether skilled or not) have little power in the decision-making process and no control over their own time. In this scenario even skilled workers become mere functionaries of the global technocapitalist machine, a situation of techno-dystopia (Kellner 1989: 216).

Gorz compares the idea of functional power (the ability to use limited skills in the productive process) with personal power (the ability to use superior knowledge of the productive process to command other workers and delegate work), to demonstrate the powerlessness of modern technical workers in influencing the decision-making process due to their functional position in the multinational capitalist system. Thus even the aristocracy of skilled workers can no longer claim to hold 'workers' power'. These workers are too concerned with maintaining their elite position to become involved in the struggle to abolish work:

> despite the implicit assumptions of liberal ideology, there are no forms of power which are not, in essence, also the power to secure and delegate. Power, by definition, is an appropriation of a position of domination, and such positions are necessarily privileged and scarce. Any occupant of such a position necessarily denies it to others.
>
> (Gorz 1987b: 56)

Gorz is, therefore, suggesting that functional power incapacitates the social mobility of disenfranchised workers to find work amongst the technical elite. Because power is finite, those holding a position of influence must seek to arrest the social mobility of others, if they want to maintain their privileged position. Gorz believes that any individual seeking power must adapt to established institutions which are designed to reinforce the 'status quo' and to negate opposition by the subjugation of individual autonomy. Like Weber, Gorz argues that this results in a situation where individuals may hold *functional* power in the capitalist machine but, even if they are skilled workers, the genuine power lies in the established institutions and the regulatory bureaucracy (Weber 1976). The skilled workers are administrators of power rather than power holders themselves. Inevitably this results in a subordination of the individual to the characteristics that the establishment requires of its administrators. Hence Gorz maintains that the logic of capital becomes pervasive not only in the economic domain but in political and social circles as well:

> The logic of capital must no longer be dependent upon the personal skills and initiatives of its servants. It must prevail whatever the abilities and individual authority of its functionaries. Naturally, the same situation is true of the mechanisms of political power. They are called upon to exercise power over people without

> allowing anyone in particular to exercise it in any personal sense. The state might be defined as a mechanism of power to which every citizen is subordinated and which, at the same time, denies personal power to everyone.
>
> (Gorz 1987b: 57)

CLASS CONFLICT AND THE STATE

Gorz's conception of the nature of state power obviously has serious implications for the nature of class conflict. After all, the administrators and servants of the established institutions do not hold power themselves, they are merely functionaries of the large bureaucratic machine. Whilst their actions may, and often do, suppress individuals and their autonomy, those administrators are not directly responsible for the outcome of their activity. The nature of the bureaucratic, hierarchical system is one where responsibility can always be devolved. The administrators are as subordinate to the power of capitalist reason as those to whom they administer, although the former reap much greater material benefit and prestige from the prevailing system. The socialist project, then, should not be aimed at replacing the administrators of the established system with a different body. Their replacement would not alter the structural inequalities of the social world. Gorz believes that unless the machinery of power is challenged and undermined, it is irrelevant who the administrators are. If the proletariat were to

> take over the machinery of domination deployed by capital, they will succeed only in producing the very same kind of domination and, in their turn, become a functional bourgeoisie. A class cannot overcome another class merely by taking its place within the system of domination. All it will thereby achieve will be a permutation of office-holders and by no means a transfer of power.
>
> (Gorz 1987b: 64)

Thus, for Gorz, the aim of socialist struggle must be to do away with the machinery of domination rather than seeking to commandeer it for emancipatory ends. Nevertheless he does realise that, in socialist society, some form of functional power will remain. The goal for socialists must be to restrict functional power to the areas where it is fundamentally necessary but, more importantly, to disassociate functional power from domination. The link between the two is not intrinsic and Gorz seeks to restrict functional power to the heteronomous sphere and, in so doing, remove the autonomous sphere of self-determining individuals from the logic of capital and the consequent relations of domination.

Gorz's arguments on the nature of power in advanced capitalist societies parallel Marxist debates about power and the state, debates that have fundamental implications for the development of socialist thought. Clearly Gorz recognises that the state, encompassing social necessity and heteronomous regulation, will have a part to play in his socialist programme. He seeks an alteration to the function of the state through the abolition of the capitalist system, rather than the abolition of the state altogether. Contrary to the views of Leninist-Marxists, who associate class power with state power, Gorz does not imply that the state should be 'smashed', a problematic idea given that some Marxists such as Poulantzas have had difficulty in actually defining the state (Hoffman 1995: 21–2; Valocchi 1991: 170). He goes beyond those theorists, such as Althusser and Poulantzas, who have outlined the 'relative autonomy of the state' (Althusser and Balibar 1970; Poulantzas 1973, 1975; Clegg *et al.* 1986: 259–97; Held 1989a: 68–70; Birch 1993: 188–94). This perspective has it that the state is necessary to protect the interests of the dominant classes but at the same time the state does not in itself hold political power which resides in social classes – in this sense it can only be relatively autonomous (Held 1989a: 69).

Gorz perceives the state to be a more neutral body of institutions which are manipulated by the capitalist class to ensure the reproduction of capitalism. Thus if the capitalist system is transformed so the state would change as well. Whilst the state presently represents the interests of capital, its function would be different in a socialist society. This view stops short of the Althusserian view that once the proletariat has seized control of the state apparatus, a new socialist apparatus will be developed which in turn will 'set in motion a radical process, that of the destruction of the state' (Althusser 1994: 109). For Gorz, a socialist society will necessitate some kind of state organisation, however this does not entail a state with hierarchical, centralised powers. In short, he believes that the functions of the state are not, by definition, implicitly linked to capitalist domination either through the class composition of the administrators (R. Miliband 1973) or by providing political unity for the dominant classes as argued by Poulantzas (Meiksins Wood 1986: 28). Because Gorz distinguishes between the theory of the state and the hierarchical domination practised by the capitalist state, his work encapsulates a greater understanding of the mechanisms of power (and the possibilities for change) than the more classical Marxists above. There is a clear alignment with the perspective of Offe who believes that the state operates as a fairly unsatisfactory arbiter between capital and labour (Held 1989a: 70–3).

The idea that received most critical attention in *Farewell to the Working Class* was the notion of the neo-proletariat which Gorz outlines in the chapter entitled 'A New Historical Subject: The Non-Class of Post-Industrial Proletarians' (Gorz 1987b: 66–74). As is usual in *Farewell*, Gorz attempts to show that the Marxian concept of the skilled worker, capable of commandeering the tools of capitalist production, is defunct. He asserts that in Marxist theory 'Class unity and class consciousness were based upon the inevitability that each proletarian would, in his or her own activity, encounter the general negation of the sovereignty of all proletarians' (Gorz 1987b: 66).

Gorz argues that capitalist development has eroded this essential relationship in Marxist theory by removing power from the social activity of the worker and by bureaucratising and technologising the productive process so that work is externalised from the worker. This differs from orthodox Marxism insofar as the alienated worker no longer has revolutionary capability due to the reification of social powerlessness through constant engagement with 'passive, pre-programmed activity' (Gorz 1987b: 67). The fact that individual proletarians have no power in the workplace, beyond the limited, pragmatic power to contest management ideas, has an inevitable effect on class consciousness. As a result, workers, who have no power within the externalised workplace, find it difficult to recognise for themselves a role as part of a unitary, subordinated class. Similarly Keane notes that 'Under pressure from quickening technical change, the workers' movement in particular loses whatever unity it once enjoyed. Not the capitalist system, but the "working class" is disintegrating' (Keane 1988: 80).

In essence, Gorz argues that class conflict is reliant upon individual workers perceiving their class identity as a means of generating the power to overcome the dominant class. If no power resides in the workplace, then class identification is unlikely. For Gorz, there is an implicit difference between class identification, in which individuals recognise opposition between the interests of employers and the exploited, and revolutionary class consciousness. Giddens has highlighted the fundamental difference between these two ideas which many followers of Marx have failed to recognise:

> Marx does not discriminate between class consciousness as perception of conflict of interest, and . . . *revolutionary class consciousness*. In contrast to conflict consciousness, this involves *a*

> *recognition of the possibility of an overall reorganisation in the institutional mediation of power and a belief that such a reorganisation can be brought about through class action.*
>
> (Giddens 1982: 164, original emphasis)

It follows that the Left must renounce the traditional goals of liberation within the workplace and seek to generate emancipatory ideas outside this alienating, heteronomous realm. In short, the impossibility of revolutionary class consciousness developing within the workplace requires reduced working hours:

> The point now is to free oneself from work by rejecting its nature, content, necessity and modalities. But to reject work is also to reject the traditional strategy and organisational forms of the working-class movement. It is no longer a question of winning power as a worker, but of winning the power no longer to function as a worker.
>
> (Gorz 1987b: 68)

Gorz reaches these conclusions by criticising the 'myth of collective appropriation' and the transcendent nature of the industrial proletariat that still remain paramount in traditional Marxian discourse. From this position, he suggests that the industrial working class has been superseded by the neo-proletariat. He contends that the proletariat, in the Marxist sense, has been defunct as a revolutionary agent for a lengthy period. The 'non-class of non-workers', on the other hand, has developed, encapsulating some features of the Marxian proletariat. Unlike the industrial proletariat, though, the neo-proletariat is not fundamentally necessary to capital and the process of industrial production. Because it is unnecessary to capitalist development, the neo-proletariat has been able to avoid the pitfalls of the proletariat in that its existence is antithetical to capitalist technologism and economic reason.

However, as Martell suggests, the exclusion of these people from the world of work may 'make them more committed than anyone else to accumulation. Material values may well be uppermost in their minds' (Martell 1994: 193). This rather speculative comment is rejected by Gorz who argues, equally conjecturally, that the externalisation of the 'non-class of non-workers' from the primary industry of capitalism has allowed it to avoid being dominated by the logic of capital. However he also suggests the logic of capital is distributed throughout capitalist society – not just at work. If this is the case then the neo-proletariat is just as likely as the proletariat to be imbued with capitalist values.

Martell continues to oppose Gorz's proclamations about the neo-proletariat with hypothetical statements to the extent that he suggests that the neo-proletariat may be more desirous of a place in the industrial system because they are alienated from it. Ironically Martell and Gorz concur that the neo-proletariat 'seem unlikely contenders for the vanguard of a future society' (Martell 1994: 193), although Gorz hopes that they may concretise their revolutionary potential as they seem to him to be the only possible agents of change.

THE NEO-PROLETARIAT

For Gorz, the membership of the neo-proletariat includes

> all those who have been expelled from production by the abolition of work, or whose capabilities are under-employed as a result of the industrialisation (in this case, the automation and computerisation) of intellectual work. It includes all the supernumeraries of present-day social production, who are potentially or actually employed, whether permanently or temporarily, partially or completely. It results from the decomposition of the old society based upon the dignity, value, social utility and desirability of work.
>
> (Gorz 1987b: 68)

It is significant that Gorz's definition incorporates such a large section of society. Conversely though, it should be emphasised that the industrial proletariat encompasses such a small portion of society that it has little in common (in traditional terms) with the rest of the 'working class'. Gorz's argument is based on his recognition that the neo-proletariat does not perceive work as a meaningful creative activity, but as an external reality which must be performed in order to earn a meagre wage to survive. Work is not undertaken because it corresponds to autonomous wants, or existential needs, or because the end product is desirable and necessary, but because work must be endured in order to survive. The drift of employment from primary to tertiary activities only accelerates this large-scale disillusionment with work. In this situation individuals tend not to define themselves in regard to their work. Keane has outlined the ambivalent character of the neo-proletariat:

> Although the non-class of non-workers is a fragmented and composite group, it is generally suspicious of established institutions (such as corporations, trade unions, political parties and state

> institutions). It experiences the whole of the existing capitalist system as 'something external, akin to a spectacle or show'. It has no single god or religion and, in definite contrast to the workers movement of the nineteenth century, has no grandiose sense of historical mission.
>
> (Keane 1988: 82)

Gorz's analysis of the neo-proletariat has major implications for the nature of socialist opposition to the contemporary system and class analysis. A lack of identification with work leads to a decrease in revolutionary class consciousness which was displayed, in Marx's time, through the powerful role the industrial proletariat played in the process of capitalist production. This class consciousness must, in Gorz's view, be revitalised by an alliance of the most disenfranchised sectors of society (the unemployed, the underemployed, and the temporarily employed), the groups in society which (to his mind) identify least with the concept of work. Furthermore, even those individuals who remain in the aristocracy of tenured, skilled workers have their work externally imposed upon them through the globalised, technocratic and bureaucratic division of labour. If these workers were to lose their place in the 'aristocracy', they would become potential recruits for Gorz's neo-proletariat because even they find little fulfilment or creativity in technocapitalism. In Gorz's words:

> Work . . . does not belong to the individuals who perform it, nor can it be termed their own activity. It belongs to the machinery of social production, is allocated and programmed by it, remaining external to the individuals upon whom it is imposed. Instead of being the worker's mode of insertion into a system of universal cooperation, work is now the mode of subordination to the machinery of universal domination.
>
> (Gorz 1987b: 71)

Contrary to Marx's plan, technologism has not facilitated the breakdown of capitalism, but rather it highlights the increased inability of the Left to combat hierarchical domination and the sterility of the majority of individuals in the face of ongoing capitalist crises. The continuing process of capitalist reproduction points to increasing technical domination and an even stronger emphasis on tertiarisation as the means to create jobs. As Gorz notes, there is an increased tendency to over-produce unnecessary goods and services which create 'whole areas of economic life [which] have the sole function of "providing work", or of producing for the sake of keeping people working' (Gorz 1987b: 71). This would merely reinforce the productivist ideology which proposes that paid labour is a fundamental prerequisite of the social system. Gorz believes that only if individuals seek to replace the logic of capital and the technical reason of productivism can emancipatory action take place:

> The realm of freedom can never arise out of material processes; it can only be established by a constitutive act which, aware of its free subjectivity, asserts itself as an absolute end in itself within each individual. Only the non-class of non-producers is capable of such an act. For it alone embodies what lies beyond productivism: the rejection of the accumulation ethic and the dissolution of all classes.
>
> (Gorz 1987b: 74)

Farewell to the Working Class, then, is an attempt to develop a theory of class conflict which comprehends the totality of social relationships which are fashioned by the economic reason of contemporary capitalism. This complex task is a break from much socialist theory which concentrates on what Meiksins calls 'the boundary question' concerning class definition (Meiksins 1986). Influential in these discussions is the work of theorists such as Wright for whom class composition is paramount and Poulantzas whose theory of the state is wholly reliant on class power (Wright 1991; Poulantzas 1975). Gorz circumnavigates these arguments and, in so doing, has left himself open to criticisms such as that developed by Hyman who insists that Gorz's 'account of the transition from occupationally conscious artisan to alienated mass worker is absurdly simplistic' (Hyman 1983: 286). Whilst this comment is not without foundation, this should not detract from the overall thrust of the Gorzian argument. His essay is primarily a critique of traditional Marxian class analysis and the reproductive power of capitalist reason rather than a socio-historic account of class relations. However Gorz's subsequent work would be more systematic in the depiction of changes in worker consciousness (Gorz 1989a).

Furthermore Gorz's discussion of the neo-proletariat is designed to encourage debate on the Left and to highlight the sterility of orthodox, class analysis in contemporary conditions. Nevertheless, Gorz's theory is not based upon the desire to wish away class conflict as Meiksins Wood would have us believe: 'What is significant about Gorz's argument is that, like other alternative visions, his rejection of the working class as the agent of transformation depends upon wishing away the need for transformation, the need to destroy capitalism' (Meiksins Wood 1986: 17–18).

On the contrary, Gorz provides a radical theory that implicitly redefines class conflict but negates the traditional working class as the agent of revolutionary change. The industrial proletariat is no longer necessary for capitalist survival because of the development of the technical division of labour. Nevertheless there does remain a collection of subordinate and exploited individuals which, according to Gorz, is still growing in number. These individuals, who were once the backbone of capitalist industry, do not play an important part in the labour process. Whilst class struggle is both justified and necessary, it must tackle the multiplicity of forms of capitalist domination through a variety of channels to illustrate the ideological, cultural, existential, and social power of capitalism. This assertion of the diversity of interest and membership in the non-class of non-workers refutes Keane's uncharacteristically erroneous claim that Gorz envisages the neo-proletariat as a 'single revolutionary group' in the Marxian tradition:

> Gorz . . . falls back upon the very questionable (Marxian) idea of a single revolutionary group which is presently passing through a vale of tears en route to a mountain paradise of freedom. In view of the highly differentiated character of temporary workers and the permanently unemployed, Gorz's belief that there is presently developing a single revolutionary subject must be rejected.
>
> (Keane 1988: 89)

At no stage did Gorz state that the neo-proletariat is becoming a 'single revolutionary subject'. He defines it as a group that no longer relates to the work ethic and is therefore opposed to the logic of capitalism. This does not mean that Gorz believes that the neo-proletariat will achieve *revolutionary* class consciousness; in the present situation, this development is most unlikely, although Gorz hopes that new social movements can encourage more radical debate in the public sphere. Nevertheless the neo-proletariat is unlikely to assume the prominent position in Gorz's theory that the industrial working class held in Marx's work. Indeed, after *Farewell to the Working Class*, Gorz rarely alludes to the neo-proletariat because the notion was so misunderstood by political commentators:

> What I was describing was a cultural change, not a political movement. I expressly insisted that the Marxist notion of a 'historical subject' has to be given up. I emphasised that there is

> no transcendent meaning of history to which to sacrifice ourselves and that, if history is to have a meaning, there must be a rupture with the prevailing productivist rationality – a rupture which cannot be brought about by any of the classes functional to capitalism, but only by their decomposition.
>
> (Gorz 1989d: 30)

The neo-proletariat, as Gorz consistently argues, is not presently a revolutionary agent. Nevertheless its disenfranchisement from all forms of power gives it the potential to become revolutionary, albeit not as an historical subject. What Gorz attempted in this original piece of work was to illuminate the problems of traditional Marxian class analysis in the current social world, in particular the myth of collective appropriation. As such, although *Farewell to the Working Class* deserves its reputation as his most controversial and heretical work, it should not be regarded as the most sophisticated theoretical exposition of Gorz's thought (Kenny and Little 1995: 291). Despite this, the impact *Farewell* has made is impressive given the limited task Gorz set himself:

> This book is an essay in the fullest sense of the word. It is an attempt to outline the perspectives and the themes around which a Left endowed with a future rather than burdened with nostalgia might re-emerge. It makes no pretence to have answered all the questions it raises.
>
> (Gorz 1987b: 1)

5

ECONOMIC REASON, FULL EMPLOYMENT AND THE IDEOLOGY OF WORK

With the publication of *Critique of Economic Reason* in 1988 (Gorz 1989a), Gorz has given theoretical substantiation to his concrete aim of reducing working hours by tracing the historical origins of the modern labour process. This book not only concretises the theoretical stance of Gorz's earlier work, but also lends an element of historical contextualisation to his innovative proposals. Characteristically Gorz's *Critique*, and the radical measures he proposes, are based upon an analysis of the condition of capitalism. From this foundation he promotes his belief in the abolition of employment as the means to achieve social emancipation.

THE IDEOLOGY OF WORK AND ECONOMIC GROWTH

Gorz argues that the technical division of labour and the finite nature of capitalist growth preclude the maintenance of full employment as the condition of normality. He observes that the desirability of full employment is being increasingly questioned by political commentators and society as a whole. As such Keane has observed that Gorz's writings challenge 'the orthodox Keynesian and neo-conservative assumption that full-time paid labour is a necessary condition of a "free" civil society' (Keane 1988: 79). Keane welcomes this perspective because less work in the arena of civil society means more free time to engage in more diverse activities. He contrasts Gorz's work with that of Dahl and Marshall but he overlooks some areas of agreement between the latter and Gorz (Dahl 1985; Marshall 1963). For instance he cites Marshall's view that 'the basic civil right is the right to work' (Keane 1988: 99), a view with which Gorz would concur except that he also accepts that there is a right not to work for capitalist employers as well. The crucial point is that promoting the right to work is not the same thing as promoting full employment – there is no regulation that the right to work entails everyone working at once for forty hours a week throughout their working lifetime.

Within the arena of political decision making though, in Britain at least, the search for full employment is an unquestioned orthodoxy (Commission on Social Justice 1994: 153–7). On the Left, little alternative is offered to neo-Keynesian discourse on this question despite widespread acceptance that this perspective is outdated (Keane and Owens 1984: 144–59). Few in Britain, with the notable exception of theorists such as Keane and Robertson (Robertson 1985; Cahill 1995: 294–309), have accepted that full employment, to the degree experienced in the 1950s and 1960s, is unattainable (and even that should be termed 'full male employment'). In Europe though, political thinkers, such as Gorz, have realised that there is a limit to the employment that can be created by capitalist growth. This theory is becoming increasingly attractive to many on the European Left who recognise that the number of people who can claim full-time paid employment is decreasing (Offe and Heinze 1992: 216–17; Coenen and Leisink 1993).

In accordance with Gorz, Offe and Heinze also criticise the benefit of full employment and justify their position with a wealth of empirical evidence. Nevertheless it is evident that social democratic political parties and trade unions appear to underemphasise qualitative arguments for a reevaluation of employment in capitalist societies, and instead continue to prioritise the quantitative achievement of full employment. Hence they ignore arguments like that of Keane who observes that 'restoring full employment through accelerating quantitative economic growth is no longer a realistic goal' (Keane 1988: 80). This raises considerable problems for trade unions given that their traditional reason for existence is to defend the rights of workers *and their work*. Consequently Coenen notes that 'the realization of the trade union's traditional objectives clashes with the reconsideration and reformulation of these objectives, and the trade union seems . . . to be little disposed as yet to overcome this deadlock' (Coenen 1993: 174).

THE FRAGMENTATION OF WORK AND THE RATIONALISATION OF THE PRIVATE SPHERE

In *Critique of Economic Reason* Gorz attempts to analyse work in capitalist societies by studying not only the heteronomous activity carried out in the public sphere, but also work performed in the private sphere for the satisfaction of individual needs, although, as many commentators have noted, this did not appear in his earlier work (Frankel 1987; Keane 1988; Sayers 1988). Gorz refers to this latter form of domestic work as 'work-for-oneself'. He realises that advanced capitalist societies can be identified by the way in which they have attempted to create an area of new growth for employment through the rationalisation and commodification of the domestic realm. Thus individuals can purchase the services of other individuals to perform their most menial or domestic tasks for them. Gorz contends that the principles of efficiency, productivity and performance should not dictate our personal behaviour in the private sphere, that is, work-for-oneself. His argument implies that the dictates of economic rationality, which attempt to save time and maximise profitability, do not provide conducive conditions for the satisfaction of domestic, individual needs. Yet these are the very principles that are beginning to govern the domestic sphere in advanced capitalism, whilst ideologists of growth have placed much emphasis on the service sector as the provider of employment that is being lost in manufacturing industries. Rather than merely noting the expansion of the service sector, Gorz questions the rationality behind the invasion of economic reason into the private sphere.

The main consequence of the capitalist attempt to colonise the domestic realm is that the self-governed area of work-for-oneself becomes open to the functionality and rationality that governs the ideology of growth and profit. Hence the space that previously constituted the 'free' time of marginalised individuals is now colonised by the agents of economic reason. In this way economic rationality is able to confer its message on individuals not directly involved with the economic and productive process – an important feature in the reproduction of capitalism when there is high unemployment.

Gorz realises, though, that individuals who are still working will not want to give up the power and prestige which their employment confers upon them. Similarly Gershuny points out that the increased competition for top technical jobs has led to 'a quite new form of social polarisation: between the money-rich / time-poor and the time-rich / money-poor' (Gershuny 1995: 43). Gershuny offers a solution in which working time is more fairly redistributed – a work-based theory which suggests that there is plenty of work around to redistribute. Gorz, on the contrary, argues that this abundance of work does not (and indeed should not) exist. In this situation individuals in full-time employment will always seek to maximise their leisure time. The easiest option for those individuals is to employ other people to perform their domestic labour, and therefore create their own leisure time. In Gorz's words the employed elite will

> purchase services and appliances which will allow them to save time even when producing these services and appliances takes more time than the average person will save by using them. They will thus foster the development, across the whole of society, of activities which have no economic rationality . . . and which only serve the private interests of the members of the professional elite, who are able to purchase time more cheaply than they can sell it personally.
>
> (Gorz 1989a: 5)

The arguments for full employment such as those which dominate socialist political discourse in the UK are ultimately flawed if they use criteria for their analysis which support the creation of jobs in the private domain. Not only does this domestic labour have no economic rationality but also it is dehumanising because it is underpaid, insecure, predominantly temporary and non-unionised. Ultimately this work prescribes the individual as a servant to those members of the professional elite who employ her/him (frequently it is women rather than men who have to undertake jobs such as cleaning). The professional elite could perform these tasks which require little personal skill or knowledge, but it is not in their interests to do so. This constitutes a division of society which marginalises many individuals and subjects them to the personal follies of the economically superior elite for whom workers perform their mundane and routine tasks. In short, Gorz argues that a sub-system is being created in which 'the economic elite will buy leisure time by getting their own personal tasks done for them, at low cost, by other people' (Gorz 1989a: 5).

Gorz contends that a 'servile class' has been created through the automation of the productive process and the commodification of the domestic realm. Furthermore, this servility is positively promoted in the political arena as parties continue to advocate the desirability of full employment. Advocates of full employment believe that any job is superior to no job regardless of how dehumanising the activity which must be performed. Whilst this may satisfy the quantitative demands of those who seek full employment or produce government unemployment statistics, Offe and Heinze argue that individual workers fail to find any creative satisfaction whatsoever in such a system:

> The gap between the imagined normality of employment and a steady job and the experienced reality of unemployment, under employment and precarious or irregular employment is widening, resulting in a growing contingent of marginalized, discouraged and powerless sections of the population, who are often called the 'new underclass'.
>
> (Offe and Heinze 1992: 2)

Like Gorz, Offe and Heinze note that this subservient work carried out in the domestic sphere disaffects individuals with the dominant system. Gorz has always viewed this disaffection as a source of emancipatory potential rather than as a liberatory force. However he realised that the imminent downfall of capitalism, predicted by Marx and his orthodox followers throughout the twentieth century, was premised upon a serious underestimation of the ability of capitalism to adapt its programme to colonise new areas for exploitation. This ongoing process finds its modern manifestation in the industrialisation and rationalisation of domesticity and leisure.

Gorz's analysis of the colonisation of the domestic sphere of work has led him to engage with the debate over payment for housework. Because he rejects the rationalisation of domestic work, some thinkers, such as Sayers and Keane, have suggested that Gorz's conclusions are 'implicitly sexist' because he allegedly does not differentiate between paid and unpaid work (Keane 1988: 81; Sayers 1991). Against this view Gorz has actively criticised domestic rationalisation as a central tenet of social reproduction because employers use this functionality to promote the idea that full-time paid employment is a fundamental necessity for society. Given that domestic labour is still primarily performed by women, the desire to submit it to economic reason would not necessarily emancipate those who perform it. The character of domestic labour is unique insofar as it is undoubtedly necessary but yet has remained economically unquantifiable. This is so because this work is not performed for economic ends but neither is it autonomous. It is a fundamental necessity, which is why Gorz categorised it as work-for-oneself. Rather than wishing to maintain the repression of women in the domestic realm therefore, Gorz advocates a social income that would be paid to all individuals who perform necessary heteronomous work on the macro-social level.

A useful example to employ in this discussion concerns childcare. The belief that childcare should be rationalised and rewarded through payment implies that the development of children can be quantified and submitted to the logic of competition, growth, and profit. Not only are these values inappropriate for the care of children but also this ethos contradicts the very nature of the development of children who, as Bowring and Connell point out, refuse 'to submit to a predictable programme of rationality, discipline, calculated obedience and perfected routine' (Bowring and Connell 1992: 4).

Gorz believes that payment for domestic labour would not involve any greater liberation for its predominantly female workers. Indeed he points to the fact that domestic tasks are already being commodified as proof in itself that this would not achieve any emancipatory aim for the women involved in the drudgery of domestic work. After all it is not surprising that in firms which specialise in domestic cleaning most of the staff are female because domestic work is wrongly perceived as women's work. Gorz reasons that instead of moving towards the incorporation of non-economic activity into the rationalised sector it is important to reverse this trend.

Undoubtedly payment for housework could lead to greater financial independence for women but this is not synonymous with emancipation. Whilst realising that participation and success in the labour market can demonstrate equal ability as males and economic independence, activity in this patriarchal arena should not be regarded as the achievement of any greater degree of emancipation. A reversal of this trend to withdraw from the industrialisation and rationalisation of work-for-oneself and the sharing of domestic tasks between men and women would enable greater space and time for creative, autonomous activities for everyone. In short, Gorz's argument is that the values of productivism are not conducive to work-for-oneself, which is not to say that domestic work is not productive in so far as it provides the temporal foundation for spending long hours working in the public sphere (Oakley 1984: 197).

The struggle to achieve payment for housework also ignores the social consequences of commodifying domestic work. Because domestic labour is viewed by many as 'women's work', the payment for this work would further ensure the restricted access of women to the public sphere. Payment for housework could accentuate the belief that 'the woman's place is in the home', resulting in the cordoning off of women in the private sphere of domesticity. Simultaneously this would ensure the prevalence of men and patriarchal conditions in civil society. Hence Gorz asserts that the domestic tasks now predominantly performed by women must be shared by men and be maintained externally from the productive process and the economic rationality promoted therein.

Certainly these menial tasks, which are often unpleasant, must be equally distributed within any partnership but they should not come under the auspices of economic reason.

In his historical analysis of the meaning of work, Gorz begins by suggesting that the conception of work as we know it is a purely modern phenomenon. He observes that although we may characterise domestic activity as work, it is performed in a fundamentally different manner than productive work in the public sphere. This is because productive work in the public sphere is allocated an economic value. The productive work in which individuals engage confers upon them an identity and value, for example as a doctor, a road sweeper or a carpenter. In short then, the modern productive process confers an economic and social value upon individuals working in the public sphere. As Oakley argues this value is not conferred on housewives despite the immense worth of their domestic work – the important point for Gorz is that conferring an economic value on this work would not be emancipatory in itself (Oakley 1984).

Gorz's advocacy of the division of society into separate heteronomous and autonomous realms has aroused much scepticism because critics believe there cannot be a binary division of society through which complex human activity can be organised. Critics argue that there would appear to be some, often ambiguous, overlap between heteronomy and autonomy which Gorz has not clarified. For instance, Keane suggests that Gorz's 'silence about unpaid forms of work also tempts him into highly romanticized accounts of life outside the sphere of the labour market' (Keane 1988: 81).

Gorz attempted to redress this omission in his early theory by using the concept of 'work-for-oneself' in *Critique of Economic Reason.* He outlined the area of domestic labour which was necessary but which was not externally dictated like heteronomous work. Thus Gorz suggested that 'work-for-oneself' was micro-social activity. Sayers, on the other hand, has argued that Gorz's idea of 'work-for-oneself' glorified an ascesis of domestic drudgery. This runs contrary to Gorz's argument which advocates 'work-for-oneself' precisely because much of the work is somewhat unpleasant and should not therefore be the means through which others earn their living.

Sayers' criticism of Gorz's theory of the dualisation of society, which he initially outlined in *Farewell to the Working Class* (1980), had some validity. In the *Critique* though, Gorz's argument becomes more sophisticated. Not only does he clarify the micro-social area of 'work-for-oneself', which is necessary without being heteronomous, but he believes that creativity and individual satisfaction can be reintroduced to production, as long as that production is small-scale and communitarian. This is a point which eludes Kellner when he argues that

> the all too sharp dichotomy between the 'realm of necessity' – that is, socially necessary labour – and the 'realm of freedom' – that is, autonomous activity outside the realm of labour – precludes the possibility of more autonomy and self-realisation *within* labour, and thus de-emphasises the importance of new work relations and organization.
>
> (Kellner 1989: 264, original emphasis)

Kellner ignores the communitarian ethos which is prevalent in Gorz's theory. Gorz believes that this ethos constitutes the means by which satisfaction can be generated for workers who perform in convivial conditions and consume the goods which they produce. What Gorz and Kellner both realise is that work within the relations of the technical division of labour precludes the self-realisation of individual workers. Nevertheless this does not mean that Gorz's prioritisation of autonomy necessarily indicates that community and self-production will not satisfy the workers involved. Indeed small-scale, communitarian production increases the likelihood that workers will be able to exercise a degree of self-determination in their work.

In the *Critique*, Gorz attempts to give historical justification to his call for the abolition of capitalist labour and full employment. Thus he seeks to demonstrate that work performed in the private sphere was the social norm in pre-capitalist societies, and, consequently, that the public sphere was the arena of social, political and cultural debate and action. He believes that even during the early industrial period, labour was primarily conducted in the private sphere. He uses the example of the early textile industry in the form of cottage industry which, although beginning to undergo the changes dictated by economic rationality, was still small-scale and personal. It was in the interests of individuals involved to minimise production costs and make their product as cost efficiently as possible. For Gorz, change came about when merchants began to dictate the productive spending patterns of small-scale industry:

> the interest for the capitalist merchants in rationalising weaving, controlling its cost and making it possible to calculate and predict this cost with precision, was by no means a new development. What was new was that at a particular point in time the

> merchants attempted to impose it on their suppliers, whereas they had previously refrained from doing so.
>
> (Gorz 1989a: 18)

Subsequently, Gorz suggests that this rationalisation of small-scale industry created a situation in which workers underwent a motivation crisis. The grounds of this motivational crisis were laid out in the nineteenth century when labour itself was no longer performed in the interests of personal satisfaction and consumption. Rather labour was colonised by economic reason which not only made these rationalised activities more organised and methodical but also ensured a shift in the meaning of 'labour'. In the words of Gorz, 'productive activity was cut off from its meaning, its motivations and its object and became simply a means of earning a wage' (Gorz 1989a: 21). Work was transformed from the arena of private needs and motivations into the essence of public sphere activity. Where individuals had come together to be creative in the interests of themselves and their communities, a new type of worker was developing. Gorz argued that this worker was the worker/consumer who did not consume what he or she produced and whose sole reason for labouring was subsistence, that is, to ensure the financial rewards necessary for survival. Furthermore the goods available for consumption were not autonomously defined but were determined by the capitalist owners:

> The economic rationalisation of work will thus sweep away the ancient idea of freedom and existential autonomy. It produces individuals who, being alienated in their work, will, necessarily, be alienated in their consumption as well and, eventually in their needs. Since there is no limit to the quantity of money that can be earned and spent, there is no limit to the needs that money allows them to have or to the need for money itself.
>
> (Gorz 1989a: 22)

These developments, which began in the late eighteenth century, motivated Marx's critique of the labour process under capitalism. This process, according to Marx, was proving extremely efficient in its maximisation of social wealth and profit but was detrimental to human species-being. Thus, whilst the new methods of production were economically beneficial to the owner of the means of production, they were fettering human, sovereign creativity and manipulating this human essence in the interest of profit. Despite this form of labour being anathema to the Marxist ideal, Marx claimed that this social labour was capable of creating the universal proletariat that was necessary for the transformation to communism. Once labour was brought into the public sphere and individuality was removed, individuals would find it easier to unite and throw off their fetters. Thus little attention was paid to the constraints on creativity and the colonisation of time that were being instituted by this new social labour.

The initial problem with the orthodox Marxist position, according to Gorz, is that the intrusion of labour into the public sphere is seen as a development in the long-term revolutionary goal. Despite this, Marx realised that there was little space within the realm of social labour for workers to recognise consciously their emancipatory potential. This being the case, a vanguard or an enlightened elite would be necessary to bring the workers to understand their universality. In the words of Gorz, describing the work of Marx in the 1840s:

> Marx is seeking to show that there is no need for communism to pre-exist in the consciousness of the proletariat for it to be realised; it is 'the movement of the real' itself. Marx does not as yet base the necessity of its advent on the internal contradictions of capitalism's development, as he was to do after 1856; he bases it on the fact that, for the proletariat, the revolution is – or will become – essential for their survival. The 'absolute inexorable necessity' in which they find themselves, of having to destroy the old society merely 'to ensure their continuing existence', serves in a sense as a transcendental guarantee of their ultimate victory.
>
> (Gorz 1989a: 25)

In opposition to Marx, Gorz argues that autonomy and individuality, which had previously characterised work in the private sphere, cannot be reinstated by positing a Marxist antithesis to economic reason. 'True' rationality will come about only through voluntary cooperation between individuals engaged in personal activity for the benefit of the community as a whole. Valid as this scenario may be, it requires a complete redefinition of work as a communal activity performed not as a subjective task but as a voluntary contribution to the community in the interests of satisfying individual needs. In essence this redefinition of the role of work involves regarding it as a private activity in the public interest. It is debatable whether such a vision could be achieved without some degree of centralised bureaucracy – a problem that Gorz faces in his discussion of the sphere of necessity (Gorz 1987b: 105–19).

However Gorz does not address the actual structure of his democratic socialism and the methods through which the state would be made accountable to local communities. Some on the Left, such as Hirst, have proffered solutions to this problem by offering the prospect of associational democracy as a means of dispersing state power (Hirst 1993; Mouffe 1993: 98–9). Hirst advocates the location of democratic powers in a variety of community associations in civil society which would render the state as an overseer of associations in a system of pluralistic representative democracy. This system is promoted as a positive step for the state which could concentrate on good government if it was freed from service provision. Hirst is aware that associationalism necessitates a higher degree of common morality and tolerance than is the case in contemporary capitalism (Hirst 1993: 118–19). This framework does provide a positive path for Gorzian policies, although Gorz's advocacy of reduced working hours would allow for greater individual participation and an even more reduced role for the state. For Gorz, 'true' rationality can be achieved only by redetermining the role of labour in the social interest, and it must be coupled by a radical diminution of the scale of advanced capitalist society. Only through a return to small-scale communities can the public sphere be rescued from the economic reason with which it has been saturated since the advent of capitalism.

Classical Marxism, on the other hand, does not require a return to small-scale society, although the state was supposed to wither away. Soviet-style communism demonstrated how difficult this process would be because it was reliant on the industrial, productivist ethic which entails a bureaucratic system partnered by a centralised state. Hoffman argues that Marxist theory on the state ultimately results in 'despotism' because of a 'schizoid malady' which results from 'an absolutist view of history; a monopolistic view of the proletariat, and a dismissive view of morality' (Hoffman 1995: 144). The deliverance of individuals from their unconscious frame of mind in the realm of necessity by a vanguard elite suggests some maintenance of hierarchical power relations. These implications of the Marxist-Leninist agenda can be avoided only by abandoning productivism and seeking to relocate work in the private sphere without diminishing its social quality. By seeking to retain the productivist utopia, orthodox Marxism is embodied by an ascesis of constraint and control. Gorz reasons that, on the existential level:

> Each individual must be able, by and in her or his work, to identify personally with the undivided totality of all (with the collective worker) and find his or her total personal fulfilment in that identification. All in all, a thoroughgoing socialisation . . . of personal

> existence must correspond to the complete personalisation of social existence, the whole of society possessing in each member its conscious subject and each member recognising in it her or his unification with all the others.
>
> (Gorz 1989a: 27)

An inherent feature of the ideology of work that still informs much socialist debate is the view that work itself is the primary activity conducted in the public sphere. This being the case, Marxism will not overcome its elements of hierarchy and authority unless it re-examines the government of the public sphere by the realm of necessity. It would appear then, to follow the thinking of Gorz, that Marxism can be rescued only by abandoning its commitment to the ideology of work and developing a politics of free time. Keane has outlined the importance of this critique of productivism to Gorz's theory:

> A politics of free time, Gorz argues, must aim at achieving a democratic civil society freed from the dominating imperatives of employment – in other words, developing a sphere of life regulated not by state institutions and/or by capitalist corporations and trade unions, but by networks of self-governing, small-scale institutions . . . whose individual members consider each other as equals and exercise their unique productive powers in their own free time.
>
> (Keane 1988: 83)

Evidently Gorz's programme would require complex organisation and the evaluation of the different tasks that individuals perform in society. This evaluation would be based upon the material and existential needs of individuals, communities and societies. Nevertheless he distinguishes this principle of social organisation from the regulation of the heteronomous sphere in advanced capitalist societies – that is, the rationalisation of tasks through economic reason.

Gorz argues that 'needs', such as excessive consumption, which are identifiable in advanced capitalist societies, do not correspond to any material aims apart from profit and growth. Furthermore, because of the unpredictable nature of the market, he argues that advanced capitalist societies require a large degree of bureaucratic regulation and hetero-organisation. The problem which Gorz identifies in the 1980s is that the industrialised world, which was characterised by the government of manufacturing industry by commodity relations, has expanded to incorporate the commodification and rationalisation of the tertiary sector (tertiarisation). Whilst fewer jobs are being created in manufacturing industry, this imbalance is redressed by unprecedented growth in the service sector. For Gorz, this signals the colonisation of private activity by the logic of economic reason.

THE EFFECTS OF TECHNICAL CHANGE

Gorz believes that whilst the sector of society governed by these regulations may have changed, the regulations governing society themselves have remained unaltered. This differentiates Gorz from post-Fordist theorists with whom he has sometimes been associated. Using the definition of post-Fordism given by Hall *et al.*, 'it [post-Fordism] signifies a qualitative shift in the organization of production and consumption, *as well as a break in the mode of regulation*' (Hall *et al.* 1992: 190, emphasis added), it is clear that Gorz cannot be regarded as a post-Fordist. However there is an unfortunate tendency in the Fordist/post-Fordist debate to locate all those such as Gorz, who argue that we must move beyond the discourse of Fordism, into the post-Fordist category. An example of such one-dimensional thinking comes from Byrne:

> Although not explicitly part of the post-Fordist 'game-show', Gorz . . . is typical of the general line. Essentially capitalism (and hence by implication capitalists) have got it all sorted out. They have found a way of defeating the industrial proletariat and proceeding with the continued growth of the system. The usual refuges for those who come to this conclusion are either in cultural journalism or dark-green, fundamentalist ecology.
>
> (Byrne 1994: 151)

Apart from being an ill-informed misrepresentation of Gorz's argument in *Farewell to the Working Class*, this passage demonstrates the limited attraction of the whole post-Fordist debate. We can accept that the arguments about the nature of work must move beyond tired Fordist categories, but this does not mean that the quantitative Fordist logic of production, growth and profit has disappeared. It has merely reappeared, repackaged by economic reason into the discourse of tertiarisation and the ideology of work. In short, although Gorz identifies the process of tertiarisation, he does not believe that the regulations governing social activity have changed *qualitatively*.

Rather than believing that the concentration on the tertiary sector characterises a fundamental change in the relations of capitalism and social reproduction, Gorz contends that this 'tertiarisation' represents a continuation of the capitalist logic of growth which does not encompass any greater degree of emancipatory potential. Current trends suggest that in the long run the development of the information age will shed more jobs than it creates if current capitalist rationality is the guiding force (Rifkin 1995: 17–20).

Gorz also argues that developments in the labour process in the West have been mirrored by the productive practices under state socialism in Eastern Europe and socialist societies throughout the world. In these cases, the ideology of work has been put forward as the means to a fulfilling existence through which individuals could realise a convergence of public and private interests. Gorz argues that this convergence is impossible and that it requires individuals to 'enjoy' their work ascetically regardless of the mundaneness of the tasks performed. In state socialist societies the state and the party have tended to maintain a productivist ethic which Gorz believes has no place in radical socialist critique:

> Soviet-style socialism thus offered a sort of caricatural magnification of the basic features of capitalism. Pursuing accumulation and economic growth as its principal goals, it attempted to rationalise this pursuit by replacing spontaneous hetero-regulation by the market with methodically programmed centralised hetero-regulation of the economy as a whole.
>
> (Gorz 1989a: 42)

This organisation could never succeed in realising the Marxist ideal precisely because the rigorous planning required a high level of functional integration of its workers. Consequently these workers were not coming together in a spirit of cooperation or solidarity. They were constituted as workers by their function in the machine and, as such, found themselves alienated from genuine social integration (Marcuse 1957: 183; P. Thompson 1984a: 62). In short, the void between public and private interest was accentuated rather than diminished. A similar rationality governed the industrial practices of state socialist societies as in capitalist nations. For Gorz, the necessary functional integration of workers resulted in social disintegration.

Gorz goes on to demonstrate why he believes that the technical division of labour in capitalist societies precludes the development of small-scale social organisation. The manufacture and use of fixed capital has ensured that individuals are alienated through their dependence on technical machinery which does not allow for self-expression and creativity. The sheer scale of modern technology, Gorz argues, can never be fully grasped by a single individual and this has led to increased specialisation amongst workers and the creation of experts and expert systems. Thus the skilled elite involved in technical, industrial employment have been constituted as experts in their own field by the tasks which they perform. As Gorz perceives individuals being allocated an identity by the activity (or lack of activity) which they perform in the public sphere, so it would seem that the hierarchical nature of advanced capitalism is defining members of the professional elite as technical experts.

Gorz argues that the specialised form of expert systems ensures that the tasks that each expert performs are useless unless they are allied with the abilities of another of the small group of professionals. In this way, not only does advanced capitalism manage to create experts whose expertise is of little personal use to them but also it ensures the inter-dependence of this small technical elite. This system almost certainly ensures that this privileged group in society will work together to maintain their supremacy over the vast majority. Furthermore the technical organisation of society ensures that most individuals will be subservient to experts in the course of their everyday existence. Gorz reaches these conclusions by reasoning that the reproduction of advanced capitalist societies is reliant on their ability to 'combine, by means of pre-established organisational procedures, an immense variety of specialised knowledge which it would be impossible for their possessors to co-ordinate through mutual understanding and conscious, voluntary self-regulated co-operation' (Gorz 1989a: 55).

The subdivision of labour has left society with armies of semi or unskilled workers who have become alienated from any self-expression in their work. The technical experts are part of a body of permanent workers who have little in common with the growing group of temporary and part-time employees who are contracted in to perform the most menial and unskilled tasks. The only satisfaction that can generally be derived from these menial tasks is the financial rewards they confer upon the worker. Whilst Sayers mistakenly argues that Gorz does not believe in the need to work (odd given that Gorz advocates the right to work as well as a right not to work at certain stages), he comes to similar quantitative conclusions as those who advocate tertiarisation – that is, any job, however demeaning, is better than no job at all (Sayers 1988: 722–44). The human need to be creative is not and cannot be satisfied in these circumstances either for the menial worker or the expert whose knowledge is too narrow and specialised to satisfy the desire for self-determination. Kellner notes how Gorz's argument is reminiscent of members of the Frankfurt School such as Marcuse and

Pollock. The comparisons with Gorz are evident when Kellner states that

> Pollock feared that in the absence of regulation and state planning, automation would increase the tendencies towards rationalisation and domination, which would widen 'the gulf between a small group of highly qualified "managers", engineers and specialists on the one hand and the vast mass of wage-earners on the other'.
>
> (Kellner 1989: 184)

Gorz has argued that employers have never really been purveyors of the need to work. Rather they have historically viewed their employees as lazy or 'allergic to work'. Sayers has failed to realise that Gorz recognises that there is indeed a need for human creativity but that the productive process has been robbed of its creative essence through the technical division of labour (Sayers 1988). Nevertheless management have created policies to placate workers through limited joint decision making, share offers, etc. – positive developments to post-Fordists but not for Gorz. He believes that this process is limited to a relatively small number of permanent, skilled workers who have formed a tenured aristocracy which is inaccessible to most other workers (Gorz 1987b: 46). Gorz argues that these policies are also doomed to failure as, although greater worker involvement can usually ensure higher productivity, this is not always accompanied by a correspondent increase in demand. In the long run, Gorz argues that it is not beneficial for either employer or employee to increase cooperative productivity given the fluctuation and impositions enforced by the free market. Ultimately he believes that employers will have to reassert their dominance over workers.

In a theoretical shift from his work in the 1960s, Gorz observes that greater worker involvement in the productive process is not necessarily an emancipatory development due to the dangers of corporatism which can lead to the deradicalisation of workers. Indeed he believes this cooperation is ultimately meaningless if the workers remain subordinate to management working under the regulations of profit and growth. According to Gorz, the only way for management to satisfy technical workers would be in the unlikely incidence that employers guaranteed their workers a job for life. In modern conditions this could really apply only to the technical elite and even then only to a limited extent. Frequently employers subcontract the unskilled and menial tasks to smaller companies. In general these smaller companies tend to have a high turnover of workers whose employment is usually temporary and insecure (Gorz 1989a: 65).

Far from being a situation which the Left should embrace, this is a scenario against which the Left must struggle harder than ever before. Changes in the labour process as a result of the technical division of labour have succeeded in fragmenting the Left and the traditional industrial working class. This has proved to be the case as the employers have given a small group of technical workers greater control over the method and process of production without actually decreasing the subordination of the majority of workers. Employers have promoted the belief that the technical elite deserve their supremacy because of their knowledge and productivity in contrast to the idleness and sterility of the traditional working class. Hence an attack on the strength of the workforce as a whole has taken place, ensuring, not only the fragmentation of the working class, but also the disunity of trade unions (Gorz 1989a: 219–42). A profound difference of interest has emerged between unions representing traditional working-class industries and new unions representing the tertiary sector. On the whole continental trade union movements, such as the Federation of Dutch Trade Unions (FNV) in the Netherlands, have been much more willing to embrace radical ideas about the way we work (Coenen 1993: 175). Similarly Keane notes how the French Democratic Confederation of Labour (CFDT) has rejected explicit advances in the direction of corporatism as the strategy for trade unions in favour of an alliance with the disadvantaged sectors in civil society. The CFDT's policy is to create solidarity with all 'workers' including those who are not working (Keane 1988: 18–19).

The CFDT have to some extent recognised the impossibility of full employment and rejected the creation of what Gorz calls 'the utopia of work'. Essentially this is the work ethic reformed and modernised to incorporate the problem of unemployment and insecurity at work. It suggests that the unemployed are lazy, that they do not want a job, that social security is too comfortable, and that the unemployed are the cause of problems in the national economy and its competitiveness. The root of this speculation is the belief that employment exists for those who genuinely want it and that more work would instigate a consumer-led recovery, although according to Kellner the notion of a consumer-led recovery is a fallacy developed by those with a blind reliance on the market (Kellner 1989: 164).

The problem for the Left, as Gorz realises, is that the ethics of productivism and full employment have been continually espoused by the trade union movement to create and safeguard jobs. Thus it is sometimes difficult to distinguish between traditional leftist ideology and neo-conservatism. Gorz believes that the Left must move away from the traditional work ethic or it will fall into the neo-Keynesian trap created by the ideology of growth. If this ethic is not abandoned we will continue to develop as a global economy built around the utopia of work:

> In such a situation, the glorification of hard work and the assertion that working and living can be one and the same thing, is an ideology which can only be held by a privileged elite which monopolises the best-paid, most highly skilled and most stable jobs and justifies doing so on the grounds of its superior abilities. The ideology of work and the ethics of effort therefore become a cover for ultra-competitive egoism and careerism: the best succeed, the others have only themselves to blame; hard work should be encouraged and rewarded, which therefore means we should not subsidise the unemployed, the poor and all the other 'layabouts'.
> (Gorz 1989a: 69)

Nevertheless Gorz realises that the history of the industrial working class demonstrates that, to some extent, it has always contained an influential skilled element who have been viewed by the Left in general as a possible, liberatory vanguard. Hence the emancipatory faith in the new technical elite that is displayed by some theorists is not without historical precedent (Mallet 1975). Other writers, such as Piore and Sabel, have been criticised by Gorz for attempting to implement a new vanguardism because they positively promote flexible specialization at work without mounting a serious challenge to the external regulation which governs flexible working (Piore and Sabel 1984; Hirst 1989: 321–8). Moreover it is relevant to point to the likelihood that flexible specialisation at work may only actually affect a relatively small group of workers. A similar point is raised by Mulgan and Wilkinson who note that 'at the bottom of the income range, flexibility is . . . more often imposed than sought – with the important difference that rewards are declining rather than rising' (Mulgan and Wilkinson 1995: 5).

As we have seen, Gorz believes that the new technical elite has little interaction with or influence on the majority of the working class. Not only do the elite work in a different sector from the traditional working class but also in many cases they actually employ the lower strata to perform their most menial tasks (i.e. work-for-oneself). This relation of dependence is unlikely to be the means through which the majority react against their oppression. Indeed menial workers are more likely to rebel against their domestic employers than to regard them as a liberatory vanguard. Furthermore it is highly questionable, as Gorz realises, whether the technical elite have even the slightest inclination to accentuate the liberation of their erstwhile equals. Indeed it would appear that the inclination to liberate this new 'underclass' would be ultimately contrary to the need of the elite to maintain its position of control. Because it is mostly skilled workers who are represented by the modern trade union movement, it is not surprising that the majority who are confined to unskilled, temporary or part-time employment find little in trade unionism to inspire confidence. A similar point is made by Keane who observes that:

> Trade unions also tend to assume that part-time workers will not support collective trade union policy, by strike action if need be. The conclusion drawn by many trade unions – that voluntary part-time employment undermines trade union solidarity and plays into the hands of employers – is arguably premature, however. Trade unions have barely begun to explore the possibilities of supplementing their collective strategies by bargaining vigorously in defence of the growing numbers of part-time employees (most of them women), and by demanding that every individual full-time employee be entitled to a right to work part-time without loss of entitlements or promotion opportunities.
>
> (Keane 1988: 93)

Another problem which Gorz alludes to in the *Critique* is that the trade union movement, in defending the rights of their present members (i.e. mainly skilled workers), is inadvertently collaborating with the employers in the maintenance of the oppression of the non-unionised majority. Trade unions, of course, are not seeking to support the conditions which maintain the subordination of the lower strata of society but in failing to interact with a wider spectrum of individual workers they are helping to substantiate the hierarchy of skilled workers. In short, trade unions must seek to incorporate unskilled, temporarily employed and unemployed individuals under their auspices if they are to proceed towards a liberatory society. Thus, by supporting a much shorter working week, they could advocate a fairer redistribution for all their members. Not only would this action increase trade union activity and influence but also it would actively undermine a system that is dependent on the fragmentation of the workers within it. Unfortunately, as Gorz demonstrates, this ethos is unlikely to become a central tenet of trade union philosophy:

> By a curious vestige of elitism, many trade unions react with great hostility to the ideas that skills can and . . . must be rendered commonplace, as if the individual's aim, and source of identity, were the possession of irreplaceable occupational skills and knowledge.
>
> (Gorz 1989a: 77)

It is not only the trade unions that are at fault in their interpretation of changing methods of production and the different working practices that these incorporate. Many on the Left, including, for example, the Labour Party in Britain, have been willing to welcome these new techniques in the belief that alienation is being overcome and that a new polyvalency is being generated in the productive process. Gorz is sceptical of these views because they fail to counteract the very essence of alienation. In short, work remains a heteronomous activity because the object of production and the means of producing the final good are not actually defined by the workers. These being the central elements of the phenomenon of alienation, it would appear to be rash to herald different productive practices as the means to the defeat of labour as a heteronomous activity.

Gorz believes that the limited autonomy that is accorded to groups of workers in the post-Taylorist workplace is a displacement of alienation because the factory is still coordinated and controlled by an external group or individual. The fragmentation of individual workers exacted by the Taylorist division of labour has been superseded by fragmented groups, linked together through technical machines. In addition, the product and means of production are still beyond the control of groups of workers. If the individual is unable to derive any genuine sovereignty in the new workplace, it is unlikely that technical methods of production will generate any positive changes in the conditions of existence of the majority of the population.

The new, technical workplace is not an arena of fulfilment for its workers as the utopia of work would have us believe. Most of the employees are technicians and maintenance workers whose essential task is to ensure the smooth and profitable running of machine technology. The factory is not a realm of 'human' creativity but a realm of humanly maintained technical achievement. As Gorz implies, a revived interest and variety in the workplace does not necessarily constitute the workplace as an arena of human fulfilment, although there may be a relatively greater degree of worker autonomy as far as decision making is concerned. Nevertheless this arena is still devoid of existential and creative autonomy (Gorz 1989a: 80).

Gorz prescribes a role for technology in assisting individuals to detach themselves from their work. He regards it as a viable means of ensuring the reduction of necessary human labour time in unpleasant tasks. Like Kellner, though, Gorz remains averse to the logic of technology that has become implanted in human relations in industrialised societies (Kellner 1989: 215). The point is to manipulate technology to achieve genuinely human aims but, as Gorz reminds us, the deployment of technology is fraught with danger:

> the superior power of technology has a price: it divorces work from life, and occupational culture from the culture of everyday life; it demands a despotic domination of oneself in exchange for an increased domination of Nature; it reduces the field of lived experience and existential autonomy; it separates the producer from the product to the point where she or he no longer knows the purpose of what she or he is doing.
>
> (Gorz 1989a: 87)

Unless technology is put to the use of humanity through the reduction of time in the realm of heteronomy it will continue to transmit its rationality into the everyday lives of the individuals who encounter it. For Gorz, technology can be effective only if it provides time and space for individuals to maximise sensual and creative pleasure – qualities that are not satisfied in the modern world of work. Human creativity is not capable of being satisfied within such a fragmented and alienating sphere as work colonised by the technical division of labour. The activities encountered are opposed to the gratification of the sensual needs of human existence. In the words of Erich Fromm, 'the social character internalises external necessities and thus harnesses human energy for the task of a given economic and social system' (Fromm 1960: 243).

Gorz is attempting to show that, whilst the nature and form of work have altered, the overriding external regulations which govern that work have remained the same. As the creative necessity of individuals is negated within the domain of work, individuals remain alienated within a system inherently designed not to correspond to human needs. The methods of ensuring this human subordination have indeed changed through the technical division of labour. As Marcuse realised, 'the individual works for himself only in so far as he works for the apparatus, engaged in activities that mostly do not coincide with his own faculties and desires' (Marcuse 1987: 45).

Although a minority of individuals may be achieving some form of autonomy and self-realisation under the conditions of advanced capitalism, it is gained only at the expense of greater repression of the vast majority. For Gorz, this is not a position in which the Left should be optimistic. Whilst the emancipatory struggle can be furthered through Gorz's radical critique, it is certainly not time for a totally new agenda. As Offe and Heinze have noted, the first stage is that capitalism must be challenged about the fallacy of full employment and the normative notion of 'being employed' must be placed under intense scrutiny (Offe and Heinze 1992: 1). Undoubtedly Gorz's work is of extreme importance if the notion of 'being employed' is to be challenged. His programme to reform trade unions is vital for socialists to develop a new understanding of work and workers. Only through such an initiative can socialism proffer a pluralist, democratic alternative that prioritises the creative self-determination of all citizens. In the words of Keane:

> Democracy . . . requires that all individuals be guaranteed the right to (periodically) withdraw from the labour market without fear of going without. Consequently, Gorz points to the need to move towards a type of post-employment civil society in which individuals would be able to choose freely whether or not (or how much) they wished to engage in paid work.
>
> (Keane 1988: 79)

THE MARKET AND THE LIFEWORLD

So what does Gorz propose as an alternative to the current state of affairs? The initial step is a difficult one to undertake. He advocates a division of society which is based upon the different social and private activities that individuals perform. This division incorporates a heteronomous sphere of economically rational work dictated by social necessity, an autonomous sphere of self-ordained activity which corresponds with individual desires, and an area of micro-social activity or 'work-for-oneself' which includes domestic work necessary for self-maintenance. However, is such a division of tasks possible? In one of his failings, Gorz does not expound exactly how activities are to be classified, although it would appear that autonomous activity and micro-social work will be self-defined. However it is not untypical of Gorz to overlook the nitty gritty in preference for the wider picture and, in this case, his view is that socialists can achieve emancipation only through an inversion of the capitalist logic of economic reason which necessitates a new politics of time.

Like Habermas, Gorz realises that the technical reason promoted in advanced capitalism has colonised the realm of autonomy and the life-world. Giddens has defined the lifeworld as 'the taken-for-granted universe of daily social activity. It is the saturation of communicative action by tradition and established ways of doing things. The lifeworld is a pre-interpreted set of forms of life, within which everyday conduct unfolds' (Giddens 1987: 232). In accordance with this, Gorz has suggested that the lived experience of most individuals 'is experienced as the lifeworld's painful absence' (Gorz 1989a: 91), due to the colonisation of the public sphere by economic reason. Thus the pervasiveness of technical domination, and the economic rationality of growth, profit and consumption which capitalist technology promotes, are the central targets in Gorz's critique of capitalism.

In order to clarify this point it is necessary to assess the meaning of economic reason and its implications for a new politics of time. Sayers has defined economic reason as

> the rationality of commodity production for the market. It is the rationality governing work which takes the form of a job, employment, work for wages. Work of this kind is purely a means to the end of exchange, of earning a livelihood – it is not undertaken to meet human needs directly, or as an end in itself.
>
> (Sayers 1991: 17)

Given the centrality of this notion to Gorz, it is worth quoting his perspective at length:

> Economically rational conduct cannot be rational in relation to religious, ethical, or existential matters. The purpose of economically rational conduct is to maximise profit and maximise efficiency, and efficiency does not tell you anything about people apart from the limits set within the scope of the rationalisation. So we cannot expect society to rationalise what is important to us as human beings; we cannot accept the idea that economic rationality is the only form of rationality. The crisis of modernity is due to the fact that we believe rationality is only one thing, and that is economic rationality. But this is an instrumental rationality, and the instruments lie outside yourself. Economic rationality says you need to reach a goal and the means of getting there are all outside yourself.
>
> (Gorz 1989c: 3)

In order to overcome the experienced deficiency of the lifeworld, Gorz suggests that a new rationality must overtake economic rationality which he believes has run its course. This corresponds with the Habermasian belief that technical interest must be subservient to the emancipatory and communicative interests (Habermas 1986). In Gorz's opinion the aim of economic reason is to make the most efficient use of the means of production in order to maximise the profit and growth which it can secure. In turn these effects of economic reason provide new goals and aims for the process to begin all over again. Thus economic reason, for Gorz, will eternally seek to make the most efficient use of time and labour and to open up new spaces where that time and labour can be consumed. This process entails the technical rationalisation of time, space and labour to extract the economic value of all human activity. Gorz insists that this specialisation and rationalisation is inappropriate for evaluating work-for-oneself and autonomous action. He therefore suggests that a different rationality must govern all activity that is not conducted in the market where economic reason is dominant – a clear indication that Gorz maintains not only the state in his alternative but also a role for the market. Ivan Illich, one of the first theorists to criticise economic rationality and professionalisation, has noted that

> Wherever the shadow of economic growth touches us, we are left useless unless employed on a job or engaged in consumption. . . . We lose sight of our resources, lose control over the environmental conditions which make these resources applicable, lose taste for self-reliant coping with challenges from without and anxiety from within.
>
> (Illich 1978: 10)

For Gorz this development is implicitly linked with the process of industrialisation for he believes economic reason became dominant when external factors, such as the market, started to dictate human activity. Although the activity that characterises economic reason has always existed, it is only recently that it has been the central determinant in human activity. Despite the fact that the market has always been essential to the growth and development of industrial capitalism, it is relatively new for it to be dictating the sovereign spheres of private human existence. In response to this scenario, Gorz has suggested that he is not opposed to the idea of the market as an institution, but merely to the dictatorship of human life by the market (Gorz 1988: 28–31). It is for this reason that he advocates a division of society so that the market can be separated from essentially autonomous forms of society which are incompatible with economic reason. Others on the Left have also been prepared to envisage a role for the market although Gorz does not go as far as contemporary 'market socialists' (Elster and Moene 1989; D. Miller 1989; Nove 1991; Roemer 1994; Pierson 1995). Whilst there are many differences between these thinkers regarding social change, they share a desire to maintain an extensive role for the market and a concern with presenting ideas which they perceive to be feasible (Van Parijs and Van der Veen 1993: 176–210).

Whereas Gorz seeks a severe limitation on the market in an arena where only socially necessary goods are produced, market socialism retains a substantial role for the market as a guiding force in society. Whilst Gorz does not engage directly with this debate, his view of the market does not quite mirror that of the traditional socialist perspective, that is, that it generates inequality, inequity, injustice, inefficiency and that it is hostile to democracy, liberty, and cooperation (Pierson 1995: 111–28). Just as Karl Polanyi's idea of socialism advocated the subordination of the economy to society, Gorz believes that market mechanisms can exist in the realm of necessity without dominating social life in general. In this sense Gorz is opposed to the market economy rather than commodity production and exchange (Gorz 1989d: 30). As long as the market operates only in the planned macro-social sector, Gorz perceives little problem. In itself this idea will be valid to those who accept his tripartite view of human activity but again it does leave him open to critics who argue that it is impossible to differentiate between spheres of activity. As a socialist vision of the role of the market, Gorz's view is more coherent than market socialism which seems to lean towards 'the "practical" wing of social democracy' and is, in effect, an extension of the social market which relies on economic growth to fund public spending (Pierson 1995: 210–11). However what is equally clear is that market socialists can champion the feasibility of their models as opposed to the radical proposals of Gorz, although 'what makes market socialism seem feasible is its attachment to the *market*, but that which makes it *socialist* is the very thing that renders it infeasible' (Pierson 1995: 211, original emphasis).

Gorz observes that human needs are no longer central to the logic of production which concentrates on profit and growth due to the influence of the market in the private sphere. The outcome of this logic has been the development of a society which construes individual needs as the desire for accumulation and the consumption of commodities. Without wishing to dehistoricise this development, Gorz is justified in equating industrialisation with an acceleration in the control of human activity by external factors. The social consequences of the manipulation of needs towards consumerism have been highlighted by neo-Marxist commentator O'Connor:

> needs construed as individual needs satisfied by commodities in fact frustrated needs for sociability, emotional intimacy, and personal integration, which, in turn, became the source of the need to escape from single living. This need was also construed as the need for commodities . . . which entered into cost of wages and salaries.
>
> (O'Connor 1984: 175)

Both Gorz and O'Connor suggest that overall control of society is exercised by the market. This has resulted in the necessity of rationalising or calculating the costs of all human activity. Thus labour value and the value of time have been quantified as individuals have evaluated how much externally regulated activity they have to perform in return for a wage. Gorz laments the eradication of genuine pleasure from productivity because work itself has become a means to ensure financial survival rather than a creative activity to satisfy human needs. In short, human fulfilment has been removed from the equation of productive activity and creativity. Consequently workers have become anonymous and homogeneous. This homogeneity springs from the necessity to use the most efficient means of production and the latest technology no matter how much it deskills the task or obliterates creativity. Gorz contends that this change comes about because survival depends on the competitive success of products in the market. Work itself is externalised from human creativity, yet the goals for which it is performed (wages) are necessary for existence. This being the case, it is little wonder that Gorz stresses the pervasiveness of economic reason. If individuals are reliant on having to negate their creativity in order to subordinate their survival to the external, competitive goals of the market, it becomes virtually impossible to free themselves from economic reason – a major problem when it comes to actually trying to change society.

TOWARDS A TRIPARTITE VIEW OF HUMAN ACTIVITY

Following these observations, Gorz has set out the criteria by which humans must behave if economic rationality is to remain the dominant factor in the way we lead our lives. Personal consumption is vital in this scenario so that individuals can weigh up the satisfaction gained in production offset against the loss of time. As soon as the products of human labour are externally defined, individuals begin to find their time consumed by the ethos of exchange rather than personal consumption. Thus creative satisfaction (individual self-realisation through creativity) is nullified by the rationality of commodity exchange and the goals of efficiency and profit which it promotes.

Gorz argues that 'work-for-oneself' resists colonisation by economic reason because it is antithetical to the mercenary impulse of economic rationality. Evidently Gorz believes that the effect of economic reason is primarily manifest in the constraint of human time. Work performed outside this rationality does not impose financial value on our time:

> The idea that people are 'wealthy' when they don't need to spend all or most of their time working and worrying about the necessities of life is as old as civilisation. You can't fit it into the logic of capitalism: it subverts the instrumental, economistic idea that wealth is more of everything except the enjoyment of life itself.
>
> (Gorz 1989d: 28)

Gorz implies that time passed in autonomous activities can evade the stranglehold of *economic* evaluation. Nevertheless this does not mean that time will therefore become free from *social* evaluation. Time, when governed autonomously, would still be allocated a value by the degree of satisfaction derived from the time consumed. Thus individuals would value their time according to the personal satisfaction they would gain from its expenditure. As Gorz realises, time, when autonomously defined, does not suddenly become value-free or abundant. Gorz merely seeks to undermine the *financial* evaluation of time because he realises that it will remain scarce even when it is autonomous. The realm of domesticity and the realm of necessity can be minimised but not eradicated, and the scarcity which these two areas impose on our time automatically ensures that autonomous time will be allocated a value. Work-for-oneself is fundamentally opposed to the regimentation of economic reason but it still defines what 'free' time we have to consume and, therefore, the value of that time. Gorz argues that a new, emancipatory politics of time must concentrate on minimising time spent in the heteronomous sphere:

> a politics of time will begin logically by *predicting the economies in hours of labour* that could result from computerization in

> the public services and administration. There could be union agreements that involve reductions in labour time, and also programs for recruitment and retraining.
>
> (Gorz 1986: 204, original emphasis)

Whatever the solution may be for abolishing economic control of time it is clear that the scarcity which characterises human conceptions of time will remain. Thus time must be perceived as a scarce commodity of which individuals must make the optimum use – an increasingly popular idea which less radical commentators have also come to address (Hewitt 1993; Mulgan and Wilkinson 1995). The limitation of economic reason and reduced working hours would not immediately free human time although it would help to counteract economic valuation of all our time. Nevertheless the focus of Gorz's argument is on liberating time from the constraints of economic reason; the fact that autonomous choices concerning how to spend time will still require evaluation is not really dealt with. This is not problematic for Gorz as this evaluation would be autonomous rather than externally defined but some examination of the value of spending time autonomously does need to be put forward if Gorz's ideas are to achieve widespread support (Zeldin 1995). Gorz's advocacy of a new politics of time, based upon a tripartite division of society, clearly imposes a qualitative differential between autonomous time and heteronomous time – a point that can be traced to E.P. Thompson's celebrated work in the 1960s (E.P. Thompson 1967: 61).

According to both Thompson and Gorz there would seem to be a totally different conception of time passed in work-for-oneself as opposed to externally dictated work governed by economic reason. In *Paths to Paradise*, Gorz criticises state socialist societies such as China for providing an ascesis of work whereby, for example, citizens are told that cleaning out latrines for sewage is a self-realising activity because it benefits the whole of society (Gorz 1985a: 64). Gorz believes that there are certain tasks which are undesirable but essential to the functioning of society. These tasks are the ones which are to be shared throughout society so that no individual has to spend all their working time in drudgery. This is the domain of necessity or heteronomy which, in Gorz's system, would still be subject to some form of economic rationality and market exchange.

Gorz's also conceives work-for-oneself as a necessary activity but one which is not within the realm of heteronomy. Essentially it is personal or micro-social. This is primarily domestic work entailing self-hygiene, childcare and maintenance of the home. Gorz suggests that these activities are and should remain separate from the economic rationality that permeates our lifeworld with the doctrine of competition and growth. This is not because this work is autonomous but because it is personal labour that we should perform ourselves to as great an extent as possible. Gorz argues that these activities do not in themselves have a market value (although one has been falsely imposed by the market) and for this reason they should not be governed by economic reason.

Gorz uses the principle of sufficiency, which corresponds with Illich's 'convivial austerity', to limit the sphere of necessity. Sufficiency is a valuable concept because it stands in opposition to the values of advanced capitalism and economic rationality. Sufficiency cannot blend with the principles of productivism, growth and profit because it encourages limits that advanced capitalism seeks to avoid. The promotion of sufficiency as a social value is problematic because the political agenda is dictated by economic reason. Gorz believes that work-for-oneself and the realm of autonomy are the only areas where sufficiency is the dominant force. However sufficiency and the creation of new needs are difficult foundations on which to base political programmes in times of excessive consumerism. Nevertheless, for Gorz, the success of economic reason in capitalist societies has been dependent on the creation of new 'needs' that have provided fresh areas for growth and profit (Gorz 1989a: 114–15).

The abolition of this productivist logic, which is fundamental to the survival of economic reason, is the forerunner of emancipation. Gorz reckons that if consumer needs can be falsely generated then the notion of sufficiency and self-limitation can also be popularised. The problem is that economic reason, as Gorz describes it, has such an interminable hold on lived experience in the realm of necessity that it will be difficult to prevent its reproduction. Again reflections of the Frankfurt School are apparent in the sense that the pervasiveness of economic reason may render it insurmountable just as the early critical theorists could perceive little of emancipatory potential under instrumental reason. Although Gorz rejects claims that his model is nihilistic, he does provide them with ammunition when he expresses how economic reason stifles opposition and spontaneity:

> this cold civilisation is able to organise itself, its cold, functional, calculated, formalised relationships, making living individuals strangers to the reified world which is nonetheless their product, and its formidable technical inventiveness going hand in hand

> with a decline of the arts of living, of communication and of spontaneity.
>
> (Gorz 1989a: 124)

Despite the pervasiveness of economic rationality which Gorz outlines, he is able to foresee an emancipatory potential within the present system. Indeed he believes the nature of the capitalist system itself is such that it creates social needs which it is incapable of satisfying. Similarly O'Connor has observed that in capitalist societies 'needs which were actually satisfied in the commodity form were necessarily frustrated in the social form. Every need fulfilled through commodities isolated the individual from society defined in the sense of social individuality, i.e. "fellowship" or "common doing"' (O'Connor 1984: 169).

Gorz points to areas such as the environment, health, education and support services which are incapable of maintaining sufficient standards through market mechanisms. These are all areas which he believes should be free from the rationalisation of economic reason and the constraints of growth and profit which characterise them presently. Whilst Gorz believes that the deprofessionalisation of these services could lead to their incorporation within the localised polity (community or associational services may replace them), he admits that 'activity directed towards economic goals has remained the driving force' (Gorz 1989a: 132). The task of socialism must be to subordinate economic reason to qualitative societal goals aimed towards autonomy and equality. Whilst this is hardly a novel suggestion within socialist theory, Gorz believes that his analysis necessarily entails the classification of which sectors of society are to be heteronomous and which will become totally autonomous, difficult though this task may be. Indeed he recognises that the division he advocates would require a difficult and complex method of 'determining which activities can be subordinated to economic rationality without losing their meaning and for which activities economic rationalisation would be a perversion or a negation of the meaning inherent in them' (Gorz 1989a: 132–3). He does add a disclaimer which acts as a rebuff to Sayers' claim that he imagines a clear division between different activities:

> It would be wrong . . . to imagine there is a clear-cut separation between autonomous activities and heteronomous work, the realm of freedom and the realm of necessity. The former does indeed have repercussions on the latter but can never subsume it entirely.
>
> (Gorz 1989a: 93)

The starting point for Gorz in this evaluation is the differentiation between types of work into those which are for exchange purposes and those which are for personal and public welfare. He observes that 'economically rational work' is work performed for a living in order to exchange it for the fruits of other people's work. Gorz does not deny that it is possible for individuals to gain some form of satisfaction in economically rational work but he believes this is a secondary factor behind survival and utility. Hence, whilst different activities may confer satisfaction on individuals, there is a line drawn between those who perform the task for enjoyment and those who perform it for exchange value. However the micro-social realm contains activity that would appear to have neither pleasure nor exchange value as the primary aim – in this sense it may be useful for Gorz also to include the idea that we work out of obligation when conducting domestic work. This may be either personal obligation or duties that we owe to those dependent on us such as children.

DEFINING ECONOMIC REASON

Economically rational work is dictated by external goals according to Gorz. Therefore whilst a task may be satisfying or pleasurable, under economic reason it must be performed for external consumption, under enforced conditions of efficiency. Gorz sets out four criteria for tasks to which economic reason is applicable:

(a) they must create use value;
(b) they must be exchangeable as commodities;
(c) they must be exchangeable in the public sphere;
(d) they must be quantifiable in terms of time and productivity to produce the greatest efficiency of labour.

(Gorz 1989a: 138–9)

These four criteria are essential because they illustrate specifically the reasoning Gorz uses to determine which forms of work can be economically rationalised and which cannot, that is, which activities should be in the realm of heteronomy and which should not. On the basis of these criteria, Gorz is able to outline his plan for a division of society. He believes that in advanced capitalist society tasks are broadly divided into two categories – commodity and non-commodity activities. Essentially this division is between tasks performed for the interests of other people and the exchange interest of the worker and tasks performed for individual well-being and personal desires.

Commodity activities include tasks such as trades (carpentry, plumbing, etc.) in which individuals are employed by others to do jobs they could not perform themselves. Thus the skill of the tradesperson is exchanged as a commodity in the public sphere. The activity of the worker is a socially acceptable task which confers upon it a use value. Furthermore each trade works under a general 'going rate' which corresponds with the productivity of labour as recognised in the public sphere. That trades are perhaps the most autonomously satisfying tasks in the public sphere ensures a level of satisfaction which is coupled with the knowledge that the task is socially useful. This leads to a level of acceptance which Gorz calls 'social insertion'. In short, there is an identity of social insertion conferred upon tradepeople which is not necessarily applicable to other forms of work. The development of these trade skills takes time to acquire and is thus virtually unattainable for individuals in full-time employment in a different area.

Gorz believes that citizenship depends upon entry to and activity within the public sphere. As such Gorz argues that 'the right to accede to the public, economic sphere through one's work is a necessary part of the right to citizenship' (Gorz 1989a: 141). Unfortunately entry to the public sphere for the majority of individuals is presently available *only* through work. Thus individuals have become reliant on the identity conferred by their work within the constraints of the market. Participation in the public sphere should not be limited to work but must include, for example, autonomous political, sporting, creative and cultural activities. These are essential forms of self-realisation which help an individual to express their sovereign identity.

The new servile labour that is being created by tertiarisation and the commodification of domestic work does not fit Gorz's criteria for economically rational work. Gorz suggests that this labour does not correspond with economic rationality because it does not create use value. His point is that domestic work is undertaken as a service when it is obvious that the employer would be capable of undertaking that labour themselves. Although these 'servants' may sell their labour in the public sphere, Gorz argues that they are employed primarily for the personal and private satisfaction of the employer; consequently servile domestic labour does not totally satisfy the second criteria of economic rationality. In the words of Offe:

> The need for all types of service labour . . . cannot be deduced from technical production functions, but must be decided on the basis of conceptions of need and criteria of normality which are

> normatively justified and always contestable. Whereas it is always possible (at a given level of technology) to specify rather precisely the quantities of raw materials and labour power required for manufacturing a certain product, the 'need' for service labour can rarely be determined with approximately the same precision.
>
> (Offe 1985: 119)

Essentially domestic labour not only condemns individuals to a menial and stigmatised existence but also confers upon them less time and access to the public sphere. Given that the principal mode of participation in the public sphere in capitalism happens through work, workers in the private sphere experience shackles on their autonomy. Clearly the ideology of full-time employment and growth is crucial in cultivating the need to create more personal time by employing individuals to perform domestic tasks. Offe concurs with Gorz's recognition that domestic work cannot be economically rationalised. He claims that 'household labour differs from wage labour in that it is normatively regulated, highly immobile and lacks a quantitative equivalence between work performed and income obtained' (Offe 1985: 72).

Furthermore Gorz, in accordance with Illich, observes that community and voluntary care services should be deprofessionalised. This category of workers includes, for example, doctors, teachers, social workers, firefighters and police officers. He believes that the caring professions, to use Sayers' term, should be rescued from the realm of the market and the logic of growth, competition and profit. Gorz believes these services should be provided in a more humane and decentralised manner by autonomous individuals in the community. As Sayers realises, Gorz rejects the definition of these tasks as economically rational because commodity relations are not applicable to the family or community. Economic reason cannot be applied to 'caring professions' because they are not necessarily quantifiable in the market. Productivity and efficiency cannot always govern the tasks to be performed in this area. Gorz's moral argument asks how can activities such as childcare, crime prevention and health care be placed under the auspices of the market and economic growth?

The quantification of these professions by successive Conservative governments in Britain since 1979 has resulted in the assessment of the value of hospitals by the number of patients they churn out, the value of schools by the number of successful students they admit, the value of the police by the number of public disorders they suppress, the value of firefighters by the number of fires they extinguish, etc. Gorz argues that this reasoning is flawed because the individual worker must be paid irrespective of their productivity. This is because 'the amount of effective work cannot be planned and does not therefore depend on the agents themselves: these agents must not have an interest in there being work for them to do' (Gorz 1989a: 143).

In short, these workers are dependent on extraneous circumstances to dictate their own productivity. Therefore some of these professions (the army, for instance) rely on a surplus of employees in case of an emergency. In times of recession, governments may have to cut the number of these employees to minimise the public sector wage bill. This can result in a situation where employees have a vested interest in the prevalence of conditions which would lead them to deploy their skills. Ultimately, it is socially unacceptable for soldiers to desire conflict so that they can avoid the perils of unemployment or for nurses to have a vested interest in people being ill in their specific hospital. In Gorz's words:

> Persons administering care must not have a personal interest in people needing their care. The money they earn should be a means of exercising their profession and not its end. Somehow, earning their living should not, so to speak, come into the bargain.
>
> (Gorz 1989a: 144)

Following Gorz's argument, the vocational desire to assist other individuals should remain the dominant factor in motivating carers and not the commercial benefits that can be accrued from that work. Gorz reasons that the correct motivation for these tasks is exemplified by volunteers. Given a vast reduction in the working week, he believes that the time would become available for individuals to learn the skills necessary to perform these tasks in the interests of the community. In essence Gorz argues for the deprofessionalisation of these caring professions to ensure that the market values, which are being thrust upon these professions in contemporary capitalism, are eliminated from the equation. It is not surprising that Gorz's thesis has aroused suspicion and criticism from the Left as well as the Right. Sayers argues that 'If these activities are made into paid professional services, they can be standardized and regularized. Provision of medical care, education and welfare can be ensured and made universal; minimum standards in these areas can be specified and enforced' (Sayers 1991: 18).

Whilst Sayers is entirely correct to point out that a variation of standard could occur with complete decentralisation and localised autonomy over welfare, his conclusion does not follow. Why should payment for these services enable standardisation? Professionalising welfare tasks does not necessarily eliminate variations in quality. Sayers' argument is based on the need for centralised control, a minimum standard so that all individuals would have an equal opportunity for the development of lifeskills and the maintenance of welfare. Whilst this is a valid objective, the mere payment of experts is no guarantee of this. It is precisely because of this failure that Gorz advocates the decentralisation and localised autonomy of welfare, a commitment he supplements with a recognition of the need for standardisation by a centralised body:

> The entire social organisation of non-economic activities (such as helping, caring, cultural and development activities) should be redefined . . . by creating a kind of synergy within a two-tiered system supported on the one hand by centralised services provided by institutions, and on the other by self-organized, co-operative services staffed by volunteers.
>
> (Gorz 1989a: 146)

Sayers' misunderstanding of Gorz's perspective leads him to misrepresent Gorz's views. Sayers advocates state intervention to provide a universal service without realising that Gorz also believes in such a system in conjunction with localised autonomy. He also criticises Gorz for celebrating voluntary services to the detriment of the present welfare state in a manner akin to the policies that the Thatcher governments (1979–90) employed to dismantle the British welfare state.

Such criticism is spurious for it ignores the motivation behind Gorz's perspective. For the latter, the welfare state is presently a bureaucratic organisation providing a minimal standard of 'support' for the socially disadvantaged underclass. Whilst this limited welfare provision is in place, capitalists can pursue competition and growth with a clear conscience. For Thatcher, the welfare state had to be dismantled to save on needless expense and to prevent a culture of welfare and dependency. There is a clear difference in motivation behind Gorz's view of the welfare state and that of Thatcher. Sayers ignores the fact that criticism of the welfare state is commonplace on the Left (Gough 1979; Offe 1984), in the apparent belief that all socialists must adhere to neo-Keynesian discourse. Where Thatcher was trying to dismantle the welfare state, Gorz is trying to find a new means of state support without the stigma and ineffectuality of the contemporary system. Where the latter feels state support to be necessary, the neo-liberals attempt to abolish it. Hence Gorz falls into neither of the categories to which Sayers assigns him, that is, the pre-capitalist regressionist intent on reverting to traditional forms of communal living or the socialist flirting with neo-liberal ideology on welfare. Both perspectives are anathema to Gorz's thought and Sayers misrepresents his work greatly in categorising him in such a way.

RECLAIMING THE PRIVATE SPHERE

In his analysis of commodity activities Gorz has attempted to show that many different forms of work exist in the work-based society. Thus it is not possible to classify all these tasks simply as 'work', especially when they do not all correspond to the criteria of work-based society (i.e. economic reason). Gorz's argument illustrates that work need not be the guiding factor governing social policy. Indeed, many pre-capitalist societies (e.g. ancient Greece) believed that work was not necessarily the major index of citizenship because work was primarily conducted in the private sphere (Gorz 1988: 29). Work has become central for Gorz because, in an economic sense, it has become the focal point of entry into the public sphere. Advanced capitalism has developed an economic hold over the domain where individuals traditionally came together to make collective decisions, whereas many pre-capitalist societies found their democratic origins in the degree to which the public sphere became an arena for social debate and action.

Gorz's perspective tends to prioritise not only the colonisation of the public sphere by economic reason, but also the commodification of relations within the private sphere. The transfer of work-for-oneself to a commercialised service sector (the process of tertiarisation) is, Gorz argues, a development anathema to the traditional ethos of industrialism, whether capitalist or socialist. Where previously domestic work was to be minimal so that individuals could spend much more time working in the economised public sphere, advanced capitalism has created a system where much of the work in society has been redeployed to the tertiary sector and the provision of domestic services. Gorz's critique of tertiarisation has extended the Habermasian critique of the colonisation of the public sphere:

> The idea is that these [domestic] tasks should occupy the greatest number of people and absorb as much working time as possible, but in the form, in this instance, of commercial services. This is because it is no longer labour that is scarce, but paid jobs. Now

> more hours of work are to be devoted to domestic tasks than they would actually take up if everyone did them for themselves. 'Making work', 'creating jobs': these are the goals of the new tertiary anti-economy.
>
> (Gorz 1989a: 155)

Gorz believes that the creation of this 'new tertiary anti-economy' is reliant upon the creation of greater social inequality. The better-paid tasks in society are performed by a few technical experts who purchase the time of the majority to conduct their domestic tasks for them. Gorz calls this the 'South-Africanisation' of society. He also mentions the theory of 'housewifisation', a term coined by Claudia von Werlhof to describe the gradual deployment of domestic tasks to a growing tertiary sector staffed by the socially disadvantaged (Gorz 1989a: 156). The result of society developing further along these lines would be the extension of heteronomy, through the creation of an elite of workers with their life built around technical work and a servile sub-class conducting the domestic tasks of the elite as a means of survival.

This heteronomous existence does not allow for the creation of a sovereign private sphere. Hence Gorz believes that the private sphere can be re-created and protected only by the disjunction of work-for-oneself and economically rational work. Furthermore Gorz claims that if individuals were to satisfy their own needs autonomously they would play a greater part in the community. Thus the private sphere is not just an individual realm but an arena where individuals can develop cooperative skills and knowledge that would enable them to perform civic tasks more effectively. Cooperation, therefore, would be a natural extension of work-for-oneself and experience in the private sphere would help individuals to find fulfilment in the public sphere. Gorz is advocating the creation of a society in which each individual would play their part due to autonomous desires for cooperation. In essence, this theory negates privatism by making the private sphere a realm of 'common sovereignty'. The crucial point to note is that Gorz envisages the achievement of emancipation through the demarcation of a wider private sphere. It is only through greater autonomous control over our actions that we can possibly come together as a liberated body. Democracy is reliant upon this individual autonomy. This is where Gorz's theory of individuality marks him out from more traditional Marxism. Gorz believes that individuals can create a liberatory society only if they have control over their own actions unburdened by excessive heteronomous work.

Gorz continues his discussion of non-commodity activities by analysing autonomous activity, that is, activities that individuals pursue to meet purely personal desires for pleasure. Autonomous actions cannot take place within the realm of heteronomy which is governed by economic reason. For Gorz, autonomous activities can be defined as those which

> are valued for and in themselves not because they have no other objective than the satisfaction and pleasure they procure, but because the action which achieves the goal is as much a source of satisfaction as the achievement of the goal itself: the end is reflected in the means and vice versa.
>
> (Gorz 1989a: 165)

According to Sayers, it is not possible to cordon off an autonomous private sphere from the market, in fact 'the whole strategy of trying to defend a private and personal sphere by restricting the public and economic sphere is characteristic of liberal individualism' (Sayers 1991: 19). He interprets Gorz's theory as anti-socialist because it tries to restrict the influence of the public sphere. This is a misinterpretation because Gorz does not seek to eradicate communication, social fulfilment and civic culture. He merely believes that individuals must be autonomous and responsible for their own actions if genuine fulfilment is to be achieved. His plan to shackle the economic rationality governing the private sphere is to promote autonomy. Certainly, as both Sayers and Gorz realise, the public sphere must provide the foundation of democratic culture. However, Sayers dismisses the importance of autonomous self-determination in the private sphere whereas Gorz prioritises it as the only means of achieving individual fulfilment autonomously. Only through such fulfilment, he argues, can individuals successfully enter the public sphere.

Influential theorists on the Left, such as Habermas, argue that the public sphere and the private sphere must be rescued from the juridification exacted upon them in advanced capitalist society (Habermas 1986: 184–5). Juridification is the process whereby the state exacts greater control over individual concerns by using institutional systems such as the law. By seeking to overcome juridification Habermas seeks to eradicate the colonisation of the lifeworld. Gorz argues that the private sphere needs to be liberated as it is currently a domain where domestic work and passive entertainment is the norm. A freed private sphere could become a realm of autonomy which could act as a springboard for self-determining individuals to enter the public sphere. There would appear to be little point in restructuring and repoliticising the public sphere if individuals remain privatistic and dependent.

The colonisation of the lifeworld, the technical division of labour, and the creation of the tertiary anti-economy all stand in opposition to the kind of emancipatory society championed by Habermas and Gorz. Will emancipatory change, though, be generated from the public sphere or the private sphere? Gorz believes that autonomy within the private sphere will enable individuals to enter the public sphere to press for a radically different agenda based upon a new politics of time. Only through the conscious unification of autonomous individuals can a politics of free time become a dominant emancipatory force in the public sphere. It is this foundation that has enabled Gorz to develop a theory of the individual which ultimately allows him to champion what appears a contradiction in terms, namely, socialist individualism.

6

TOWARDS SOCIALIST INDIVIDUALISM?

Given his theoretical grounding in the existentialist tradition, it is not surprising that Gorz has prioritised the development of individual autonomy. From the preceding analysis it is apparent that the concept of the individual has become sovereign in his emancipatory project. The notion of the individual has achieved greater prominence in socialist debate in recent times due to social fragmentation and the prevalence of the ideology of individualism in advanced capitalist societies. Indeed many socialists have used the theory of Marx to justify their concentration on the individual (Forbes 1990; Leonard 1984; Tucker 1980).

MARXISM AND THE INDIVIDUAL

It is possible to link Gorz's perspective on the individual with 'Marxian individuation'. As Schaff and MacPherson have emphasised Marx was an 'individualist' (Schaff 1970; MacPherson 1962). Indeed, Tucker notes that 'there can be little dispute over whether Marx is an individualist, for he places great value on the achievement of autonomy' (Tucker 1980: 65). It is the failure to recognise that Marx was an individualist that blinds critics to the neo-Marxian originality of Gorz's theory. Cranston, for instance, believes there is a sharp dichotomy between Marxism and existentialism and rejects claims that Marx was concerned with the individual:

> Existentialism as it is commonly understood, and certainly as it is expounded by Sartre, entails an extreme form of individualism, whereas Marxism has no more conspicuous feature than its rejection of individualism – its belief that man must be seen in terms of the social whole or the common humanity.
>
> (Cranston 1976: 217)

Not only does Cranston simplify the complexity of Sartrean existentialism, but also he confuses Marx's critique of liberal individualism (which Gorz shares) with a rejection of the primacy of the individual. A more valid point is made by Miller who recognises that 'Marx himself highly valued the elaboration of human individuality as a progressive aspect of historical development' (J. Miller 1979: 3). Although Gorz reserves considerable criticism for Marx in certain areas, he regards Marxism as irreplaceable as an instrument of analysis (Gorz 1987a). Indeed it is pertinent, in attempting to display the Marxian as well as the existential roots of Gorz's theory of the individual, to refer to the words of Marx and Engels (in *The German Ideology*) who claimed that communists

> are very well aware that egoism, just as much as self-sacrifice, is in definite circumstances a necessary form of the self-assertion of individuals. Hence the communists by no means want . . . to do away with the 'private individual' for the sake of the 'general' self-sacrificing man.
>
> (Marx and Engels 1970: 104–5)

Despite the aforementioned comments that Marxism is not anti-individualist, those on the Left who cherish the agency of the individual may still be characterised as 'liberals'. Against those socialists who have adopted a fresh approach to correspond with 'new times' (Hall and Jacques 1989), more traditional Marxist thinkers have enveloped themselves in the dogmatic defence of socialist collectivity (Meiksins Wood 1986; Pepper 1993). Gorz's interest in the individual does not adhere to either of these schools of thought. Gorz asserts the sovereignty of individual autonomy as the means to combat the prevalence of social isolation in advanced capitalist societies. This, he believes, is the only way that autonomous individuals can unite to mobilise their emancipatory potential through a new politics of time. Viewed in this perspective, Gorz can be presented as a theorist of the individual – a portrayal that characterises his work more effectively than more conventional presentations of Gorz as a utopian, a Green, a theorist of class or a theorist of work.

It is apparent that the Gorzian theory of the individual does not fit comfortably with either side of the individualism/collectivism dichotomy. Unlike those who have adopted a new individualist approach, Gorz's perspective emerges from a self-consciously radical analysis which is primarily concerned with highlighting the non-satisfaction of individual, existential needs, and the consequent lack of time and space for autonomy, in the conditions of advanced capitalism. Simultaneously Gorz is opposed to the dependence on collectivism which characterises much Marxist literature, and his theory is constantly resonant with existentialist reflections on freedom. Many commentators, such as Cranston, overlook the priority that Marx gave to individual emancipation:

> Existentialists lay great stress on the isolation, the solitude, the 'abandonment' of the individual; and no existentialist writer has stressed this more than Sartre . . . but Marxism regards individualism as a 'delusion of theory' and holds that man's true nature is social.
>
> (Cranston 1976: 213)

Gorz, on the other hand, is aware that individual freedom was prominent in Marx's work. Marx's critique of 'liberal individualism' did not eliminate the question of individual autonomy from socialist theory. The roots of Gorz's critique of liberal individualism can be clearly observed in the work of Marx who Forbes suggests 'has wrongly been seen as an "anti-individual" thinker. Although very antagonistic to liberal individualism in his approach to the question of the individual in society, Marx was not a philosophical anti-humanist who denied the significance of the individual' (Forbes 1990: 220). Similarly Miller argues that 'Marx . . . relied on an understanding of history and human agency that linked the pursuit of material interest with the ideal of individual emancipation' (J. Miller 1979: 143). Rather than reducing socialism to collectivism, Gorz recognises that a theory of societal liberation requires the emancipation of the individual:

> The question immediately raised is that of the past history of the individual, for there is no other subject than the individual subject; that is clear even in Marx. We must look at the question of the history of the individual subject's relationship to the body, to the environment, to society, and whether this relationship can ever be formed in such a way that I can view it as 'my own'.
>
> (Gorz 1989b: 274)

Clearly though Gorz envisages socialism as a system which can actually realise liberal goals – a view which mirrors that of Mouffe, for instance, who argues that we should try to develop 'liberal socialism' (Mouffe 1993: 90–101). Mouffe cites the work of Norbert Bobbio as a seminal expression of how positive proposals for democracy can be furthered by a constructive dialogue between liberals and socialists within the framework of representative democracy (Bobbio 1987). Clearly this is a different agenda from that of Gorz who desires the liberation of time so that individuals can participate more actively in the way they lead their lives whereas Bobbio reconciles himself with some of the deficiencies of liberal democracy in the name of realism. However it is important to note the similarity between their programmes when it comes to the primacy of the individual as the essential agent. Mouffe notes, though, that Bobbio's defence of individualism tends to cloud the vicissitudes of contemporary capitalism that have been engendered by the dominant ideology of individualism, although she agrees with his defence of representative democracy (Mouffe 1993: 95).

So, following Mouffe's assertion that we need to maintain the importance of the individual agent without supporting liberal individualism, we can see a role for Gorz in the formation of socialist individualism. As I have already observed, Hirst's notion of associational democracy may be one framework for pluralistic socialism (a point with which Mouffe concurs), but it appears as a system where the state (including parliament) maintains a position in which the arbitrary use of power over groups and associations could remain. Gorz's theory is equally concerned with the empowerment of individuals within associations as well as democratising the state–association relationship. Viewed in this way, the ideas of Mouffe and Hirst can be regarded as a step along the path to Gorzian socialism. Moreover their ideas suggest that a simple division between individualism and communiatrianism is not sufficient in the development of socialism. Mouffe's concluding remarks provide an incisive analysis of the task ahead:

> It is . . . in its questioning of individualism and in its contribution to the formulation of a new approach to individuality that restores its social nature without reducing it to a simple component of an organic whole, that the socialist tradition of thought can still play an important role.
>
> (Mouffe 1993: 100).

PRIVATISM AND SOCIAL ISOLATION

Gorz consistently refers to the problems of developing individual autonomy in the context of contemporary capitalism. This problematic development is also of vital importance to contemporary theorists such as Habermas and Giddens (Giddens 1991; Habermas 1986). These writers highlighted the barriers to the satisfaction of individual existential needs which are created by the domination of capitalist societies.

Rather than seeking to explain this capitalist reproduction through the ideological incorporation of the masses as theorists such as Mandel have done (Mandel 1982: 29), thinkers such as Habermas and Offe have noted how there is little space for oppositional action and critical thought to develop due to the manipulation of individual time, space and resources in advanced capitalism. They argue, in accordance with Gorz, that individuals are not ideologically duped into accepting the ideas of the dominant forces in society, but rather that individuals do not have the power or resources to counteract the pervasive logic of capitalism. The major sources of this manipulative power work through 'the colonisation of the lifeworld' (Habermas) and the forms of privatism that have been analysed by Williams and Held as well as the theorists mentioned above (Williams 1983: 7–18; Held 1982: 153–60). This theoretical tradition recognises that the explanation of social reproduction requires a much greater investigation of human psychology than the more mechanical and simplistic deployment of the notion of false consciousness.

Only through an analysis of social isolationism can the reproductive power of capitalism be explained and the subsequent implications for individual autonomy be outlined. Hence an examination of Gorz's theory of individual autonomy requires an explanation of the forms of ontological domination developed by the forces of capitalism. This is essential to the clarification of Gorz's ideas and it is a task which he himself has prioritised from his early work in the 1950s through to his later writings.

Ideology-centred theorists wrongly interpret privatism as an extreme or peculiar form of individualism. Thus the failure of most individuals in contemporary capitalism to find space for the development of self-identity in civil society is viewed as a manifestation of a widespread desire for individuals to seek significance and ontological security in the private sphere. The conclusion of such an analysis must have it that individuals choose to adopt the privatistic ethos rather than being forced into the private sphere by the inadequacy of the public sphere in satisfying ontological needs. Lasch disagrees with those who regard privatism as an ideological choice:

> When personal relations are conducted with no other object than psychic survival, 'privatism' no longer provides a haven from a heartless world. On the contrary, private life takes on the very qualities of the anarchic social order from which it is supposed to provide a refuge. It is the devastation of personal

> life, not the retreat into privatism, that needs to be criticised and condemned.
>
> (Lasch 1979: 27)

This analysis fits comfortably with Gorz's theory. Not only does Lasch refute the notion of false consciousness but also he undermines an ideology-centred approach to the analysis of privatism. In essence, 'ideology-centred' theorists, such as Althusser, believe that the prominence of privatism is a manifestation of the ideological success of capitalism in persuading individuals that the source of self-identity is to be found in the private sphere. After all he believes that ideological state apparatuses (the church, the school, etc.) ensure '*subjection to the ruling ideology*' and that '*it is in the forms and under the forms of ideological subjection that provision is made for the reproduction of the skills of labour-power*' (Althusser 1994: 104, original emphasis). This theory is ultimately flawed because it is not grounded in the lived experience of individuals but in the desire to explain social reproduction through the myth of false consciousness. In short, theorists like Althusser insist that the search for identity in the private sphere is an ideological decision taken by individuals to satisfy their needs in alienation from other individuals *because they have been indoctrinated by the capitalist system.* Gorz's contention, in accordance with Lodziak's ideas, is that an analysis of privatistic motivation must be grounded in individual experience rather than ideology (Lodziak 1988).

A third perspective has been suggested by Abercrombie, Hill and Turner who state that the 'economic and political subordination of people makes ideological incorporation increasingly redundant' (Abercrombie *et al.* 1994: 164). Thus they question the number of people who are actually supportive of the dominant ideology in advanced capitalist societies and the power of ideological state apparatuses to create false consciousness (Abercrombie *et al.* 1980). To take their arguments further though, we must focus on the lived experience of privatised individuals and differentiate between privatised existence and a commitment to individualism. Again the comments of Lasch are relevant in understanding the nature of privatism:

> Experiences of inner emptiness, loneliness, and inauthenticity are by no means unreal or, for that matter, devoid of social content. . . . They arise from the warlike conditions that pervade . . . society, from the dangers and uncertainty that surround us, and from a loss of confidence in the future.
>
> (Lasch 1979: 27)

The ideology of individualism, a powerful tool of the neo-liberal right, stands in opposition to Lasch's theory. The former is an extremely convenient way of explaining the failures and misfortunes of individuals in satisfying their needs. The ideology of individualism promotes competition between people and excessive growth and consumption. Thus, by promoting privatistic individualism and a lack of social responsibility, the outcome of individual actions can only be laid at the feet of that individual. It cannot be denied that contemporary neo-liberal thought is characterised by an increased emphasis on this ideology.

However many socialists argue that reliance upon the ideology of individualism is problematic because it devolves responsibility from society to the individual when it is apparent that advanced capitalism is characterised by the increased powerlessness of the individual (Mobasser 1987: 119–28). The primary problem for thinkers who wish to dissociate the phenomena of privatism and individualism comes with the idea that because individuals are privatistic, they are also following the ideology of individualism. This suggests that individuals are privatistic because they have made an ideological decision to be so. These ideas can be inferred from statements such as 'the dominant current in the political culture of contemporary Britain runs from collectivism to individualism and thence to privatism' (Papadakis and Taylor-Gooby 1987: 15). On the contrary, privatism is not an ideology; it is an objective reaction to social conditions when the public sphere holds no space for the development of autonomous self-identity and ontological security. In such a situation it is understandable that individuals will seek to resolve the search for meaning and identity through relationships in the private sphere such as those within the family.

In accordance with Habermas, the prevalence of privatism should be understood as a practical syndrome rather than as an ideological commitment to individualism. The main forms of privatism that Habermas outlined in his early work, in particular *Legitimation Crisis* (1976a), were the concentration on the family and career as the agents of social significance (family-vocational privatism) and abstinence from the political domain (civic privatism) which complements the former. In the words of Lodziak:

> The encouragement of an orientation toward family and career is at one and the same time an encouragement away from the development of an active interest in politics. The system thus steers people into civic privatism or political abstinence. From time to

> time we are invited to register a vote in electoral contests amongst parties whom we are to entrust with 'bigger' matters while we get on with our own lives, exercising consumer choice and pursuing careers.
>
> (Lodziak 1988: 13)

INDIVIDUALISM AND MOTIVATION: THE POLITICS OF LEGITIMATION

Habermas initially believed that the legitimation of capitalism was reliant on the state satisfying individuals' needs. This, he believed, was the means through which capitalism gained its reproductive power (Habermas 1976a). Capitalism encouraged individuals to seek significance through a devotion to one's family and job and individuals were discouraged from engaging with the political arena. Hence, if individuals concerned themselves with their private needs, the running of society was left to those experts maintained by the power of capital. In such a system, Habermas believed, capitalism held reproductive power through the political abstinence of the majority. In this situation radical mobilisation around socialist goals was unlikely to occur. Habermas believed that the private sphere had successfully satisfied the perceived needs of the population and therefore capitalist society had gained the consent of its members. In short, capitalism encouraged the prevalence of privatism to acquire legitimacy.

However the conflict of interests between labour and capital and the increased public spending budget in the 1970s meant that there was extreme pressure on the state to satisfy individual needs. What became apparent was the contradictions in the role of the state as on one hand it was concerned with providing conducive conditions for capital accumulation, whilst on the other it faced a demand for services and spending from the population (Offe 1984). Habermas believed that this contradiction led to a crisis of legitimacy for the state which could not satisfy the demands of both capital and labour. In turn, this threatened capitalist reproduction. Although these ideas contain valuable analysis of the crisis of capitalism, Habermas was to refine them in later writings (Habermas 1984; Narr 1984).

The most obvious criticism of the early Habermasian approach was that it supposed that capitalist society needed consent and legitimacy to secure its reproduction. Following the breakdown of 'Keynesian consensus' in the late 1960s and early 1970s, Habermas believed the system to be in crisis because it could no longer rely on the loyalty of society. Nevertheless capitalism survived and it continues to reproduce itself in the face of social unrest on a global scale. As Habermas was to realise, this suggests that the capitalist system does not require the consent of its members to reproduce itself and that the failure to overcome capitalism is the result of two central factors. Firstly, as Habermas himself pointed out, the failure to overthrow capitalism was a question of individual motivation in terms of acquiescence rather than of legitimation. Furthermore, as Gorz has emphasised, the lack of resources held by the majority of the population serves to reinforce the subservience of individuals to the system and discourages oppositional action.

Beetham provides a further criticism of the Habermasian notion of legitimation crisis. He argues that the notion of crisis is loosely applied in the sense that public unrest ultimately tends not to be directed at the rules and organisation of the economic or political system. Rather it tends to focus on governmental authority which is altogether different from a crisis of the state because the latter suggests fundamental disagreements regarding the rules of the political order (Beetham 1991: 169). He points to the experience of the 1980s when, in Britain for example, a government committed to neo-liberal policies came into power which sought to eliminate the sources of 'legitimation crisis' by relinquishing governmental commitment to high levels of public spending. However Beetham's point can be taken a step further in an era when the arena of politics is held in much distaste and there is a prevalent negative view of politicians regardless of which party they belong to. In this situation individuals are likely to turn their backs on politics and political activism and essentially they withdraw any engagement with the political process. This trend can be identified in the small number of individuals who bother to turn out for elections – the point is clear, civic privatism is rife.

Habermas and Gorz predicted two possible outcomes of this situation. One might be that individuals could react against civic privatism and social isolation by entering into greater political activity against the system through new social movements; this would amount to individuals re-entering the public sphere. The more likely result, though, was that more individuals would be driven further into the private sphere in the search for significance. In essence, a new form of privatism would develop which Lodziak has termed 'self-maintaining privatism' (Lodziak 1986: 178–84). This new privatism was characterised by the struggle of individuals to achieve self-identity and esteem when left to their own powerless, private sphere in the absence of any kind of fulfilment in the public domain. This type of privatism, which is increasingly prevalent, complements and accentuates the effects of civic and family-vocational privatism in devolving responsibility from the system to the individual.

Nevertheless some individuals do indicate a degree of commitment to the ideology of individualism promoted by the capitalist system. These individuals can be said to be engaging in self-seeking or mobile privatism which is manifest through excessive consumption and pre-occupation with status as a gauge of human value (Habermas 1976b; Lodziak 1986: 175–84). It would be a mistake to overestimate the number of people actively involved in an ideological commitment to self-seeking privatism but, as Lodziak has observed, this form of privatism is the closest correlation there is between privatism and the ideology of individualism. Furthermore, individuals practising mass consumption are actively involved in self-maintaining privatism simultaneously, precisely because excessive consumerism is no substitute for self-esteem, ontological security or a degree of autonomy. This serves only to increase the pressure on personal and familial relationships which tend to provide the only areas where the slightest degree of self-esteem and reciprocal love can be sought. Consumerism, as Gorz has realised, is distinctive because its 'pleasures' or effects are short-lived, passive and asocial. According to O'Connor:

> 'Consumers' remain irreducibly human beings who constitute themselves as historical subjects as well as objects of the consumption process. In short, the commodity form of need satisfaction, together with the wage form of labour, means that to the degree that needs are satisfied in the 'individual' form, they are frustrated in the social form.
>
> (O'Connor 1984: 20)

Following O'Connor and Gorz, it is pertinent to note that the identity conferred by consumer activity is at best transient and unstable and cannot be emancipatory. Even individuals who find satisfaction in self-seeking privatism do not necessarily satisfy existential needs when they consume luxury, material goods. Existential needs which satisfy the desire for security and positive identity are on an entirely different plane from material needs or wants. The latter can never satisfy the human desire for autonomy, self-determination, and reciprocal love. Nevertheless, as Lasch observes, it is important to note that consumer activity has become a prominent mode of attempting to gain some private pleasure in the face of the competitive logic that governs the public sphere in late capitalist societies: 'The pursuit of self-interest, formerly identified with the rational pursuit of gain and the accumulation of wealth, has become a search for pleasure and psychic survival' (Lasch 1979: 69). As such socialists cannot merely dismiss consumerism as evidence of false needs, they must question how these 'needs' are created and perpetuated and, more importantly, develop a strategy to reverse these trends.

Gorz's dualisation of society seeks to expand the private sphere and, therefore, to create an arena where the private satisfaction of existential needs becomes a possibility. In essence, Gorz attempts to create a private sphere that does not reflect the growth, accumulation and consumption of the public sphere in advanced capitalism. He does not deny the necessity of collective, human interaction for individual self-identity but he does suggest that there are possibilities within the private sphere for individuals to develop ontological security and maintain a relatively stable identity. In short, the private sphere can yield satisfaction for individuals but it must be delivered from the atomisation of contemporary privatism. As Horkheimer suggested, 'the emancipation of the individual is not an emancipation from society, but the deliverance of society from atomisation' (Horkheimer 1974: 135).

DEVELOPING THE EMANCIPATORY INTEREST

Gorz argues, in accordance with Marcuse's advocacy of the pleasure principle, for the maximum pleasure to be derived from the different sectors of society created by his dualisation:

> Vitality, joie de vivre, creature comforts; joy in beauty and artistic creation or joy in liberating action: all may come together in the same person – this remains the ideal – but not at the same moment. This is why the differentiated organization of time – days, weeks, years and so on – has always existed. The ideal is an existence in which one can move smoothly between planes without having to sacrifice or subordinate any one of them.
>
> (Gorz 1989b: 276)

Gorz emphasises that the traditional area for social interaction and the formation of self-identity (i.e. civil society) has been eroded and colonised by the logic of capitalist growth. This is the trend which Habermas has referred to as the 'colonisation of the lifeworld' which is linked to his theory of the different 'interests' which help to reproduce societies (Habermas 1987: 356). These are the technical, communicative and emancipatory interests. The first alludes to the tendency of societies to seek control over nature through the production of goods and the development of technology. Communicative interest refers to the interactive structures of society which allow individuals and institutions to communicate thereby aiding the technical interest. Finally there is the emancipatory interest which encompasses the desire of individuals to achieve self-liberation through power struggles using both language and technology. It is the interaction between these three interests which, according to Habermas, enables the production and reproduction of societies.

In line with both Marcuse and Gorz, Habermas argues that contemporary technocapitalism is distinguished from previous, social organisation by the manner in which the technical interest has become the governing factor in social reproduction (Marcuse 1978). This has occurred to the detriment of the other interests (communicative and emancipatory) and signifies the marginalisation of communication and struggles for autonomy. Essentially Habermas is asserting that the logic and rationality of technical domination has taken control of not only the state and the economy but also everyday life in the private sphere. Hence, as Offe has realised, state policy towards areas such as health and education, which was previously governed by the principle of necessity, has come to be identified with rationalisation and maximum efficiency; both of which are characteristics of the technical interest. Offe believes that the bridge between the individual and the state has broken down (Offe 1984).

Following Habermas and Offe, communication in the public sphere is essential for democratic politics, yet this has been precluded by the excessive influence of the technical interest. The public sphere, that is, the arena of political decision making, has become increasingly colonised by technical rationality. Thus, whilst civic privatism has been identified as a barrier to self-liberation, it should be noted that the agenda of political debate has been saturated by the logic of technical growth, thereby making the political domain unattractive to many individuals. Just because individuals abstain from political activism does not mean that they do not hold strong political beliefs and commitments. It is public structures organised around the technical interest which bar entrance to the political arena, not the political acquiescence of individuals to the ideas and interests of the dominant class. The origins of this theory lie in the work of Marcuse who, like Gorz, believed that the inversion of technical reason could provide emancipatory potential (Kettler 1976: 27).

For Marcuse, Habermas and Gorz, the suppression of technical reason is vital if self-determination and collective action are to become politically viable. Essentially technical 'progress', and its effects on social relations, have ensured that the capitalist system no longer requires legitimation from the population. In essence, the state has not been conferred with authority by the population but, on the contrary, is able to govern without genuine input from the members of advanced capitalist societies. Thus the state administers to people in the interest of capital: it does not express the public interest. As Keane has persistently argued, democracy and public opinion rarely figure in political argument precisely because the public sphere is depoliticised, institutionalised and rationalised along external principles to accountability and representation (Keane 1988). In a situation such as this, it is not surprising that most individuals are not motivated to seek satisfaction of existential needs in such a depoliticised public sphere. Thus, the tendency to regard the private sphere as the source of self-actualisation is accelerated (Habermas 1984: 20).

For Habermas, the economy and state have become detached from the lifeworld and are no longer controlled by or subject to political debate in the public sphere. On the contrary, the 'system' has achieved a position in which it dictates to or colonises the private and public spheres. This has led to an erosion of the values and traditions that were previously identified with the lifeworld. Thus, the inter-personal relationships which characterised activity within the public sphere have been increasingly replaced with the values of technical reason. The prioritisation of the technical interest, and the civic privatism that it encourages, results in an abolition of the communicative interest. Habermas uses this eradication of the communicative interest to explain why individuals tend to seek solace in the private sphere. The consequent, social isolationism that privatism creates not only impedes oppositional activism but also positively assists what Gorz sees as technofascist social control. Habermas alludes to the effects of these developments on Germany in a style very reminiscent of Gorz:

> The end of the work-based society . . . is throwing up problems which so far have not been properly analysed. But they are experienced as problems by everyone . . . the Federal Republic is moving towards a 'split' society, with a productive core of the employed, and an expanding margin of the poorly fed and neglected, who are forced into subcultures and ghettos. The decisive political question of the next few years will be whether

this process can be kept out of the public gaze, or will become the focus of political confrontations.

(Habermas 1986: 141)

The correlation with Gorzian theory is quite obvious at this point. Although both Habermas and Gorz hope that this division of previously integrated sectors within society becomes the focus of political confrontation, the opposite appears to be the case. Technocapitalism seems capable of shrouding this existential crisis within the productivist political agenda which it has created. Thus, the reproduction of capitalism does not at present appear to be under threat, even though it is hardly legitimised by the population. The problems and crises that Habermas outlines are apparent and they fit comfortably with another feature of the colonisation of the lifeworld that Giddens has concentrated upon – the pervasive powers of surveillance held and used by technocapitalist states. These are used to maintain social control and alienate any form of radical discourse or active mobilisation that could be subversive (Giddens 1985: 302–10; Held 1989a: 142). Members of the parliamentary British Labour Party and trade unionists have been subject to close surveillance even though the majority of them hardly represent a threat to the contemporary, political 'status quo'.

Both Gorz and Habermas attempt to analyse the emancipatory possibilities of the private sphere, although Habermas eventually prioritises the rejuvenation of the public sphere to realise the emancipatory potential. Gorz stresses that under-socialisation (the absence of traditional socialising agents) creates a situation in which the individual can achieve self-definition in the private sphere (Gorz 1985a: 65–6; Narr 1984: 36). Essentially these theorists believe that the changing nature of the agents of socialisation, such as the family, education and work, lead to the possibility that individuals will not be socialised into traditional roles to the extent that they were previously. This leaves a gap which individuals could use to define their identity in a manner that is not decided by the traditional agents of socialisation in capitalist society (especially work). Of course, this does not mean that all under-socialised individuals will necessarily develop radical consciousness – rather it is merely an identification of the potential that exists.

Gorz argues that the breakdown of the nuclear family has led to a possibility that more individuals can seek their identity outside the constraining limitations of being a father or a mother, a 'breadwinner' or a 'housewife'. Nevertheless this possibility has never materialised as individuals continue to seek identity and significance in the private sphere. The socialisation gap has tended to be filled by the trivia of the mass media rather than an emancipatory self-identity. This tendency towards the passive consumption of media images accentuates the emphasis on social isolation and hinders the development of autonomous agency. According to Narr:

> this type of development of informational and communicative techniques destroys the integrity of social spheres as well as that of individuals themselves. Individuals possess no controlling criteria, no controlling information, no controlling communication; they can in fact reduce the complexity in the quantity of information and communication only by placing trust in this complexity. That is its primary sense.
>
> (Narr 1984: 43)

Keane and Giddens are quick to point out that individuals are not simple receivers of the messages purveyed by the media and that there is emancipatory potential within the new information era (Giddens 1984: 16; Keane 1991). Similarly Habermas sees positive, liberatory signs in the electronic media, not surprising given his long-term desire to resurrect the communicative interest:

> The mass media belong to these generalized forms of communication. They free communication processes from the provinciality of spatiotemporally restricted contexts and permit public spheres to emerge, through establishing the abstract simultaneity of a virtually present network of communication contents far removed in space and time through keeping messages available for manifold contexts. These media publics hierarchize and at the same time remove restrictions on the horizon of possible communication . . . they considerably strengthen the efficacy of social controls. But tapping this authoritarian potential is always precarious because there is a counterweight of emancipatory potential built into communication structures themselves.
>
> (Habermas 1986: 390)

Like Gorz, Habermas is quick to highlight the liberatory possibilities of some forms of capitalist technical development. Nevertheless it is apparent that communication structures are more often used for authoritarian, social control as opposed to the transmission of radical ideas. Moreover, alternatives to the flood of pre-packaged electronic media trivia, such as the heightened activism of social movements, do not appear to have surpassed passivity as guiding influences in the 'socialisation gap'. Again, social isolation is reinforced by the media structure which actively encourages privatism despite the inherent emancipatory/authoritarian contradictions that Habermas exposes. Moreover control of the media has ensured that it has been a primary agent in the growth and pervasiveness of the materialist perception of needs.

OBSTACLES TO SELF-DETERMINATION: THE MANIPULATION OF NEEDS

The constant search for emancipatory potential is a theme that both Habermas and Gorz discuss. Gorz does not concur with the optimism that characterises the Habermasian proposals, which suggests that Gorz may have a stronger grasp of the difficulties in creating a desirable alternative to the conditions of advanced capitalism. Without this, it is impossible for individuals to achieve ontological security and self-determination in the realm of autonomy. Gorz believes that the key barrier to the development of self-determination is the manipulation of individual needs by the state economic system:

> The demand for self-determination, for autonomy, can today only be expressed negatively: through a withdrawal into the family and private life. Work and society remain the realm of heteronomy. The importance of strengthening the micro-social communities in which we live and work lies precisely in the fact that they provide the missing but necessary mediation between the spheres of the private individual and society as a whole. Liberated time is only meaningful if people can use it in shaping social relations and modes of co-operation.
>
> (Gorz 1989b: 297)

Marx's theory of the manipulation of needs, which has been revitalised by Heller and, more recently, by Lodziak, incorporates a persuasive analysis of the nature of power (Heller 1976; Lodziak 1995). For Heller, the Marxist notion of the manipulation of needs manifests itself in contemporary capitalism through excessive consumerism:

> Capitalism is the pimp that by constantly producing new objects creates an unending stream of new needs which make people prostitute themselves. The numerical growth of needs will never be able to become *true* wealth, because it is merely a *means* serving an alienating force, alien to individual human beings, i.e. the expansion of capitalist production.
>
> (Heller 1976: 50)

Lodziak's construction of the manipulation of needs thesis is invigorated by the use of the ideas of Gorz, Giddens and Habermas. The manipulation of needs theory tackles the needs of individuals in the pursuit of autonomy on an experiential level. Lodziak challenges the idea that individuals have internalised the dominant ideology and therefore reproduce this consciousness in their actions. Thus, in accordance with Seve, he seeks to break the consensual link between action and consciousness (Seve 1978: 321). In essence, this disjunction undermines the dominant ideology thesis because it recognises that the acquiescent behaviour of most individuals to the dominant system does not correspond to an ideological verification of the dominant beliefs. Other commentators like Mann have also noted widespread ideological indifference amongst the majority of the population rather than an incorporation of the dominant ideology (Mann 1982: 373–95).

Essentially, Lodziak is trying to scale down the emphasis given to ideology in contemporary socialist theory. The manipulation of needs thesis seeks to redress this imbalance. There are three central points in this thesis which can be a useful addition to Gorzian theory, although Gorz himself does not refer to the manipulation of needs directly:

1 Human action does not directly represent consciousness but is a result of the resources available and not available to individuals in the satisfaction of experienced needs.
2 The scope of individual action is severely impaired by the fact that the capitalist economy and the state control most of the available resources in society.
3 Employers and the state manipulate their resources to form structures of domination which are reproduced by actions which do not conflict with these structures but reinforce them.

(Lodziak 1995)

In accordance with Lodziak, Gorz attempts to show how individual action is curtailed by the control of resources by dominant groups. This is vital for social reproduction because the system ostensibly attempts to satisfy the basic, material needs of most individuals whilst simultaneously blocking the development of potentially emancipatory, existential needs. Because resources are held and controlled by small, dominant groups in society, most individuals are compelled into relations of dependency on others to obtain the resources for mere survival. Predominantly, as Gorz constantly emphasises, this dependency on others is linked to a system of employment which is organised to satisfy the employer's need (profit) rather than that of the employee (survival). Essential to this analysis is the idea of the structuration of time and needs outlined by Giddens, an idea that also underpins Gorz's advocacy of a new politics of time (Giddens 1984). Because employers and the state control resources, individuals are forced to sell their time to employers to gain their own resources for survival. This system consumes time which could be used for the development of needs that go beyond basic survival, such as existential needs.

Therefore the manipulation of needs theory incorporates the notion that human action is limited by the time and resources available to act. Hence, the time spent in employment for the satisfaction of basic needs impedes the time available for emancipatory action and the satisfaction of existential needs. As Gorz argues, the structuration of time limits the sphere of human action outside the heteronomous realm and therefore restricts the possibility of the satisfaction of needs that go beyond survival. Similarly Heller observes in her analysis of Marx, 'beyond survival needs' cannot be satisfied in the same way that basic needs are satisfied in advanced capitalist societies:

> spiritual and moral needs, those that relate to the collectivity, are the opposite of necessary needs. Such needs [spiritual and moral] will not be fixed – at least in the future – by their position in the division of labour, because they are *individual* needs (they cannot be expressed by any average), and because their satisfaction is not purchasable.
>
> (Heller 1976: 34, original emphasis)

This manipulation of needs and time generates a situation in which fragmented leisure time, all that is left outside of the heteronomous realm, is increasingly directed towards passive electronic entertainment and consumption. Lodziak argues that there is no alternative to the dominant system that can be actualised by powerless individuals engulfed in the isolation of privatism (Lodziak 1986). In this state of affairs individuals tend to acquiesce pragmatically to the prevailing conditions, rather than act against them in limited circumstances which would threaten their survival. For instance, individuals actively striving to work twenty hours per week, to allow time for greater existential autonomy, may lose their job, their means of basic survival, to be replaced by individuals prepared to renounce their autonomy and work forty hours per week.

Manipulation of needs theory also recognises that individuals can experience needs without choosing to satisfy them, even survival needs. Again this corresponds with Seve's belief that there is a disjunction between consciousness and action. This suggests that there are many consciously experienced needs which individuals do not or cannot satisfy due to a lack of material resources and time. In the contemporary system, most of these unsatisfied but experienced needs tend to be existential needs, given that we are aware of the limits to our range of action due to lack of resources. In conditions where there is a stark choice between spending time gaining the resources for basic, survival needs through work, and forgoing basic needs to satisfy existential needs (cultural, erotic, aesthetic, etc.), individuals will generally try to find work. Gorz insists that a reduction in work time, coupled with a social wage, can release time and resources for individuals to satisfy 'beyond survival needs'.

It is possible then, within the framework of Gorz and Lodziak, to outline three specific categories of human needs. Firstly, there are basic survival needs; these include the material and biological necessities required for the maintenance of life. Secondly, there are structurally imposed needs which are generated by the systematic organisation of society. Thus, through the satisfaction of survival needs, other needs are generated such as welfare, transport, and consumer goods to save time and space. Finally there are what Gorz and Marcuse refer to as existential needs. This category refers to the desires for identity, significance and esteem which go beyond mere survival. In socialist debates this is the category which attracts the most controversy, although, as Geras has observed, Marx argued that the nature of the individual encompassed a broad desire for self-determination (Geras 1983: 98–100).

Gorz, in agreement with Heller, argues that existential needs cannot be universally defined because the meaning of culture, love, friendship and beauty differs between individuals. Nevertheless, Gorzian theory recognises that the only way for existential needs to be satisfied is for those needs to be autonomously chosen by the individual concerned. Thus, those activities which are likely to derive the greatest satisfaction and meaning are those which are autonomously defined and executed, thereby yielding the most self-expression. In a style akin to Gorz, Lodziak argues that autonomy is impeded by the manipulation of needs through the structuration of time and the inequality of resources:

> The needs of autonomy, ontological security and a sense of significance derive from the need for meaning. The satisfaction of survival and meaning is mediated through the satisfaction of structurally-imposed and system-generated needs, which are historically variable. In addition to the structurally-imposed

> needs already mentioned . . . money and time can be viewed as structurally imposed in advanced capitalist societies.
>
> (Lodziak 1992: 8)

Lodziak is obviously aware that the time spent satisfying survival and structurally imposed needs severely impinges on the sphere left over for the satisfaction of existential needs. Soper observes how this creates a general powerlessness, an apathetic acquiescence which corresponds with the Habermasian conception of privatism:

> If you are deprived of food, you feel the pangs of hunger; if you are deprived of love or of opportunities for creative activity, or of the space and time that are preconditions of any self-development, you do not so much feel the loss as lose the power to feel – you become the victim of a vicious regress, caught up in a process that numbs sensitivity in the very act of depriving it.
>
> (Soper 1981: 184)

Gorz's understanding of the manipulation of needs theory in advanced capitalist society correlates closely with that of Lodziak and Soper. Gorz realises that the capitalist class manipulate the subordinated sector of society through the exchange of surplus labour into surplus goods. As such, he argues that individuals are constituted as potential consumers whose individual needs are limited to buying goods and services that keep advanced capitalist economies afloat. In essence, Gorz believes that individuals do not satisfy their existential needs, but the needs of capitalist reproduction:

> *People must be prevented from choosing to limit their working hours so as to prevent them choosing to limit their desire to consume.* A growing number of wage earners must work and earn *beyond their felt needs*, so that a growing proportion of income may be spent on consumption determined by no need. For it is such optional, superfluous consumption, which can be directed, shaped, manipulated according to the 'needs' of capital more than to individuals' needs. *It is to the extent that consumption frees itself from felt needs and exceeds them that it can serve production, that is, serve the 'needs' of capital.*
>
> (Gorz 1989a: 119, original emphasis)

Gorz's manipulation of needs theory is based on the realisation that the manipulation of resources is necessary for social reproduction. Socialism must, then, submit the economy and the state to rigorous, critical analysis. This implies a rejection of the explanation of social reproduction through false consciousness and the indoctrinating power of the electronic media. The central determinant which characterises Gorz's theory is his experiential analysis of the nature of power and the imbalance of resources in the conditions of advanced capitalism. In short, this imbalance precludes the possibility of the development of individual autonomy. Without autonomous power, individuals are unable to concretise the emancipatory potential that Gorz identifies.

In the final analysis, Gorz attempts to discover arenas for the rebirth of critical, emancipatory thought. This, he realises, is difficult to achieve within a system whose power relations are actively engaged in minimising the development of radical critique. Hence if these power relations, governed by the allocation of resources, are not challenged, then autonomy and consequently emancipation may not be achieved. Similarly, Adorno stated that 'freedom means to criticise and change situations, not to confirm them by deciding within their coercive structure' (Adorno 1983: 226).

Gorz's discussion of existential needs, individuality, critical thought and individual autonomy is dynamic and thought-provoking but he does not go into sufficient detail in his discussion of needs. If socialists are to substantially base their proposals on needs and the priority of satisfying them, then they need a more specific typology of human needs than Gorz provides. Recently thinkers of the Left have made more substantive discussion of needs a priority, particularly in relation to the concept of abundance (Doyal and Gough 1991; Van Parijs 1993; Soper 1993). Of these contributions the most rigorous is that of Doyal and Gough who offer a universal programme of needs and, importantly, give over much space to need-satisfaction. It is a comprehensive theory which negates Kymlicka's claim that 'the [Marxist] needs principle does not compete with liberal theories of equality, for it is simply at a less-developed stage of formulation' (Kymlicka 1990: 186).

At the most basic level Doyal and Gough outline three multifaceted dimensions of basic needs: physical health; autonomy of agency; and critical autonomy which are designed to facilitate the greatest possible degree of participation and liberation (Doyal and Gough 1991: 151–77). Due to his failure to deal with needs in detail, we can only infer that this programme of needs corresponds closely to Gorz's notion of human needs. The important point that Doyal and Gough raise which is also central to Gorz's thesis is that there can be human needs which can be satisfied in different ways by separate individuals. What

Marxist theorists tend not to emphasise is the fact that, given the resources, individuals may still choose not to satisfy needs. If the aim of socialism is to provide individuals with the means of satisfying their needs, including time and resources for autonomous activities, we must be equally aware that not all individuals will use their resources in the appropriate manner. Nonetheless the goal of enabling individuals to exercise self-determination cannot be emancipatory if individuals are coerced into spending their resources in a specific way – that would constitute the kind of social engineering that is antithetical to Gorz's liberatory aims.

As Gorz observes, it is the manipulation of time, needs and resources in advanced capitalist societies that ensure their reproduction. Only through a new politics of time which prioritises existential autonomy over the economic logic of capital, can Gorz's vision of a truly emancipated socialist society become a political reality. In Gorz's words:

> A new utopia is needed if we are to safeguard what the ethical content of the socialist utopia provided; the utopia of a society of free time. The emancipation of individuals, their full development, the restructuring of society, are all achieved through the liberation from work. A reduction in working hours will allow individuals to discover a new sense of security, a new distancing from the 'necessities of life' and a form of existential autonomy which will encourage them to demand more autonomy within their work, political control of its objectives and a social space in which they can engage in voluntary and self-organised activities. (Gorz 1989a: 101)

7

UTOPIANISM AND WELFARE

Theses for a future left

There is a long history of utopian thought in the socialist tradition stretching back to Saint-Simon, Owen and Fourier which has been resurrected in more recent times by a range of Western European authors (Geoghegan 1987). Gorz is probably the best-known contemporary utopian socialist and this is one of the reasons why his work has achieved such notoriety. Utopianism is a vibrant method of challenging the accepted political order and questioning orthodoxy within political traditions but, unfortunately, it is also too readily dismissed by defenders of dominant or popular ideas. Importantly though, even popular ideas usually entail an element of utopianism such as the glorification of the market as the panacea for all our ills in neo-liberal theory (Geoghegan 1987: 3–4). In the light of this, it is disingenuous to ignore ideas on the basis that they do not correspond with the prevailing political climate.

Gorz has attracted much criticism from commentators for the more prophetic or utopian elements in his work, or those policy ideas he has extrapolated from his socialist individualism (Frankel 1987; Giddens 1987). Moreover even commentators who defend the concept of utopia have fundamentally misunderstood the idea of the neo-proletariat and classed Gorz's theory as 'absurd' (Levitas 1990: 196–7). These comments have been primarily aimed at the 'utopia' he outlined in *Ecology as Politics* (1987a), but reference has also been made to the iconoclastic critique that Gorz expounded in sections of *Farewell to the Working Class* (1987b) and *Paths to Paradise* (1985). In these works, Gorz set out to demonstrate the sterility of traditional socialist theory when applied to the specific conditions and contradictions of advanced capitalism. He believed that the purpose of utopianism was 'to liberate the imagination to the possibilities of change' (Gorz 1987a: 42).

THE USE OF UTOPIA

Essentially Gorz maintained that classical Marxism was outdated and that socialists could ground their claims in realism only by developing a revitalised alternative to advanced capitalism. As such, he argued that the Left must seek to create new avenues for change, rather than paying lip-service to the myths of collective appropriation and the innate historical role of the revolutionary proletariat. The most recent exposition of these ideas has been *Capitalism, Socialism, Ecology* (1994).

Evidently Gorz's work corresponds with the criteria for utopianism that Geoghegan has outlined:

> The classic utopia anticipates and criticizes. Its alternative fundamentally interrogates the present, piercing existing societies' defensive mechanisms – common sense, realism, positivism and scientism. Its unabashed and flagrant otherness gives it a power which is lacking in other analytical devices. By playing fast and loose with time and space, logic and morality, and by thinking the unthinkable, a utopia asks the most awkward, the most embarrassing questions.
>
> (Geoghegan 1987: 1–2)

Gorz does not attempt to replace orthodox Marxist ideas with a new 'truth' but instead attempts to encourage a greater degree of self-criticism on the Left. Utopianism is a powerful means of developing this critique as it can avoid the prescriptive and prophetic elements of Marx's concept of history. Nevertheless, as Geoghegan has noted, rather than seeking to dehistoricise Marxism, Gorz's intention is 'to avoid the authoritarian utopianism implicit in some types of Marxism. The model is to stimulate individual creativity in readers, not establish some kind of binding norm' (Geoghegan 1987: 128).

In this very limited task, Gorz succeeds, although his perception of the role of the state is ambiguous (Frankel 1987: 59–63). What is apparent from his writings is the lacuna between socialist theory and the practice of traditional socialist parties and institutions. This refutes the taunts of utopianism levelled at Gorz from the orthodox Left because the former attempts to reunite socialist theory and practice. His account of the bankruptcy of traditional theory involves a persuasive argument for the necessity of redeveloping socialism to engage with the specific contradictions of advanced capitalism. Only through such a reassessment, he argues, can the Left lay claim to the realism which is necessary for the concretisation of socialist theory. In the words of Bauman:

> The utopian function of the socialist project can be retained, in the circumstances, only on the condition that its critical edge is directed against *all* reality. Since this reality encompasses sectors styled as socialist, socialist *utopia* must take a critical stance toward socialist *reality* as well as capitalist reality.
>
> (Bauman 1976: 130, original emphasis)

What is also apparent in the 'utopian' elements of Gorzian theory is the debt he owes to Marx. He is undoubtedly selective in his use of Marx; in fact, some of his criticisms are particularly vitriolic, especially in *Farewell to the Working Class.* Nevertheless his work is firmly grounded in the Marxian tradition, a point emphasised by the constant recourse to *Grundrisse* in *Paths to Paradise.* Grint notes that Gorz pushes a 'rather heretical form of Marxism [which] actually has strong resonances with Marx's critique of the commodification of all relations' (Grint 1991: 205). As Geoghegan argues, Gorz's place in the Marxian tradition is much clearer than that of other so-called 'post-industrial utopians' such as Rudolf Bahro whose theory also originated from the socialist critique of Marxism (Geoghegan 1987: 133).

Frankel's critique of Gorz (along with Toffler, Jones and Bahro) characterises his work as utopian in the negative sense that his beliefs are held to be unrealisable. He rejects post-industrial visions on the grounds that 'they remain pious wishes if not linked to concrete plans of action and organization' (Frankel 1987: 18). In his more recent work Gorz provides a refutation of this criticism by outlining a plan of action for trade unions and an economic structure through which reduced working hours could be facilitated and a citizen's wage imposed (Gorz 1989: 219–42; 1994: 102–17). The question remains as to whether the absence of a clear strategy for change in Gorz's early work was a major failing. After all he was trying to free the Leftist imagination rather than construct the post-industrial socialist prototype. Moreover, as Smart notes, Frankel's criticism is equally applicable to 'most social theorists who have sought critically to analyse the present and comment on the future – a long list' (Smart 1992: 67).

It seems that the negative accusation of utopianism is often bandied about loosely just as Marx and Engels employed a historicist optimism in their scientific socialism that has survived the test of time no better than the early utopian socialists that they derided. The point is not to ridicule Marx and Engels for their 'vision', precisely because their work has provided a great deal of stimulation for political theorists and activists since it was written. What Gorz provides is a 'utopia' which is firmly grounded in the transformation of concrete political, social and economic structures and, as Hoffman notes, 'democracy . . . involves a "utopianism" embedded in the world of reality' (Hoffman 1995: 14).

The other forum in which the concept of utopianism has recently been prominent is in the modernity/post-modernity debate. As utopianism is a mode of thought which presents us with holistic visions at the end of the political horizon it can be portrayed as an extension of 'the project of modernity'. If we swallow the post-modernity thesis that the era of modernity has come to an end, then it is possible to make the argument that we have also reached a post-utopian phase (Mishra 1993). However Mishra's proclamation of 'the end of utopia' is problematic, not least in his narrow definition of utopianism which he equates with historicist ideologies such as Marxism, democratic socialism and neo-conservatism. Whilst he is justified in pointing to difficulties facing these traditions, Mishra throws the utopian baby out with the ideological bath water when it seems that both retain relevance to the contemporary era.

Mishra regards the aforementioned ideologies as both historicist and evolutionary grand narratives which have failed and consequently lost credibility (Mishra 1993: 18–19). In their absence he leaves us with a post-modern inertia devoid of ideological conflict in which social policy is reduced to 'micro-politics'. This appears to underestimate the amount of conflict that welfare capitalism generates. Just because the system has not collapsed as Marxist theorists predicted does not mean that welfare capitalism has won a mythical battle with Marxists, democratic socialists and neo-liberals. Rather there is continuing opposition to welfare capitalism typified by the work of Gorz whose 'utopian' theory offers a new dimension for the stagnating traditions of Marxism and democratic socialism. Moreover the fact that Gorz's work is proving increasingly influential suggests that the Left has not stagnated to the extent presented by Mishra and the continued prominence of neo-liberalism in the political arena points to some health on the Right. This appears to negate Mishra's rather uncritical acceptance of the post-modernity thesis and highlights the likelihood of continued vigorous conflict over the existence and future of welfare capitalism.

Interestingly Mishra points to some of the trends which are central to Gorz's theory, most notably, the end of full employment and the inadequacy of the Keynesian welfare state in this scenario. The fact that they concur on these developments adequately demonstrates that conflict remains regarding welfare capitalism. It also clarifies the fact that Mishra's identification of utopianism as a purely modernist form of thought is rather simplistic. Similarly Frankel believes that the post-industrial utopians he analyses all 'adhere firmly to the tradition of the European Enlightenment' (Frankel 1987: 180). Smart, on the other hand, points to the strand of anti-modernism in Bahro's work and contrasts this with Gorz's search for 'an essentially orderly totality' which serves the point that not all post-industrial utopians are servants of the project of modernity (Smart 1992: 108). Nevertheless it seems apparent that Gorz does retain a modernist perspective which might explain his sympathy with Alvin Toffler's modernist work despite their differences. Ultimately, though, it is difficult not to concur with Frankel, who argues that it is lax to loosely categorise diverse thinkers as 'modern' or 'post-modern', which is a common trend amongst those who argue that we have moved into a post-modern era such as Mishra (Frankel 1987: 182).

Klein offers a slightly different perspective on social policy, although he agrees with Mishra that Marxist utopias are now redundant and that Offe, Gough and O'Connor overestimated the crisis of the welfare state (Klein 1993: 10–11). Habermas has clarified the problem that orthodox Marxism faces, that is, that it is unrealistic to create a welfare programme which relies on Marx's idea of social labour because 'that utopia has lost its point of reference in reality: the power of abstract labour to create structure and give form to society' (Habermas 1989: 53). This does not mean that the radical Left is defeated as Mishra and Klein believe. Rather as Habermas indicates we must create socialist programmes (or utopias) in which social labour is relinquished. Gorz's advocacy of a separation between autonomy and heteronomy in his theory provides exactly the impetus which Habermas yearns for – whether it is perfect or realisable is up for debate but, as Geoghegan notes, at least it exists (Geoghegan 1987: 133).

AUTONOMY IN A POST-INDUSTRIAL AGE

One of the central ideas in *Farewell to the Working Class* which has attracted substantial criticism is Gorz's proposal for a dualisation of society. By this he means that because there are specific, necessary and unpleasant tasks that must be undertaken for the day-to-day running of society, two distinct spheres of human existence should be identified – the heteronomous and the autonomous spheres. The heteronomous sphere would be the domain of all work deemed necessary for the survival and well-being of society and this work would be undertaken by all of the able population. Consequently, through the equitable distribution of these tasks amongst the working population, more 'free' time would be created for everyone. This time would constitute the realm of autonomy – an arena for social interaction, individual creativity and localised production. What is apparent from even this brief overview of Gorz's ideas on the dualisation of society is that centralised planning for the coordination of the different sectors of society would persist. In short, the dualisation of society would necessarily rely on some degree of state organisation, although because much would be organised on a local community basis, it would be possible to run much heteronomous work through local associations.

Geoghegan and Frankel have both emphasised the tension between this commitment to a role for the state and Gorz's dominant libertarian ideas. Whilst this is undoubtedly a valid criticism, it is not one Gorz has ignored for he constantly refers to the essential subordination of the heteronomous sphere to the autonomous sphere. His point is that heteronomy cannot be totally eradicated, therefore, it must be highly organised, and simultaneously minimised so that it can be subservient to the liberatory realm of autonomy. As Grint notes:

> Gorz is more concerned to retain a 'necessary' degree of advanced technology and 'other-directed' or heteronomous work, since only such a structure can provide the level of material production which we have now become accustomed to, and without which the creation of a sphere of autonomous, or 'self-directed' work would be impractical.
>
> (Grint 1991: 25)

This outline entails a role for the state which is fundamentally opposed to its role in liberal democratic societies and the highly centralised authoritarian states of Eastern Europe. The role of the state in Gorz's programme is to ensure that individuals have as much autonomous time as possible. For Gorz, the concept of individual autonomy questions the function of the state in liberal democracies:

> the cohesive workings of society appear to be assured, for good or ill, by a quasi-subject, the state. But the state is not a real subject: it is no one. In itself it is no more than an administrative machine, controlled by no one and incapable of formulating a general will which everyone may be called upon to express. The limits, dysfunctions and weaknesses of the capitalist state mean that society is always imperfectly cohesive and, as a result, that more or less substantial areas of indeterminacy and freedom will remain.
>
> (Gorz 1987b: 77)

Given this account of the role of the state in capitalist societies, Gorz goes on to criticise the way in which the state functions in state socialist societies. The latter are programmed and organised so that individual activity is subordinated to and determined by an external, collective goal which is often saturated by productivist heteronomy. Obviously neither scenario is particularly attractive to Gorz, although he does envisage a state sector that is organised and regulated. The problem for Gorz, and other radical and heretical socialist thinkers, is in identifying and defining the collective goal to which heteronomous activity should be directed.

It is neither the productivist industrialism of monolithic 'Marxist' states nor the 'authoritarian statism' of contemporary capitalist societies that guide the Gorzian ideal, but rather the complete suppression of the state by sovereign, human autonomy. This implies that the state should be concerned with the coordination of minimal, social necessity which cannot be produced by individuals or communities due to the scale of production. The work of Nove has been prominent in the debate over the importance of the scale of production in the phase of socialist transition:

> The bigger the unit in which he [the worker] is working, the more he is likely to feel alienated, remote from management decisions, a minor cog in a big machine. He [Gorz] is surely right that this question of scale, rather than just ownership, can be decisive.
>
> (Nove 1983: 199)

Gorz's programme also connotes a complete disjunction between the two sectors of society so that the subordination of the realm of heteronomy can be ensured. As many critics have implied, this clear identification of distinct spheres is highly problematic (Sayers 1991: 19; Frankel 1987: 60). In defence of Gorz, Cunningham notes that he 'aims to show that in socialism there are potentially antidemocratic structures (of the state) and a reason to maintain them (to plan)' (Cunningham 1987: 125). Once again there is a correlation between Gorz's thesis and the work of Marcuse in the 1960s. Both sought to minimise social necessity to maintain a distinct area of individual autonomy. In Marcuse's words:

> Complete automation in the realm of necessity would open the dimension of free time as the one in which man's private *and* societal existence would constitute itself. This would be the historical transcendence toward a new civilization.
>
> (Marcuse 1986: 37)

Gorz seeks to impress upon the reader that his programme for change would not result in what Keane terms a 'land of Cockayne' (Gorz 1989d). Gorz constantly stresses that the collective goal of his 'utopia' would not be attractive to all. Thus, due to the element of heteronomy and state planning, Gorz's utopia would not be a 'photograph of everyone's preferences' (Gorz 1987b: 78). Furthermore, Gorz is anxious to emphasise that a pluralistic political debate between 'a multiplication of decision-making centres' upon a collective goal will, if applied, necessitate planning and, therefore, a state sector but that this does not entail the creation of a general will to which every individual would be subservient:

> it is wrong to make it everyone's patriotic, civil or political duty to equate the objectives of the plan with his or her personal fulfilment. For that is to require an unconditional identity between individual and state, and an abandonment of the specificity and autonomy of all values and activities not related to politics and the economy. From being 'soldiers of production' in the capitalist economy, individuals end up as soldiers permanently mobilised to serve a plan presented to them as the emanation of 'the general will'.
>
> (Gorz 1987b: 79)

Clearly this has implications for our conception of human liberty. It is clear that Gorz believes that we have considerable obligations as citizens, many of which could be rather unpleasant. However it appears that our most important duty is to maximise the liberty of other citizens by sharing necessary work around as equitably as possible. Gorz goes to great lengths to emphasise his dissatisfaction with liberal views of 'individual freedom' and his distaste for bourgeois individualism that fuels his desire for a comprehensive analysis of human autonomy. For instance, Gorz is well aware of the problems that confront human autonomy through the liberal individualist idea of freedom typified by passive consumption in the private sphere. Gorz's conception of individual autonomy is formed in opposition to possessive individualism and the ethic of consumption. Gorz argues that the privatistic impulse of advanced capitalist societies constitutes the private sphere as

> a sphere of sovereignty wrested (or to be wrested) from a world governed by the principles of productivity, aggression, competition, hierarchical discipline etc. Capitalism owes its political stability to the fact that, in return for the dispossession and growing

> constraints experienced at work, individuals enjoy the possibility of building an apparently growing sphere of individual autonomy outside of work.
>
> (Gorz 1987b: 80)

Gorz states that oppositional potential within this private sphere can develop only if the content of that sphere is perceived as a positive alternative to capitalism. In *Critique of Economic Reason*, Gorz realises that the 'colonisation of the lifeworld' by the technical reason of modern capitalism renders the development of opposition in the individualistic private sphere problematic (Gorz 1989a: 173–9; Habermas 1984: 20). Nevertheless this does not refute Gorz's original suggestion that the private sphere has become an arena where individuals seek a sovereign, creative autonomy. Gorz's argument is persuasive because he demonstrates that creative human activity is now primarily and minimally exercised in the private sphere, with the arena of work experienced as a heteronomous externality which has little correlation with sovereign, individual creativity. Unfortunately, individuals must enter the domain of heteronomous work to gain the resources necessary for achieving any degree of autonomy in the private sphere (i.e. wages). Gorz is conscious that activity within the private sphere is not, in contemporary conditions, oppositional or liberatory:

> The priority of the post-industrial left must therefore be to extend self-motivated, self-rewarding activity within, and above all, outside the family, and to limit as much as possible all waged or market-based activity carried out on behalf of third parties (even the state). A reduction in work time is a necessary but not a sufficient condition. For it will not help to enlarge the sphere of individual autonomy if the resulting free time remains empty 'leisure time', filled for better or worse by the programmed distractions of the mass media and the oblivion merchants, and if everyone is thereby driven back into the solitude of their private sphere.
>
> (Gorz 1987b: 87)

For Gorz, the sphere of influence of heteronomy, in the form of the state, must be minimised if any form of individual autonomy is to develop. Contrary to Marx, he believes that 'it is impossible that individuals should totally coincide with their social being' (Gorz 1987b: 90). There is, he argues, a realm of activity which is incapable of corresponding to human needs for creative and aesthetic pleasure. As such these heteronomous activities should be separated and clearly differentiated from sovereign, autonomous activities. Hence Gorz believes that Marx's attempt to create a link between heteronomous necessity and the 'social being' of workers is unrealistic. Following Gorz's argument, Marxism is flawed because it seeks conformity and uniformity between citizens and work, an idea that has no place in Gorz's socialism. This is a self-consciously moral argument and is aimed at dismissing the conformist rules of contemporary capitalist and socialist societies which gauge human value and responsibility by adherence to pre-conditioned social norms such as work. Gorz believes that these conditions should decline in importance in any attempt to formulate a liberatory, socialist theory. Socialism which concedes its morality to technical and productivist dictates can never succeed in generating individual autonomy because the essence of human existence is automatically sacrificed to conformist economic goals.

Gorz perceives that the creation of a general will dictated by heteronomous goals inevitably leads to a negation of human subjectivity in both capitalist and state socialist societies. With this submission of individuality and morality to the logic of economic growth, the possibility of a socialist morality recedes. Only with the subordination of immoral, productivist requirements can a morality develop with the primary aim of increasing and encouraging autonomous individual action. Nevertheless, as has been emphasised, heteronomous necessity will remain in Gorz's scenario but it must be limited and subservient to the moral goals of autonomy. As Gorz himself realises, these recommendations do not differ greatly from the aims Marx expounded in his later work (Gorz 1987b: 95). Van Parijs points to evidence in both the *1844 Manuscripts* and *Critique of the Gotha Programme* that Marx envisaged the process of disalienating human activity 'by giving work an ever smaller place in life and by making it less and less like work' (Van Parijs 1993: 235). This point has been substantiated by Hirsch who perceives a link between Marx's aims and Gorz's work:

> Gorz sees the expansion of the sphere of individual autonomy and the limitation of the sphere of necessity (both economic and political) as the primary goal of revolution in post-industrial society. . . . Economic values would be subordinated to non-economic values and the ultimate goal of Marx's thought would be achieved: the extinction of political economy as such. Thus Gorz retains a utopian vision of communism.
>
> (Hirsch 1982: 241–2)

The value of this type of social dualisation lies in the possibility of individuals undertaking a critical assessment of the tasks they perform rather than merely doing jobs according to externally dictated requirements. This definition of autonomy goes beyond mere freedom of agency to encompass the freedom of people to make political choices about how they actually spend their time – in this sense it is not just autonomy but *critical* autonomy (Doyal and Gough 1991: 68–9). Gorz foresees a freedom of movement for individuals between the different sectors of society that will incorporate a social obligation coupled with a creative autonomy. Identity would no longer be conferred upon individuals by the heteronomous tasks they are required to perform, as is the case in contemporary capitalism. The immoral link between paid labour and social identity would thus be eliminated without socially necessary tasks being eradicated. To this extent Gorz argues that

> The point, then, is not to abolish heteronomous work, but only to use the goods it supplies and the way in which they are produced in order to enlarge the sphere of autonomy. It will serve that purpose all the better if it supplies the autonomous sphere with the greatest possible number of efficient convivial tools, and if the amount of heteronomous work required of each individual is reduced to a minimum.
>
> (Gorz 1987b: 101)

Gorz asserts that as much heteronomous production as possible should be taken out of the state sector and transferred to small- and medium-scale productive units. This would eliminate 'external necessities' that are needed to administer large-scale production and the state apparatus in general. This process would also facilitate the dualisation of society into two distinct spheres – one governed by the laws of material necessity (heteronomy) and the other by self-determined action (autonomy). Gorz suggests that

> The existence of a state separate from civil society, able both to codify objective necessities in the form of law and to assure its implementation, is thus the essential prerequisite to the autonomy of civil society and the emergence of an area outside the sphere of heteronomy in which a variety of modes of production, modes of life and forms of cooperation can be experimented with according to individual desires.
>
> (Gorz 1987b: 112)

Again, the necessity of regulation within Gorz's plan is evident. He continues to emphasise the functionality and degree of planning that would be required for the implementation of a dualised society. He also realises that this regulated sector of society, the realm of heteronomy, would be characterised by the non-human codification of human activity. The realm of heteronomy, in Gorz's programme, would be governed by a legal framework that was unconcerned with spontaneity or reciprocal human relations. It is precisely because Gorz wishes to develop a dominant sector of complete autonomy that he outlines this codified, regulated sphere. Only by assessing the role of the state through strict controls on state power, can society ensure that it does not colonise civil society and the realm of autonomy. Hence Gorz argues that to prevent planning and regulation dominating all social activity, it is necessary to organise a small, heteronomous arena in which codified behaviour is essential. Not only would this facilitate a drastic reduction in work time, but also it would encourage individuals to appreciate autonomous time which was not regulated and which was governed by spontaneous human relations. According to Gorz: 'The problem facing a "post-industrial socialism" is therefore the abolition not of the state but of domination. Law and domination, the state apparatus and the apparatus of domination need to be dissociated from one another' (Gorz 1987b: 115).

THE POVERTY OF SOCIAL DEMOCRACY AND NEO-LIBERALISM

Gorz elaborated these themes in 1983 with the publication of *Paths to Paradise* (Gorz 1985a). This book is primarily an investigation and vitriolic indictment of what he terms 'living-dead capitalism'. It analyses Keynesian economics and the inadequacies of the social democratic Left in Europe, the advent of the micro-electronic revolution and concludes with a justification of reduced working hours and a wage for life. It never quite reaches the startling originality of *Farewell to the Working Class*, but it is a systematic analysis which gives economic as well as political credence to the theory set out in *Farewell*. It is littered with references to Marx's *Grundrisse* and helps to locate Gorz's position within the Marxian tradition. The utopian foundation of the book is set out in the preface where he asserts that 'there are times when, because the social order is collapsing, realism consists not of trying to manage what exists but of imagining, anticipating and initiating the potential transformations inscribed in present changes' (Gorz 1985a: vii).

The proposals for a future left in *Paths to Paradise* are concretely grounded in Gorz's critique of advanced capitalism. Because he believes this system to be in crisis, he asserts the need for socialist theory to outline an emancipatory alternative which requires a complete restructuring of the relations and institutions of contemporary capitalist society. His point is that when socialism attempts to utilise capitalist structures for its own ends, it is as flawed as the capitalism it has succeeded. Only by advocating a political theory radically opposed to the preceding order can socialism acquire the credibility needed to safeguard its survival. Hence Gorz criticises those theorists and activists on the Left who retain outdated productivist solutions to the problems that the crisis of capitalism and neo-Keynesian economics have created (Brown 1994). He recognises that many trade unions and 'Labour' parties continue to posit economic growth as the means to counter recession, poverty and inequality (Gorz 1989a: 219–42). These ideas, which have been bankrupt since the economic downturn in the 1960s and the 1974 oil crisis, have no place in Gorzian theory. In his own words, 'future socialism will be post-industrial and anti-productivist or it will not be' (Gorz 1985a: 3). Moreover this post-industrial future will be based upon individual self-limitation and a more austere way of life which necessitates a rejection of high growth, productivist policies in socialist economics (Gorz 1993; Smart 1992: 96).

Drawing upon his experiences as an economics journalist and political editor of *Les Temps Modernes*, Gorz goes on to give a detailed description of the failure of Keynesian regulation and its weaknesses in countering the imbalances of the contemporary crisis. He stresses that socialism which has utilised a neo-Keynesian discourse has succeeded only in giving the New Right the grounds to launch an ideological offensive against socialism. Gorz suggests that the crisis of Keynesian capitalism is identifiable in two tendencies – over-accumulation and under-consumption. The former is defined as 'investment of amounts of capital in excess of what can be made profitable by the sale of realisable production at market price' whilst the latter is evident in the 'inability of part of the population to satisfy its potential demand because of lack of purchasing power' (Gorz 1985a: 7). In attempting to redress these imbalances, capitalism has been forced to deal with the increasing necessity of welfarism and taxation for public investment. Gorz argues that this entails a large degree of 'external regulation' by the state to counter the obvious inability of the market to regulate itself in the interests of human welfare – a fact that even contemporary social marketeers appear to accept. This has led to an uneasy coalition of free market ideology with state intervention and regulation to counteract the inadequacy of the market – an idea which Offe has dealt with at great length (Offe 1984). Until the 1960s this uneasy coalition was manageable but it began to break down because

> Keynesian regulation can work only during times of high profits, of strong potential growth, and thus of strong propensity to invest. It can regulate and sustain economic growth, but cannot alone, create the conditions for it. It cannot instigate growth when a long cycle of accumulation comes to an end, and when, through market saturation, labour shortage and exhaustion of the resources of technological progress, the rate of profit falls and a long downward cycle begins.
>
> (Gorz 1985a: 8)

This inherent weakness of Keynesianism, which has been apparent since the 1960s, explains Gorz's belief that capitalist development and the neo-Keynesian policies it has adopted have reached their limit. He concludes that 'the welfare state . . . must therefore be understood as a substitute for society' (Gorz 1989a: 186).

Gorz argues that the failure of the Left to look beyond economic growth for the panacea to the crisis of capitalism has perpetuated the ideological assault of the New Right on neo-Keynesian socialist economics. As Ralph Miliband has argued, the current impasse of socialism is linked, to a large extent, with the failure of Left governments in the 1960s and 1970s to understand the crisis and to construct a different theoretical approach (R. Miliband 1973, 1984). For Gorz, socialist theory must now be based on a rejection of the productivism which is dominant in Keynesian economics because 'infinite growth of material production is a material impossibility. Growth will always reach a structural limit: its specific sources are never inexhaustible' (Gorz 1985a: 12). This belief is obviously antithetical to the perception of commentators such as Kumar who has suggested that radical socialists

> did not question the basic belief that the industrial societies had solved the oldest problem of them all, that of scarcity and want. Keynes' prediction of the 1930s seemed to have been borne out: the economic problem would be solved within the century.
>
> (Kumar 1978: 195)

On the contrary, Gorz has revealed why the structural failures of Keynesian economics have created a situation where renewed growth is unlikely through demand or investment. Meanwhile liberal democratic regimes still maintain the primacy of individual consumption as the key to economic regeneration. The privatisation of health and education in Britain has led to a clearer differentiation between the privileged minority and the subordinated majority. Gorz asserts that medical and educational advancements have become similar to other forms of consumption because technical advancements are available only to the minority that can afford them. Gorz believes that, despite these technical advancements:

> social inequality does not diminish, because every time the dominated classes advance, privilege is re-established at a higher level, thus devaluing their gains. So 'progress' in health and education becomes almost entirely illusory. The extension of education or the rise in so-called health costs no longer corresponds to any real progress.
>
> (Gorz 1985a: 18)

The answer to these problems, according to Gorz, for both Left and Right is the reduction of social costs. The only means of adequately approaching this problem for the Left is to seek collective answers to these public, social difficulties and to react against the possessive individualism which permeates the consumerist rhetoric of the neo-liberalism. To address the minimalisation of social costs a return to production according to necessity rather than profit is required. This entails what Gorz calls the 'socialisation of production decisions' and the 'social control' of production itself. In other words he is advocating the adjudication of the value of a product according to the side-effects and social costs that product may induce through pollution and waste, for instance. Gorz believes this logic would facilitate the decentralisation of consumer goods so that they could be produced within communities aware of the social costs incurred by producing a specific good. This development could be achieved only by a systematic break with the capitalist ideology of consumption. Only through an inversion of the idea of 'progress through consumption' can social problems be collectively solved. Therefore, Gorz is advocating a complete ideological transformation of society to encourage collective problem-solving rather than individual, consumerist solutions:

> Dissatisfaction, the endless search for 'more' and 'better', is not born of the autonomous awareness of lack or inadequacy but of the existence of supposed improvements which the market supplies to a minority. So collective control of supply, and thus of

> decisions about social production, is the key to an egalitarian transformation of the model of consumption and to a corresponding expansion of non-market, autonomous production.
>
> (Gorz 1985a: 24)

This solution to the reduction of social costs is obviously anathema to the productivist logic of capitalism. Gorz is at pains to demonstrate the means by which neo-liberals would attempt to lower social costs and the effects these policies would have on public sector institutions such as health, education, transport, and housing. He suggests that the New Right relies upon micro-technology to assist what Attali has called the production of demand (Attali 1981). This entails the use of computers to service individual health and education needs rather than the doctor or the teacher. The economic lifeblood of capitalism would rely upon consumers 'creating demand' for the technical capacity to interact with sophisticated computers.

On an existential level this results in the dehumanisation of individual and collective problems and the ultimate victory for an instrumentalised, technological society. Furthermore the profit made from this rationalisation of human problems gives little incentive for capitalist society to seek to solve those problems. If the greatest profit is made by the use of computers to tackle the existential problems that capitalist structures have created, then why should capitalists eradicate this profitable source of revenue at its origin. As Gorz insists:

> this marks the extension of the sphere of capitalist production to encompass activities formerly belonging to the (re) production of the labour force. The cost of this (re) production (maintenance, training, socialisation, health care) is sharply reduced while part of the network of services previously paid for by social contributions or taxes is shifted on to the individual. Industrialising these services thus reduces compulsory deductions and increases individual purchases of new forms of commodities.
>
> (Gorz 1985a: 26)

The consequences of such a development, which are already apparent to some degree, are that production and consumption are externally determined by an economic system without attention to human need. The most profitable goods are produced and then consumers are created for these products:

> the boundary between production and consumption, people and commodities, gets blurred. Commodities produce the people

> who are needed to get commodities consumed and produced. Individuals, consumers themselves, become commodities, produced or self-produced and sold at a profit.
>
> (Gorz 1985a: 28)

Whilst the advent of micro-electronics has accentuated this tendency towards the technologisation of human relations, Gorz believes that the micro-electronic revolution heralds an opportunity for socialism to challenge the instrumental reason of capital. In addition he believes that micro-electronics do not exclude self-management of time and activity as was the case with large-scale technology. Moreover Gorz asserts that new technology does not automatically lend itself to the regeneration of capitalist accumulation. His belief is grounded in the fact that capitalists utilising micro-technology do so automatically at the cost of variable capital (labour). Opportunities for socialism exist because exchange value can no longer be linked to labour time and thus, Gorz argues, 'wages can no longer depend on the amount of work performed, nor the right to an income on having a job' (Gorz 1985a: 30).

REDUCED COSTS, REDUCED WORKING HOURS

Essentially Gorz believes that the micro-electronic revolution encourages the abolition of work – a situation that requires a reinterpretation of socialist theory. The problem for Gorz and other radical socialists is how to manage and control these fundamental changes in the interest of socialism. As Bauman has noted, capitalism is capable of incorporating the egalitarian impulses that motivate socialism, into its programme:

> this 'egalitarian impulse', by itself, does not necessarily lead to socialist conclusions. Late capitalism has managed to accommodate this impulse and to translate it, under the aegis of economic growth, into a defused and harmless pursuit of a higher standard of living, which may, but does not necessarily, come into direct confrontation with the principle of unequal distribution.
>
> (Bauman 1976: 118–19)

The problems that the micro-electronic revolution creates for capitalism highlight the contradictions in, and crisis of, the system. Whilst highly profitable capital is replacing older, fixed capital and variable capital, it is apparent that with the decrease of labour, purchasing power gained through wages from working is also eroded. Gorz notes that 'automation abolishes workers: equally it abolishes potential buyers'

(Gorz 1985a: 31). It is apparent that this development has led to a tertiarisation of labour whereby a small technical elite of experts administer technology whilst a majority floats between unfulfilling, uncreative employment in the service sector (Gorz 1988: 30). Whereas he noted with distaste in the 1960s and 1970s that individuals were imbued with a social identity through their job, Gorz now believes that the advent of micro-electronic technology has created a situation where people are disaffected with work and do not seek identity through it, with the exception of the dwindling number of professionals (Gorz 1985a: 33).

Gorz's argument is similar to that of Giddens insofar as they both assert that the expert elite maintain their knowledge as a means of domination and social status (Giddens 1991). A central element in the Gorzian plan is the socialisation of knowledge. He believes that micro-technology facilitates this development because it is apparent that full-time, lifelong work for all is unrealistic and its continuing prominence in the political domain is no more than an ideological fraud. Alec Nove believes that Gorz overestimates the emancipatory potential of technological development:

> He [Gorz] goes a little too far, perhaps influenced by Ivan Illich, in his belief in do-it-yourself as the basis of producers' satisfaction; in his version the state's industries should aim at providing the means for all kind of domestic production. . . . *No doubt such things are desirable, but many citizens are both unattracted by and incapable of technology in the home.*
>
> (Nove 1983: 199, emphasis added)

Taking Nove's point, it would seem that individuals must become aware of the potential for change, the possibilities that a policy of reduced working hours could engender – a line of thought which has always characterised Gorz's work. It is not unreasonable to suggest that people may be attracted to a plan in which everyone has the right to work and it is highly feasible that this right will be even more attractive if it is accompanied, as is necessary, by a reduction in working hours (Leisink and Coenen 1993: 13). Lipietz makes the important point that 'reduced working hours . . . means working less so that everyone can work, or in fact, . . . everybody working so that people can work less' (Lipietz 1992: 84). Nevertheless this emancipatory rationale rarely enters political and economic debates which are subsumed within the outdated ideology of work. Simultaneously the work ethic promoted by the logic of productivist capitalism continues to subordinate human creativity through the colonisation of human time and needs. Nevertheless Gorz perceives this manipulation of the population as an opportunity for the exploited majority to align themselves with socialist theory based around the rejection of work and the identity it confers upon individuals. This, he believes, would counter a situation in which

> the unemployed are socially marginalised, even when they are the majority. . . . They are deemed to be socially inferior and inadequate and effectively denied all social participation and activity. They remain outcasts and objects of resentment, begrudged whatever charity society grants them. A stratification which repudiates equal rights and justifies itself through quasi-racist hatred and contempt – this is the price we pay for the preservation of the labour elite's hegemony.
>
> (Gorz 1985a: 36)

Whilst the unemployed are marginalised, Gorz argues that modern, technical innovation continues to erode human labour in the tertiary sector as well as amongst the elite of experts. The long-term trend points towards the abolition of more formal employment, thus increasing the ranks of the socially marginalised. Although Gorz is justified in citing the potential of this numerically strengthened group of individuals for seizing upon a new political agenda, the problem arises as to how this underclass of individuals is to achieve the power and resources to challenge the structurally ingrained domination of the elite (Himmelstrand *et al.* 1981).

Generally the elite experiences difficulties in maintaining its privileged position. It has to create demand for the goods it produces when increasingly people are being robbed of their traditional means of funding their consumption – wages. For this reason employment must be created regardless of its usefulness or necessity. Furthermore, marginalised individuals must be paid for these meaningless tasks to enable them to consume. Gorz suggests that the consequences of these developments for capitalists are that

> people must be paid to consume the products supplied. Consumption must be put on a par with work and must be rewarded accordingly. Individuals must be paid in relation to their consumption of non-material goods insofar as this consumption is also productive: they produce themselves to meet the requirements of the goods they consume. Commodities buy their

> consumers so that the latter, by the very act of consumption, become what society needs them to be.
>
> (Gorz 1985a: 36)

Gorz argues that this scenario, which is coming into being before our eyes, does not correspond to a preservation of the capitalist system but is simply a complex effort to maintain power in the hands of the technocratic elite. The aim of this technocracy is to control the needs, time and abilities of the majority. It is a form of domination by a system of which the technical elite are managerial administrators rather than owners or 'masters'. Thus Gorz suggests controversially that 'we are much closer to a totalitarian society run by a technocracy with a quasi-military hierarchy than to bourgeois capitalist society' (Gorz 1985a: 39).

BASIC INCOME AND THE FUTURE OF WELFARE

From the basis of this critique of technocapitalism, Gorz goes on to formulate his strategy for 'a way out of capitalism'. Perhaps not surprisingly his proposals for future liberation have received much more critical attention than his rigorous analysis of contemporary capitalism which he elucidates in the first part of *Paths to Paradise* and in his later work.

The central element of Gorz's plan for a socialist solution to the crisis of capitalism is the implementation of an income for life in the form of a social wage. In recent years there has a boom in literature on the idea of a basic income, particularly in France, Germany and the Netherlands (Van Parijs 1992a; Coenen and Leisink 1993; Lipietz 1992; Gorz 1994). The simplest definition of basic income is 'an income unconditionally paid to all on an individual basis, without means test or work requirement' (Van Parijs 1992b: 3). This idea fits comfortably with Gorz's advocacy of reduced working hours because it 'is granted by virtue of an unconditional entitlement, and the idea that any income from other sources will come on top of the basis it provides' (Van Parijs 1992b: 4). As we shall see Gorz provides a very specific view of basic income, but it is pertinent to note that he realises that a social wage could be incorporated within a technocratic capitalist system:

> the right to an income independent of a job is thus no guarantee of freedom, equality and security. It can be easily accommodated within an elitist technocracy and/or a system of totalitarian control reaching into our intimate relation with ourselves.
>
> (Gorz 1985a: 40)

The essence of this argument is that contemporary capitalism is abolishing work, yet this alone does not facilitate liberatory change although it may provide opportunities for change. The micro-electronic revolution has, he argues, changed the material conditions and nothing more. Gorz realises that the concept of a basic income is open to manipulation by those on the Right who seek to maintain the social and political dominance of an employed elite (Gorz 1992). One variant of basic income which typifies this approach is negative income tax which was advocated by Milton Friedman as a transitory means to abolish state welfare in the longer term (Van Parijs 1992: 30).

The strand of Gorz's theory which many commentators unfortunately ignore is his advocacy of reduced work hours which not only is based on the right of each individual not to work full-time, but also incorporates the *right of everyone to work*. Gorz does not defend the life of passive indolence and uncreativity advocated by Lafargue, for instance (Keane 1988: 83). He believes that, even in the heteronomous sphere, there may be some activity which individuals find fulfilling if it is organised cooperatively:

> The guarantee of an income independent of a job will be emancipatory or repressive, from the Left or the Right, according to whether it opens up new spaces for individual and social activity or whether, on the contrary, it is only the social wage for compulsory passivity.
>
> (Gorz 1985a: 40)

The point of this argument is that the Right could manipulate an income for life to ensure social control and passivity by paying very low sums to marginalised individuals who are otherwise unemployed. This is possible because the renewed interest in basic income is derived from the fact that 'the social and economic significance of work has gradually come under increasing pressure' (Vilrokx 1993: 205–6). Against this possibility, Gorz argues that socialists must prioritise economic citizenship:

> access to work in the public sphere is essential to economic citizenship and to full participation in society. In complex modern societies, the participation in the social process of production is an essential factor of socialization and of membership in socially formalized communities and groups, even if working time is reduced to less than half the present average.
>
> (Gorz 1992: 182)

Gorz believes that a social income designed by the Left must be based on radically different principles. The basic income must entail the right of every individual to a social wage corresponding to a minimum amount of socially necessary labour over the course of that individual's life. According to Gorz's calculations this minimum amount of labour counts as twenty thousand hours over a lifetime. Furthermore he emphasises the right of every citizen to organise their work time around their own autonomous time and activity. Hence the twenty thousand hours could be distributed as ten years of full-time work, twenty years of part-time work or, the most likely alternative, forty years of intermittent work. Similarly Offe has observed that

> the option of discontinuous participation in employment would cease to be considered second best (due to the unavailability of 'full' employment) and would instead be seen as the most-preferred alternative – even under conditions where full employment was thought to be feasible.
>
> (Offe 1992: 75–6)

Gorz is aware that considerable organisational difficulties would arise in implementing such a system, although this is, to some extent, a natural by-product of complex modern societies. It is not unfeasible to suggest that Gorz's utopia could require less regulation than contemporary capitalism given recent technological developments. Nevertheless he is attempting to inspire debate rather than provide solutions to all the social problems created by the crisis of capitalism. The system he advocates would prioritise the subordination of waged work to other social activity as 'Waged work will cease to be the primary activity but, through the guaranteed income for life which it provides for all, it will remain the economic basis for a limitless variety of possible activities without economic objectives or economic logic' (Gorz 1985a: 42).

However it is important to address the various criticisms that are rightly or wrongly levelled against the idea of basic income. The most common objection is that basic income is not affordable. Adriaansens and Derckson point out that 'basic income would be too expensive, because non-working adults who do not receive social security (mainly housewives) would also be entitled to it' (Adriaansens and Derckson 1993: 201). The first answer to this point is that basic income is advocated so that economic citizenship is conferred on those who are currently excluded such as 'housewives' even though this may increase taxation. Secondly, a number of commentators have shown that there are a number of options available for raising the necessary revenue which would not lead to very high income tax rates. For instance Desai argues that for a basic income of £50 per week, half the money would be paid for by the abolition of most existing benefits coupled with a modest increase in the higher band of income tax, the abolition of tax concessions such as mortgage interest relief and the extension of VAT to some zero rated goods (Desai 1995: 2). This is not necessarily the best way to fund basic income but it does show that we cannot dismiss it out of hand as unaffordable. The debate has already begun as to an appropriate taxation strategy and this dialogue needs a wider stage (Steiner 1992; Carling 1992; Van Parijs 1993).

A second objection to basic income theory is that some individuals will work hard to supplement their own income and create the wealth to pay for the basic income of others who may be lazing around content with their standard of living (Taylor-Gooby 1991: 198; Adriaansens and Derckson 1993: 201). Although the degree of welfare scrounging is overplayed by neo-liberal theory, it is relevant to point out that some individuals may not fully contribute to the community. For this reason Lipietz warns that a high basic income would discourage people from working (Lipietz 1992: 97). This is why Gorz advocates a citizen's wage, which implies not only the right to and the right not to work, but also the obligation to do some socially necessary work. In the words of Coenen and Leisink, 'a libertarianism that grants rights but imposes no obligations leaves the issue of social responsibility towards the community as contingent' (Leisink and Coenen 1993: 19). This negates the criticism that basic income 'discharges citizens from the duty to take part in the social division of labour' (Adriaansens and Derckson 1993: 201). Indeed, as Lipietz points out, it is up to collective societal decisions to provide individuals with the opportunity to show solidarity by giving them the right to work (Lipietz 1992: 99).

The basic income debate is still in its infancy with all of the commentators above providing useful insights. The absence of substantive empirical data on the costs of basic income is now starting to be addressed, with Gorz at the forefront in his evaluation of the economic policies necessary for reduced working hours and a citizen's wage (Gorz 1994). It is important now to clarify Gorz's perception of the latter with particular reference to the concept of political obligation which provides an interesting adjunct to Gorz's dominant libertarian theme.

WORK AND THE CITIZEN'S WAGE

The central feature of Gorz's plan for an income for life is that rather than accentuating individual dependency apparent in the contemporary welfare system, the citizen's wage is actively designed to eliminate the subordination of the individual to the state. There is, he believes, a stark choice to be made between an income for life and an escalation of present welfarism precisely because modern capitalist growth does not facilitate sufficient labour to sustain consumption at desired levels for capitalists. Essentially his argument is for social income to be paid to individuals as citizens rather than workers. Only through such a system could the liberation of the realm of autonomy come about and the domination of that realm over heteronomy be facilitated. The concept of citizenship is paramount in Gorz's notion of a basic income, which differs from those that totally dissociate work and income (Baker 1992; Jordan 1992):

> excusing people from working by securing them an income anyway is not a way of giving them full membership of their society. You cannot become a member of any community if you have no obligation whatsoever towards it. Being a member of a group means that you can rely on the others, but also that they can rely on you. There can be no inclusion without reciprocal obligations.
>
> (Gorz 1992: 184)

It is clear that Gorz's notion of citizenship requires an acceptance that justice entails an element of 'fair-play' in the sense that reciprocity is the basis of his social contract (Horton 1992: 89–90). Obligation for Gorz is necessary to maximise the liberty and autonomy of everyone, in this sense it is what Dunn calls 'an obligation of prudence' of which he notes 'if it is to be genuinely obligatory for all, there must be real advantages for each and every subject in his own political subjection' (Dunn 1989: 41). For Gorz this advantage lies in the liberation of time which encompasses the development of autonomy and self-determination. Thus whilst individuals have reciprocal duties to maximise the autonomy of their peers, they also have the liberty to spend the majority of their time as they please. Although his theory has an obvious deontological element, it is equally clearly teleological as well. To an extent then Gorz's perception of obligation overcomes the polarity between deontology and teleology which Dunn believes to be irresolvable (Dunn 1989: 41). Indeed, as Horton believes, it is difficult to differentiate between specific types of theory of obligation, although he does do so himself as an analytical tool (Horton 1992: 80). Gorz's perspective goes beyond obligation with regard to respect for others, and presses for individual citizens to recognise their role in increasing the welfare of all citizens (Plant 1991b: 207).

Of course critics of Gorz ask how the distribution of wealth required for the basic income is to be organised. Gorz believes that his system does not create major organisational problems nor does it imply the kind of centralisation that Keane and Geoghegan have identified (Keane 1988: 88; Geoghegan 1987). In simple terms, he suggests that the citizen's wage is most easily funded by taxing automated production so even the tax changes advocated by Desai above may not be necessary. Gorz cites this example:

> In 1983, Japanese employers proposed that robots should pay union dues. It would make much more sense if they were to pay social contributions, per unit of output, varied like VAT according to the model of consumption which is to be promoted.
>
> (Gorz 1985a: 45)

Gorz is advocating a system of 'political pricing' which differs little from the current system of taxation and subsidy. Following Marx, automation eradicates market laws and the law of value. In such a system, Gorz believes that society has to prioritise certain areas and this can be achieved only by an evaluation of the worth of production through political pricing to ensure the well-being of the community. Thus the more production of a good damaged the environment for example, the more taxation the owners of the factory would have to pay per unit of production (Lipietz 1992: 125–6).

These changes, though, can emerge only from a social desire for change and a new politics of time. This would require collective action from unions and community groups to prioritise the standardisation of work so that multi-talented individuals could move unproblematically between different areas of heteronomous work (Gorz 1989a). This would enable individuals to self-determine their twenty thousand hours over a lifetime and hence facilitate a more emancipated society. By the standardisation of work Gorz means that trades and skills must be as simplified as possible so as to make them completely accessible to everyone through lifelong learning (Commission on Social Justice 1994). The priority must be to make technology highly efficient thereby enhancing the capability of socialising the productive process. This, Gorz believes, is the only means of reversing the trend towards the increasing professionalisation of the elite minority and the parallel marginalisation of the unskilled majority:

> Automation and computerisation can be emancipatory only if they standardise and simplify even more tasks and functions than in the past – if, in other words, they enable everyone, after a universal basic education, to acquire a wide, adaptable range of qualifications, independently and swiftly. Only then can work which is reduced for all and shared by all become a right for all: the right to make and feel ourselves useful to society.
>
> (Gorz 1985a: 47)

Clearly Gorz realises that technology can facilitate emancipation only if it is organised in the interests of liberation and pluralistic democracy. He believes that technology must be developed to eradicate quantitative, economic logic in the autonomous sphere and that technology must be subordinated to non-economic goals such as the liberation of human time, self-ordained human activity and individual self-determination. It is apparent that Gorz's dualisation of society would actively ensure that *within the heteronomous sphere*, individual autonomy would not be dominant. This is perhaps inevitable, but it is not particularly important to Gorz because of his subordination of heteronomy to the autonomous realm. In any case, even in the realm of necessity, cooperative work between individuals in a community may be fulfilling:

> there is no a priori reason why friendship, creativity, comradeship, generosity and festivity should not be given a place within heteronomous work. But the fact remains that they have been forcibly excluded from it, and that there is now neither time nor place for workers to share non-economic and non-market values and relationships, to bring together work, life and culture. And if workers lack that experience even outside work, it is hard to see how they would struggle to incorporate non-economic values within it.
>
> (Gorz 1985a: 49)

Gorz's vision of a socialist society suggests that the domains of economic and non-economic values would be qualitatively and quantitatively differentiated. Gorz believes that a reorganisation of society around a new politics of time would help to alleviate the most dehumanising aspects of heteronomy. That may well be the case, but heteronomy will, in all likelihood, remain unsatisfactory and external. Nevertheless Gorz is aware of this probability when he argues that 'we must not expect that heteronomous work – work whose form and objectives are externally determined by the organisation of production on a national or continental scale – can ever be totally abolished or transformed into autonomous activity' (Gorz 1985a: 50).

Self-management and smaller, more autonomous work groups can restore a greater degree of self-expression to the heteronomous sphere but they cannot eliminate the inherent functionality of externally defined tasks. This is so because the organisation of production at a macro, transnational level can never truly represent the desires of individuals at a community level. Gorz argues that the realm of heteronomy, which is inescapable, must rely upon procedural rules and norms which will necessitate the minimalisation of creative human spontaneity. Certainly self-management within the sphere of heteronomy is to be encouraged, but it will not be able to conquer the complexity of global production and the universal rules which such a large-scale plan intrinsically implies. For Gorz, the nature of heteronomous work can be improved to make it more fulfilling but as long as the work performed is externally dictated it will remain impoverishing for the autonomy of the worker:

> Oppressive hierarchies, laboriousness, monotony, boredom – all these can be eradicated, and the workplace can become a place of mutual exchange, co-operation and harmony. But such a liberation of work relations is not the same as autonomy of work itself or workers' self-determination (or self-management) of its overall purpose and content.
>
> (Gorz 1985a: 52)

Gorz's thesis is that the struggle for self-management in the workplace is justifiable but only as part of a broader struggle in the overall quest for socialism. Capitalism can be surpassed only by prioritising a needs-based theory of value rather than the dominant productivist ethos which is primarily used by capitalists as a means of social control. The sphere of necessity is inescapable but it does not have to hold a sovereign position in the order of human activity. Gorz's proposals for reduced working hours will be liberatory only if existential needs are given a privileged position over external, market-defined necessities. Furthermore Gorz believes that the abolition of the compulsion to work will encourage more individuals to find the productive process enjoyable and self-realising precisely because the tasks involved will be engaged in voluntarily, even if they are designed on a social scale. Gorz differentiates, though, between necessary production carried out autonomously and that carried out in the heteronomous realm in the hope (perhaps overly optimistically) that individuals will favour the former:

> necessities produced in your free time always have a different status from those which have to be produced. Precisely because the latter are guaranteed to all by society, the former are extras which you make for the sheer pleasure of creating them by yourself, indulgences, not things which you couldn't do without. Bread and cakes you bake yourself are not the same as those you buy; handmade clothes and shoes have a different appeal from those made in a factory.
>
> (Gorz 1985a: 60)

To conclude it may be useful to comment on the citizen's wage in the light of the burgeoning literature on citizenship which has become increasingly prominent in recent years (Andrews 1991; Meehan 1993; D. Miliband 1994; Mouffe 1993; Oliver and Heater 1994). Gorz's work is not a regular feature in these debates despite the contribution he has made in cognate areas. In some ways his concentration on economic rights as the basis of autonomy in a socialist society may be unattractive to those whose concentrate on civil, political and social rights. Coote, for instance, maintains that we cannot achieve economic and social rights without having political rights (Coote 1994: 61). But how can we exercise political rights effectively if we do not have the economic wherewithal to influence structures of power? Gorz's perspective is that civil and political rights are important but without economic autonomy they become unrealisable. Even those of a less radical persuasion than Gorz have recognised that

> If we believe that we have a right to the protection of civil and political rights, then we cannot draw a distinction between civil and political rights on the one hand, and social and welfare rights on the other, because the latter involve resource constraints in the way that the former do not.
>
> (Plant 1991a: 56)

Plant is of the belief that Marxists maintain class conflict to the denigration of debates over citizenship, yet clearly there are thinkers such as Gorz who have developed a more sophisticated approach whilst still retaining a place (however vague) in the Marxist tradition (Plant 1991a: 53). He is correct to point out that ideas of citizenship have to cross class barriers but of course Gorz's presentation of reduced working hours is designed to do this. So much so that his ideas on time, formulated since 1980, are now appearing slightly diluted in mainstream debates (Hewitt 1993; Demos 1995).

Gorz's stress on individual obligations and responsibilities as well as autonomy has marked out a highly original position. For instance he shows that the prioritisation of autonomy does not necessarily lead to the kind of liberal individualism which eschews a communitarian approach to politics. In other words, a developed theory of autonomy which recognises the limits as well as the benefits of the concept need not surrender coherent citizenship as Oliver and Heater believe. Gorz provides a view of autonomy which encompasses the 'legal and moral obligations of citizenship, and thus the development of a mature effective citizenry' (Oliver and Heater 1994: 69).

THE SOCIALIST UTOPIA: TOWARDS A NEW POLITICS OF TIME

Following Gorz's argument, it is likely that necessities would be produced autonomously as well as within the realm of heteronomy. Precisely because the creation of these goods would be self-ordained and the produce self-consumed, it is likely that individuals would derive satisfaction from their production. Hence it is apparent that Gorz does not advocate a reduction in work time in the interests of being idle. On the contrary, it is precisely so individuals can determine their own activity whether that function is necessary or not. The ability to move between different sectors of society and activity, thereby using a complex variety of talents and abilities, provides the very fabric of human existence. The only means of achieving this scenario, for Gorz, is reduced working hours, in other words, socialist theory needs to adopt a new politics of time. He cites Glotz to justify this point:

> A new politics of time: this is not a side issue from some sectional struggle, but a humanist idea which transcends social divisions. It would be the most important objective in the programme of a political movement which would not be ashamed to claim emancipation as its goal.
>
> (Glotz 1987, cited in Gorz 1989a: 190)

Gorz's notion of a new politics of time has received strong criticism from Giddens who contends that

> Although Gorz's remarks are written in an attitude of tough-minded realism, they must rank among the least compelling of

> the various diagnoses he offers in his book. Gorz's 'dual society' is more unrealistic and naive than the conceptions of democracy which he rejects.
>
> (Giddens 1987: 295)

This reaction is fairly typical of the reception that Gorz's work received in the 1980s, although his last two major books can be viewed as a major rebuff to those who portrayed him as an idealist (Gorz 1989a; 1994: 102–17). Although Giddens is not totally unsympathetic to Gorz's project, it is apparent that he remains within a theoretical school that is resistant to a radicalisation of socialism through 'utopianism'. In Europe this road to renewal has been adopted by Gorz, and others such as Habermas, who perceive 'utopianism' to be the main avenue for socialist change (Habermas 1986). Within Britain only the likes of Robertson (1985) and Keane have realised the value of this theoretical approach:

> Just as nearly every utopian island is shrouded in fog, so Gorz's utopian socialism is often lacking in clarity and definition. Gorz, therefore, does not pretend to have answered all of the many questions his books raise. He is concerned rather to mount an attack on what he describes as the prevailing nostalgia and unimaginative attachment, especially within the socialist tradition, to the goal of 'restoring' full employment.
>
> (Keane 1988: 79)

Nevertheless, Giddens' critique characterises the general reception of Gorz's utopian ideas, especially when he states that 'any sort of political programme based mainly upon such proposals would be a risky and short-sighted undertaking' (Giddens 1987: 296). The failure to engage with the radical kind of proposals that Gorz advocates has serious implications for the development of any new political programme. This is the precise reason why Gorz has been so heretical, for he realises the necessity of self-criticism on the Left. Criticisms of Gorz, such as those of Giddens, limit the possibility of such self-criticism arising within socialist theory and only assist the dominant hegemonic position that neo-liberal ideology and discourse hold in contemporary, mainstream, political debate. In the words of Geoghegan:

> His [Gorz's] assertion that the utopians are the realists in our society cannot be repeated too often. Coming as it does from one who has always had a sharp eye for the realities of advanced capitalist society, it is particularly valuable. He has also sat down

and constructed his own vision of a future society – something which can only be to the good. His alternative may appear flawed or repugnant to some, but it is at least there and can in turn stimulate others to adopt, amend or replace it.

(Geoghegan 1987: 133)

CONCLUSION

Since the 1950s Gorz has concentrated on the identification of emancipatory potential for the individual. In this sense there is a common theme throughout Gorz's work, running from *The Traitor* to his more mature writing. Gorz's originality lies in his prioritisation of individual autonomy against the collectivist tendency in classical Marxism. In contemporary socialist debate, Gorz can be located alongside the latest generation of critical theorists, such as Habermas and Offe, who have also been prepared to question the dominant orthodoxy in the Marxian tradition.

Undoubtedly work and the labour process hold a central position in Gorz's theory. Through an ongoing analysis of the technical division of labour and the micro-electronic revolution, Gorz has identified the potential for a dynamic socialist programme in which a new politics of time is sovereign. Although Gorz has constantly elucidated the reasons why socialists should abandon the utopia of full employment and neo-Keynesian discourse, the Left still tends to regard him as a heretic. Nevertheless it is likely that Gorz will continue to champion the reduction of working hours and a new politics of time as prerequisites for emancipatory change.

Furthermore it is likely that Gorz will continue to engage in dialogue with political ecologists. In his most recent book, Gorz has returned to the ecology question more explicitly than he has done since 1975 (Gorz 1994, 1987a). In all likelihood he will remain an important figure in eco-socialist debate which, by and large, is concerned with the incorporation of ecological goals into an anthropocentric, socialist project. His work challenges not only dominant Leftist ideas, but also political ecology which remains an uneasy ally of socialism. Along with the likes of Raymond Williams and Hans Magnus Enzensberger, Gorz should be regarded as one of the few theorists who recognised the importance of the red/green interface at an early stage.

As a theorist who constantly raises issues that are anathema to traditional socialist debate Gorz is widely considered to be a 'post-industrial utopian'. This utopianism, as Geoghegan and Keane have argued, should be regarded as a positive development in the struggle for a new, emancipatory politics. Gorz's recommendations for a politics of free time and his prioritisation of individual autonomy and self-determination are grounded in the lived experience of individuals in advanced capitalist societies. As such, the negative, simplistic connotations of 'utopianism' should not detract from the overall thrust of Gorz's theory which is based on the political reality of advanced capitalism. In Europe, at least, the development of emancipatory utopianism is becoming more acceptable in socialist debates, although this theoretical tradition is generally treated with suspicion in Britain (Anderson 1980). It is probable, then, that Gorz's influence in continental Europe will be greater than in Britain which is generally constrained within a more, traditional ideological straitjacket.

This study has been concerned to challenge conventional interpretations of Gorz's work. Gorz's eclectic sources, his idiosyncratic style and the ubiquity of his theory when viewed in its entirety, resist the type of categorisation to which he has been subjected. In presenting Gorz as a theorist of individual emancipation or as a socialist individualist, it is possible to identify a consistent theme in his work since the 1950s. From his roots in existential philosophy and his critique of Marxism, Gorz has developed an enduring analysis of the labour process, the technical division of labour, class conflict and the ecology question. In his treatment of all these themes the emancipation and self-determination of the individual remains paramount.

From this basis Gorz has attempted to formulate a liberatory programme that embraces a diverse range of groups and individuals who could unite to challenge the pervasive power of advanced capitalism. Rather than concentrating on the factory as the site of socialist politics, Gorz seeks to engage with cultural groups, trade unions and community organisations. His aim is not to subsume small-scale collectives within a centralised, bureaucratic party. On the contrary, he wishes to maintain the localised, spontaneous nature of cultural and community groups. This reiterates Gorz's advocacy of student/worker unification in the run up to the 1968 uprising in Paris. Now Gorz intends to embrace an even wider scope of groups incorporating 'new social movements'. Nevertheless he recognises that this will require dialogue between social movements, trade unions, and a variety of disenfranchised sectors of society:

> The inadequacy of an analysis that relies principally on the cultural resistance to the 'colonization of the lifeworld' contained in the 'new social movements', is that these movements do not consciously and concretely attack the domination of the economic rationality embodied in capitalism. These movements are certainly anti-technocratic, that is, directed against the cultural hegemony of the leading stratum of the ruling class, but they only strike at the cultural assumptions and social consequences of the relation of domination, not, however, at their economic-material core. The new social movements will become the bearers of socialist transformation when they ally themselves not only with the 'modern worker' but also with the contemporary equivalent of the disenfranchised, oppressed and immiserated proletariat – that is, with the post-industrial proletariat of the unemployed, occasionally employed, working short-term or part-time, who neither can nor want to identify themselves with their employment or their place in the production process.
>
> (Gorz 1990: 42)

This passage highlights Gorz's theoretical programme and helps to clarify the direction in which his work will move in the future. Gorz's critique of the labour process is likely to diversify further than before and his work will continue to promote dialogue between the new social movements, trade unions and cultural and community groups. Nevertheless the emancipatory potential of individual autonomy remains his paramount theoretical objective. Thus, the critique of economic reason and the advancement of a new politics of time are the central elements in Gorz's programme.

In line with Offe, Gorz is assuming a prominent role in the debates over welfare and the basic income. As employment becomes increasingly scarce in advanced capitalist societies, these areas of socialist concern will become more important. Gorz's work has already become influential in socialist discourse on both welfare in general and, more specifically, the basic income debate (Gorz 1992; Coenen and Leisink 1993; Van Parijs 1993). Again this debate in socialist theory is most prominent in France, Germany and the Netherlands but, as European integration continues, British political theorists will have to engage with these new areas of political thought and social policy. It is in this context that Gorz's work can be seen to be both original and stimulating.

To conclude, it should be apparent that Gorz has staked out an iconoclastic and highly original perspective within the socialist tradition.

His work is distinctive in its fusion of theory and political realism. Gorz is clearly committed to the advancement of socialist critique to correspond with the specific conditions of advanced capitalism. His work is directed towards a new generation of socialist thinkers who have grown up within the contradictions of capitalism in the late twentieth century. For Gorz, socialism must renew itself through the self-criticism of traditional socialist objectives as much as through a critique of capitalism:

> If a socialist movement does not focus on cultural, interpersonal, community life as intensively as it does on working life, it will not be able to succeed against the capital-realizing leisure and culture industry. It only has a chance if it consciously insists on the creation of expanding free spaces for the development of a many-sided, communicative, everyday culture and everyday solidarity liberated from commodified relations of buying and selling.
>
> (Gorz 1990: 45)

Gorz has provided a framework for discussion and an opportunity for socialists to advance alternative economic thinking which is not shackled by neo-Keynesian orthodoxy (Gorz 1994). However, whilst he provides the bones of the new debate, there is not yet sufficient flesh on them for socialists to advance a thorough programme for change. Gorz's ideas are important and deserve appropriate treatment but his most important legacy, if it can be achieved, will be the liberation of the socialist imagination. He has thrown down a gauntlet to the exponents of socialist orthodoxy to embrace the ethic of self-criticism, to think what was previously unthinkable, and it is imperative that a new generation of socialist theorists pick it up.

BIBLIOGRAPHY

Abercrombie, N., Hill, S. and Turner, B (1980) *The Dominant Ideology Thesis*, London: Allen & Unwin.

—— (1994) 'Determinacy and Indeterminacy in the Theory of Ideology', in S. Zizek (ed.).

Adorno, T. (1983) *Negative Dialectics*, New York: Continuum.

Adriaansens, H. and Derckson, W. (1993) 'Labour Force Participation, Citizenship and a Sustainable Welfare State in the Netherlands', in H. Coenen and P. Leisink (eds).

Allen, S. and Smith, C. (1974) 'Race and Ethnicity in Class Formation: a Comparison of Asian and West Indian Workers', in F. Parkin (ed.).

Althusser, L. (1971) *Lenin and Philosophy and Other Essays*, London: New Left Books.

—— (1994) 'Ideology and Ideological State Apparatuses (Notes towards an Investigation)', in S. Zizek (ed.).

Althusser, L. and Balibar, E. (1970) *Reading Capital*, London: New Left Books.

Anderson, P. (1980) *Arguments within English Marxism*, London: New Left Books.

Anderson, P. and Blackburn, R. (eds) (1965) *Towards Socialism*, London: New Left Books.

Andrews, G. (ed.) (1991) *Citizenship*, London: Lawrence & Wishart.

Arato, A. and Gebhardt, E. (eds) (1978) *The Essential Frankfurt School Reader*, Oxford: Blackwell.

Aronson, R. (1977) 'The Individualist Social Theory of Jean-Paul Sartre', in *New Left Review* (ed.).

Attali, J. (1981) *Les Trois Mondes*, Paris: Fayard.

Bahro, R. (1982) *Socialism and Survival*, London: Heretic.

—— (1984) *From Red to Green*, London: Verso.

—— (1986) *Building the Green Movement*, London: Heretic.

Baker, J. (1992) 'An Egalitarian Case for Basic Income', in P. Van Parijs (ed.).

Baran, P. and Sweezy, P. (1968) *Monopoly Capitalism*, Harmondsworth: Penguin.

Bauman, Z. (1976) *Socialism and the Active Utopia*, London: Allen & Unwin.

Beetham, D. (1991) *The Legitimation of Power*, London: Macmillan.

Benson, L. (1974) 'Market Socialism and Class Structure: Manual Workers and Managerial Power in the Yugoslav Enterprise', in F. Parkin (ed.).

Berger, J. and Kostede, N. (1982) 'Review of A. Gorz, Abschied vom Proletariat: Jenseit des Sozialismus', *Telos*, 51, Spring, 230–3.

Birch, A.H. (1993) *The Concepts and Theories of Modern Democracy*, London: Routledge.

Bobbio, N. (1987) *The Future of Democracy*, Cambridge: Polity Press.

Bocock, R., Hamilton, P., Thompson, K. and Waton, A. (eds) (1980) *An Introduction to Sociology*, London: Fontana.

Boggs, C. (1995) *The Socialist Tradition*, London: Routledge.

Bookchin, M. (1980) *Towards an Ecological Society*, Montreal: Black Rose.

—— (1980–81) 'Review of A. Gorz *Ecology as Politics*', *Telos*, 45, Winter, 177–90.

—— (1982) *The Ecology of Freedom: The Emergence and Dissolution of Hierarchy*, Palo Alto, CA: Cheshire Books.

—— (1986) *The Modern Crisis*, Philadelphia, PA: New Society.

Bosquet, M. (Gorz) (1972a) *Capitalism in Crisis and Everyday Life*, Hassocks: Harvester.

—— (1972b), 'The Prison Factory', *New Left Review*, 73, May–June, 23–34.

Bowring, F. and Connell, M. (1992) 'Autonomy, Heteronomy and the Phenomenology of Domestic Labour: A Reply to Gorz's Critics', unpublished manuscript, Nottingham Polytechnic, October.

Braverman, H. (1974) *Labor and Monopoly Capitalism: The Degradation of Work in the Twentieth Century*, New York: Monthly Review Press.

Brown, G. (1994) 'The Politics of Potential: A New Agenda for Labour', in D. Miliband (ed.).

Burrows, R. and Loader, B. (eds) (1994) *Towards a Post-Fordist Welfare State?*, London: Routledge.

Byrne, D. (1994) 'Planning for and against the Divided City: a Case Study of the North East of England', in R. Burrows and B. Loader (eds).

Cahill, M. (1995) 'Robertson', in V. George and R. Page (eds).

Carling, A. (1992) 'Just Two Just Taxes', in P. Van Parijs (ed.).

Carter, A. (1993) 'Towards a Green Political Theory', in A. Dobson and P. Lucardie (eds).

Caute, D. (1964) *Communism and the French Intellectuals 1914–1960*, London: André Deutsch.

—— (1973) *The Fellow Travellers: A Postscript to the Enlightenment*, London: Quartet.

Chiodi, P. (1976) *Sartre and Marxism*, Hassocks: Harvester.

Clegg, S., Boreham, P. and Dow, G. (1986) *Class, Politics and the Economy*, London: Routledge & Kegan Paul.

Coenen, H. (1993) 'The Concept of Work in the Trade Unions: Towards a Debate on Economic Rights', in H. Coenen and P. Leisink (eds).

Coenen, H. and Leisink, P. (eds) (1993) *Work and Citizenship in the New Europe*, Aldershot: Edward Elgar.

Cohn-Bendit, D. and Cohn-Bendit, G. (1968) *Obsolete Communism: The Left-Wing Alternative*, London: André Deutsch.

Commission on Social Justice (1994) *Social Justice: Strategies for National Renewal*, London: Vintage.
Connerton, P. (ed.) (1976) *Critical Sociology: Selected Writings*, Harmondsworth: Penguin.
Coote, A. (1994) 'Deciding about Rights', in D. Miliband (ed.).
Cranston, M. (1976) 'Jean-Paul Sartre: Solitary Man in a Hostile Universe', in A. De Crespigny and K. Minogue (eds).
Cunningham, F. (1987) *Democratic Theory and Socialism*, Cambridge: Cambridge University Press.
Dahl, R.A. (1985) *A Preface to Economic Democracy*, Cambridge: Polity Press.
Davies, H. (1988) *Sartre and Les Temps Modernes*, Cambridge: Cambridge University Press.
Debray, R. (1968) *Revolution in the Revolution*, Harmondsworth: Penguin.
De Crespigny, A. and Minogue, K. (eds) (1976) *Contemporary Political Philosophers*, London: Methuen.
Demos (1995) 'The Time Squeeze', *Demos Quarterly*, 5 (whole issue).
Desai, M. (1995) 'Basic Instinct to Spring the Benefits Trap', *Observer*, 13 August.
Dickson, D. (1974) *Alternative Technology and the Politics of Technical Change*, London: Fontana.
Dobson, A. (1990) *Green Political Thought*, London: Routledge.
—— (1993) 'Critical Theory and Green Politics', in A. Dobson and P. Lucardie (eds).
Dobson, A. and Lucardie, P. (eds) (1993) *The Politics of Nature: Explorations in Green Political Theory*, London: Routledge.
Doyal, L. and Gough, I. (1991) *A Theory of Human Need*, London: Macmillan.
Drover, G. and Kerans, P. (eds) (1993) *New Approaches to Welfare Theory*, Aldershot: Edward Elgar.
Dunleavy, P. and O'Leary, B. (1987) *Theories of the State: The Politics of Liberal Democracy*, London: Macmillan.
Dunn, J. (1989) 'Political Obligation', in D. Held (ed.).
Eccleshall, R., Geoghegan, V., Jay, R., Kenny, M., MacKenzie, I. and Wilford, R. (1994) *Political Ideologies: An Introduction*, London: Routledge.
Eckersley, R. (1992) *Environmentalism and Political Theory: Towards an Ecocentric Approach*, London: UCL Press.
Elster, J. and Moene, K.O. (eds) (1989) *Alternatives to Capitalism*, Cambridge: Cambridge University Press.
Enzensberger, H.M. (1988) *Dreamers of the Absolute*, London: Radius.
Ferris, J. (1993) 'Introduction: Political Realism and Green Strategy', in H. Wiesenthal (1993).
Forbes, I. (1990) *Marx and the New Individual*, London: Unwin Hyman.
Frankel, B. (1982) 'On the State of the State: Marxist Theories of the State after Lenin', in A. Giddens and D. Held (eds).
—— (1987) *The Post-Industrial Utopians*, Cambridge: Polity Press.
Fromm, E. (1960) *Fear or Freedom*, London: Routledge.
Garaudy, R. (1970) *Marxism in the Twentieth Century*, London: Collins.
—— (1971) *The Whole Truth*, London: Fontana.
Geoghegan, V. (1987) *Utopianism and Marxism*, London: Methuen.

George, V. and Page, R. (eds) (1995) *Modern Thinkers on Welfare*, Hemel Hempstead: Harvester Wheatsheaf.
George, V. and Wilding, P. (1994) *Welfare and Ideology*, Hemel Hempstead: Harvester Wheatsheaf.
Geras, N. (1983) *Marx and Human Nature: Refutation of a Legend*, London: Verso.
Gershuny, J. (1995) 'Time Keynesianism', *Demos Quarterly*, 5, 42–4.
Giddens, A. (1982) 'Class Structuration and Class Consciousness', in A. Giddens and D. Held (eds).
—— (1984) *The Constitution of Society*, Cambridge: Polity Press.
—— (1985) *The Nation-State and Violence*, Cambridge: Polity Press.
—— (1987) *Social Theory and Modern Sociology*, Cambridge: Polity Press.
—— (1991) *Modernity and Self-Identity*, Cambridge: Polity Press.
Giddens, A. and Held, D. (eds) (1982) *Classes, Power and Conflict: Classical and Contemporary Debates*, London: Macmillan.
Glotz, P. (1987) 'Die Malaise der Linken', *Der Spiegel*, 51.
Goodin, R.E. (1992) *Green Political Theory*, Cambridge: Polity Press.
Gorz, A. (1959) *La Morale de l'histoire*, Paris: Editions du Seuil.
—— (1963) 'Common Market Agriculture', *New Left Review*, 23, January–February, 55–7.
—— (1965a) 'Work and Consumption', in P. Anderson and R. Blackburn (eds).
—— (1965b) 'Le Test vietnamien', *Les Temps Modernes*, 228, 1921–4.
—— (1965c) 'Sartre and Marx', in *New Left Review* (ed.).
—— (1967) *Strategy for Labor*, Boston, MA: Beacon, first published 1964.
—— (1968) 'The Way Forward', *New Left Review*, 52, November–December, 47–66.
—— (1969) 'The Pompidou Regime', *New Left Review*, 58, November–December, 29–31.
—— (1970a) 'What were the Lessons of the May Events?', in C. Posner (ed.).
—— (1970b) 'Détruire l'université', *Les Temps Modernes*, 285, 1553–8.
—— (1970c) 'Immigrant Labour', *New Left Review*, 61, May–June, 28–31.
—— (1972) 'Technical Intelligence and the Capitalist Division of Labour', *Telos*, 12, Summer, 27–41.
—— (1973) 'The Tyranny of the Factory: Today and Tomorrow', *Telos*, 16, Summer, 61–7.
—— (1975) *Socialism and Revolution*, London: Allen Lane, first published 1967.
—— (ed.) (1976a) *The Division of Labour*, Hassocks: Harvester.
—— (1976b) 'On the Class Character of Science and Scientists', in H. Rose and S. Rose (eds).
—— (1977a) *Fondements pour une morale*, Paris: Galilee.
—— (1977b) 'Sartre and the Deaf', *Telos*, 33, Autumn, 106–8.
—— (1982) ' What, Then, is Freedom? Reply to Bahro', *Telos*, 51, Spring, 126–7.
—— (1983) 'The Reconquest of Time', *Telos*, 55, Spring, 212–16.
—— (1985a) *Paths to Paradise / On the Liberation from Work*, London: Pluto Press, first published 1983.

—— (1985b) 'Against Confusing Autonomous Activity with Wage Labour', *Telos*, 64, Summer, 123–4.

—— (1985c) 'The American Model and the Future of the French Left', *Socialist Review*, 84, 101–7.

—— (1986) 'The Socialism of Tomorrow', *Telos*, 67, Spring, 199–206.

—— (1987a) *Ecology as Politics*, London: Pluto Press, first published 1975.

—— (1987b) *Farewell to the Working Class: An Essay on Post-Industrial Socialism*, London: Pluto Press, first published 1980.

—— (1987c) '(S)He Who Doesn't Work Shall Eat All the Same: Tomorrow's Economy and Proposals from the Left', *Dissent*, 34, 179–87.

—— (1987d) 'Reshaping the Welfare State', *Praxis International*, 6, 1.

—— (1988) 'Making Space for Everyone', *New Statesman / Society*, 25 November, 28–31.

—— (1989a) *Critique of Economic Reason*, London: Verso, first published 1988.

—— (1989b) *The Traitor*, London: Verso, first published 1958.

—— (1989c) 'World of No Workers', *Guardian*, 9 December, (*Weekend Guardian*).

—— (1989d) 'A Land of Cockayne?', interview with J. Keane, *New Statesman / Society*, 12 May, 26–31.

—— (1990) 'The New Agenda', *New Left Review*,184, November–December, 37–46.

—— (1992) 'On the Difference between Society and Community, and Why Basic Income Cannot by Itself Confer Full Membership of Either', in P. Van Parijs (ed.).

—— (1993) 'Political Ecology: Expertocracy versus Self-Limitation', *New Left Review*, 202, November–December, 55–67.

—— (1994) *Capitalism, Socialism, Ecology*, London: Verso, first published 1991.

Gough, I. (1979) *The Political Economy of the Welfare State*, London: Macmillan.

Gould, C. (1988) *Rethinking Democracy: Freedom and Social Cooperation in Politics, Economy, and Society*, Cambridge: Cambridge University Press.

Grahl, B. and Piccone, P. (eds) (1973) *Towards a New Marxism*, St Louis, MO: Telos Press.

Green Party of Ireland (1989) *Communism and Capitalism – One Down, One to Go: Towards a Sane Economy*, Dublin: Green Party of Ireland.

Grint, K. (1991) *The Sociology of Work*, Cambridge: Polity Press.

Grundmann, R. (1991) *Marxism and Ecology*, Oxford: Clarendon Press.

Habermas, J. (1976a) *Legitimation Crisis*, London: Heinemann.

—— (1976b) 'Theorem of Motivation Crisis', in R. Bocock *et al.* (eds) (1980).

—— (ed.) (1984) *Observations on the Spiritual Situation of the Age*, Boston, MA: MIT.

—— (1986) *Autonomy and Solidarity: Interviews*, London: Verso, edited by P. Dews.

—— (1987) *Theory of Communicative Action*, Cambridge: Polity Press.

—— (1989) *The New Conservatism*, Cambridge: Polity Press.

Hall, S. (1985) 'Authoritarian Populism: A Reply to Jessop *et al.*', *New Left Review*, 151, May–June, 115–24.

Hall, S. and Jacques, M. (eds) (1989) *New Times: The Changing Face of Politics in the 1990s*, London: Lawrence & Wishart.
Hall, S., Held, D. and McGraw, A. (eds) (1992) *Modernity and its Futures*, Cambridge: Polity Press.
Hardin, G. (1968) 'The Tragedy of the Commons', *Science*, 162, 1243–8.
Hay, P.R. (1988) 'Ecological Values and Western Political Traditions from Anarchism to Fascism', *Politics*, 8:2, October, 22–9.
Hazareesingh, S. (1991) *Intellectuals and the French Communist Party: Disillusion and Decline*, Oxford: Clarendon Press.
—— (1994) *Political Traditions in Modern France*, Oxford: Oxford University Press.
Held, D. (1982) 'Critical Theory and Political Transformation', *Media, Culture and Society*, 4, 153–60.
—— (1989a) *Political Theory and the Modern State*, Cambridge: Polity Press.
—— (ed.) (1989b) *Political Theory Today*, Cambridge: Polity Press.
—— (ed.) (1993) *Prospects for Democracy*, Cambridge: Polity Press.
Heller, A. (1976) *The Theory of Need in Marx*, London: Allison & Busby.
Hewitt, P. (1993) *About Time: The Revolution in Work and Family Life*, London: Rivers Oram Press.
Himmelstrand, U., Ahrne, G., Lundberg, L. and Lundberg, L. (1981) *Beyond Welfare Capitalism*, London: Heinemann.
Hirsch, A. (1982) *The French New Left: A History and Overview*, Montreal: Black Rose.
Hirst, P. (1989) 'After Henry', in S. Hall and M. Jacques (eds).
—— (1993) 'Associational Democracy', in D. Held (ed.).
Hoffman, J. (1995) *Beyond the State*, Cambridge: Polity Press.
Horkheimer, M. (1974) *Eclipse of Reason*, New York: Continuum.
Horton, J. (1992) *Political Obligation*, London: Macmillan.
Horvat, B., Markovic, M. and Supek, R. (eds) (1975) *Self-Governing Socialism*, New York: International Arts and Science Press.
Howard, D. and Klare, K. (eds) (1971) *The Unknown Dimension: European Marxism since Lenin*, New York: Basic Books.
Hulsberg, W. (1988) *The German Greens*, London: Verso.
Hyman, R. (1983) 'André Gorz and his Disappearing Proletariat', *Socialist Register*, London: Merlin Press.
Hyman, R. and Price, R. (eds) (1983) *The New Working Class? White-Collar Workers and their Organizations*, London: Macmillan.
Illich, I. (1973) *Tools for Conviviality*, New York: Harper & Row.
—— (1978) *The Right to Useful Unemployment*, New York: Marion Boyars.
Johnson, R.W. (1981) *The Long March of the French Left*, London: Macmillan.
Jones, C. (ed.) (1993) *New Perspectives on the Welfare State in Europe*, London: Routledge.
Jordan, B. (1992) 'Basic Income and the Common Good', in P. Van Parijs (ed.).
Judt, T. (1986) *Marxism and the French Left*, Oxford: Oxford University Press.
Keane, J. (1988) *Democracy and Civil Society*, London: Verso.
—— (1991) *The Media and Democracy*, Cambridge: Polity Press.
Keane, J. and Owens, J. (1984) *After Full Employment*, London: Hutchinson.
Kellner, D. (1989) *Critical Theory, Marxism and Modernity*, Cambridge: Polity Press.

Kenny, M. (1994) 'Ecologism', in R. Eccleshall *et al.*

Kenny, M. and Little, A. (1995) 'Gorz', in V. George and R. Page (eds).

Kettler, D. (1976) 'Herbert Marcuse: The Critique of Bourgeois Civilisation and its Transcendence', in A. De Crespigny and K. Minogue (eds).

Kitschelt, H. (1994) *The Transformation of European Social Democracy*, Cambridge: Cambridge University Press.

Klein, R. (1993) 'O'Goffe's Tale', in C. Jones (ed.).

Kumar, K. (1978) *Prophecy and Progress*, Harmondsworth: Penguin.

Kymlicka, W. (1990) *Contemporary Political Philosophy*, Oxford: Oxford University Press.

Laclau, E. and Mouffe, M. (1985) *Hegemony and Socialist Strategy*, London: Verso.

Lasch, C. (1979) *The Culture of Narcissism*, London: Abacus.

Lefebvre, H. (1975) 'Elements for a Sociology of Self-Management', in B. Horvat *et al.* (eds).

Leisink, P. and Beukema, L. (1993) 'Participation and Autonomy at Work: a Segmented Privilege', in H. Coenen and P. Leisink (eds.).

Leisink, P. and Coenen, H. (1993) 'Work and Citizenship in the New Europe', in H. Coenen and P. Leisink (eds).

Leonard, P. (1984) *Personality and Ideology: Towards a Materialist Understanding of the Individual*, London: Macmillan.

Levitas, R. (1990) *The Concept of Utopia*, Hemel Hempstead: Philip Allan.

Lipietz, A. (1992) *Towards a New Economic Order: Postfordism, Ecology and Democracy*, Cambridge: Polity Press.

Lodziak, C. (1986) *The Power of Television*, London: Pinter.

—— (1988) 'Dull Compulsion of the Economic: The Dominant Ideology and Social Reproduction', *Radical Philosophy*, 49, Summer, 10–16.

—— (1992) 'The Manipulation of Needs Thesis', unpublished paper, Nottingham Trent University.

—— (1995) *Manipulating Needs: Capitalism and Culture*, London: Pluto Press.

McLellan, D. (1979) *Marxism after Marx*, London: Macmillan.

McNall, S.G., Levine, R.F. and Fantasia, R. (eds) (1991) *Bringing Class Back In: Contemporary and Historical Perspectives*, Boulder, CO: Westview Press.

MacPherson, C.B. (1962) *The Political Theory of Possessive Individualism*, Oxford: Clarendon Press.

Mallet, S. (1975) *The New Working Class*, Nottingham: Spokesman.

—— (1983) 'The New Working Class', in R. Hyman and R. Price (eds).

Mandel, E. (1982) *Introduction to Marxism*, London: Pluto Press.

Mann, M. (1973) *Consciousness and Action among the Western Working Class*, London: Macmillan.

—— (1982) 'The Social Cohesion of Liberal Democracy', in A. Giddens and D. Held (eds).

—— (1983) 'A Sceptical View of the New Working Class', in R. Hyman and R. Price (eds).

Marcus, L. (1992) 'An Invitation to Life: André Gorz's *The Traitor*', *New Left Review*, 194, July–August, 114–20.

Marcuse, H. (1957) *Soviet Marxism*, London: Routledge and Kegan Paul.

—— (1972a) *An Essay on Liberation*, Harmondsworth: Pelican.

—— (1972b) *Counter Revolution and Revolt*, Boston, MA: Beacon.
—— (1978) 'Some Social Implications of Modern Technology', in A. Arato and E. Gebhardt (eds).
—— (1986) *One Dimensional Man*, London: Ark.
—— (1987) *Eros and Civilization*, London; Ark.
Marglin, S. (1976) 'What do Bosses do?', in A. Gorz (ed.).
Marshall, T.H. (1963) *Sociology at the Crossroads and Other Essays*, London: Heinemann.
Martell, L. (1994) *Ecology and Society*, Cambridge: Polity Press.
Marx, K. and Engels, F. (1970) *The German Ideology*, London: Lawrence & Wishart.
Meadows, D.H., Meadows, D.L., Randers, J. and Behrens, W.W (1972) *The Limits to Growth*, New York: Universe.
Meehan, E. (1993) *Citizenship and the European Community*, London: Sage.
Meiksins, P. (1986) 'Beyond the Boundary Question', *New Left Review*, 157, May–June, 101–20.
Meiksins Wood, E. (1986) *The Retreat from Class: A New 'True' Socialism*, London: Verso.
Miliband, D. (ed.) (1994) *Reinventing the Left*, Cambridge: Polity Press.
Miliband, R. (1973) *The State in Capitalist Society*, London: Quartet.
—— (1984) *Capitalist Democracy in Britain*, Oxford: Oxford University Press.
Miller, D. (1989) *Market, State and Community: Theoretical Foundations of Market Socialism*, Oxford: Clarendon Press.
Miller, J. (1979) *History and Human Existence: From Marx to Merleau-Ponty*, Los Angeles: University of California Press.
Mishra, R. (1993) 'Social Policy in the Postmodern World', in C. Jones (ed.).
Mobasser, N. (1987) 'Marx and Self-Realisation', *New Left Review*, 161, January–February, 119–28.
Mouffe, C. (ed.) (1992) *Dimensions of Radical Democracy: Pluralism, Citizenship, Community*, London: Verso.
—— (1993) *The Return of the Political*, London: Verso.
Mulgan, G. and Wilkinson, H. (1995) 'Well-being and Time', *Demos Quarterly*, 5, 2–11.
Narr, W.-D. (1984) 'Towards a Society of Conditioned Reflexes', in J. Habermas (ed.).
New Left Review (ed.) (1977) *Western Marxism: A Critical Reader*, London: New Left Books.
Nove, A. (1983) *The Economics of Feasible Socialism*, London: Allen & Unwin.
—— (1991) *The Economics of Feasible Socialism Revisited*, London: Allen & Unwin.
Oakley, A. (1984) 'Domestic Work', in K. Thompson (ed.).
O' Connor, J. (1973) *The Fiscal Crisis of the State*, New York: St Martin's Press.
—— (1984) *Accumulation Crisis*, Oxford: Blackwell.
Offe, C. (1984), *Contradictions of the Welfare State*, London: Hutchinson, edited by J. Keane.
—— (1985) *Disorganized Capitalism*, Cambridge: Polity Press.
—— (1992) 'A Non-Productivist Design for Social Policies', in P. Van Parijs (ed.).

Offe, C. and Heinze, R. (1992) *Beyond Employment: Time, Work and the Informal Economy*, Cambridge: Polity Press.
Oliver, D. and Heater, D. (1994) *The Foundations of Citizenship*, Hemel Hempstead: Harvester Wheatsheaf.
Ophuls, W. (1977) *Ecology and the Politics of Scarcity*, San Francisco: Freeman.
Pahl, R.E. (ed.) (1988) *On Work: Historical, Comparative and Theoretical Approaches*, Oxford: Blackwell.
Papadakis, E. and Taylor-Gooby, P. (1987) *The Private Provision of Public Welfare*, London: Wheatsheaf.
Parkin, F. (ed.) (1974) *The Social Analysis of Class Structure*, London: Tavistock.
Parsons, H. (1978) *Marx and Engels on Ecology*, Westport, CT: Greenwood.
Pateman, C. (1970) *Participation and Democratic Theory*, Cambridge: Cambridge University Press.
Pepper, D. (1984) *The Roots of Modern Environmentalism*, London: Routledge.
—— (1993) *Eco-socialism: From Deep Ecology to Social Justice*, London: Routledge.
Phillips, A. (1991) *Engendering Democracy*, Cambridge: Polity Press.
Pierson, C. (1991) *Beyond the Welfare State?*, Cambridge: Polity Press.
—— (1995) *Socialism after Communism: The New Market Socialism*, Cambridge: Polity Press.
Piore, M. and Sabel, C. (1984) *The Second Industrial Divide*, New York: Basic Books.
Plant, R. (1991a) 'Social Rights and the Reconstruction of Welfare', in G. Andrews (ed.).
—— (1991b) *Modern Political Thought*, Oxford: Blackwell.
Porritt, J. (1986) *Seeing Green*, Oxford: Blackwell.
Porritt, J. and Winner, D. (1988) *The Coming of the Greens*, London: Fontana.
Posner, C. (ed.) (1970) *Reflections on the Revolution in France: 1968*, Harmondsworth: Penguin.
Poster, M. (1975) *Existential Marxism in Post-War France*, Princeton, NJ: Princeton University Press.
Poulantzas, N. (1973) *Political Power and Social Classes*, London: New Left Books.
—— (1975) *Classes in Contemporary Capitalism*, London: New Left Books.
Reader, K. (1987) *Intellectuals and the Left in France since 1968*, London: Macmillan.
Rifkin, J. (1995) 'The End of Work as We Know It', *Demos Quarterly*, 5, 17–20.
Robertson, J. (1985) *Future Work*, London: Gower.
Roemer, J. (1994) *A Future for Socialism*, Cambridge, MA: Harvard University Press.
Rose, H. and Rose, S. (eds) (1976) *The Political Economy of Science*, London: Macmillan.
Ryle, M. (1988) *Ecology and Socialism*, London: Radius.
Sartre, J.P. (1974) *Beyond Existentialism and Marxism*, London: New Left Books.
—— (1989) 'Of Rats and Men', in A. Gorz (1989b), 1–33.
Sayers, S. (1988) 'The Need to Work', in R.E. Pahl (ed.).

—— (1991) 'Gorz on Work and Liberation', *Radical Philosophy*, 58, Summer, 16–19.

Schaff, A. (1970) *Marxism and the Human Individual*, New York: McGraw-Hill.

Seale, P. and McConville, M. (1968) *French Revolution 1968*, London: Heinemann.

Seve, L. (1978) *Man in Marxist Theory and the Psychology of Personality*, Hassocks: Harvester.

Smart, B. (1992) *Modern Conditions, Postmodern Controversies*, London: Routledge.

Soper, K. (1981) *On Human Needs: Open and Closed Theories in a Marxist Perspective*, Hassocks: Harvester.

—— (1993) 'The Thick and Thin of Human Needing' , in G. Drover and P. Kerans (eds).

Steiner, H. (1992) 'Three Just Taxes', in P. Van Parijs (ed.).

Stephens, J. (1979) *The Transition from Capitalism to Socialism*, London: Macmillan.

Supek, R. (1975) 'The Sociology of Workers' Self-Management', in B. Horvat *et al.* (eds).

Taylor-Gooby, P. (1991) *Social Change, Social Welfare and Social Science*, London: Harvester Wheatsheaf.

Thompson, E.P. (1967) 'Time, Work, Discipline and Industrial Capitalism', *Past and Present*, 38, 56–97.

—— (1980) 'Notes on Exterminism: The Last Stage of Civilization', *New Left Review*, 121, May–June, 3–32.

Thompson, K. (ed.) (1984) *Work, Employment and Unemployment*, Milton Keynes: Open University Press.

Thompson, P. (1984a) *The Nature of Work: An Introduction to Debates on the Labour Process*, London: Macmillan.

—— (1984b) 'The Labour Process and Deskilling', in K. Thompson (ed.).

Tokar, B. (1987) *The Green Alternative*, San Pedro, CA, R. & E. Miles.

Touraine, A. (1974) *The Post-Industrial Society*, London: Wildwood House.

Tucker, D.F.B. (1980) *Marxism and Individualism*, Oxford: Blackwell.

Valocchi, S. (1991) 'The Class Basis of the State and the Origins of Welfare Policy in Britain, Sweden and Germany', in S.G. McNall *et al.* (eds).

Van Parijs, P. (ed.) (1992a) *Arguing for Basic Income: Ethical Foundations for a Radical Reform*, London: Verso.

—— (1992b) 'Competing Justifications for Basic Income', in P. Van Parijs (ed.).

—— (1993) *Marxism Recycled*, Cambridge: Cambridge University Press.

Van Parijs, P. and Van der Veen, R.J. (1993) 'Universal Grants versus Socialism', in P. Van Parijs (ed.).

Vilrokx, J. (1993) 'Basic Income, Citizenship and Solidarity: Towards a Dynamic for Social Renewal', in H. Coenen and P. Leisink (eds).

Wall, D. (1990) *Getting There: Steps to a Green Society*, London: Green Print.

Weber, M. (1976) *The Protestant Ethic and the Spirit of Capitalism*, London: Allen & Unwin.

Weston, J. (ed.) (1986) *Red and Green: The New Politics of the Environment*, London: Pluto Press.

Wiesenthal, H. (1993) *Realism in Green Politics: Social Movements and Ecological Reform in Germany*, Manchester: Manchester University Press, edited by J. Ferris.
Wilde, L. (1994) *Modern European Socialism*, Aldershot: Dartmouth.
Williams, R. (1983) 'Problems of the Coming Period', *New Left Review*, 140, July–August, 7–18.
—— (n.d.) *Socialism and Ecology*, London: Socialist Environment and Resources Association.
Wissenburg, M. (1993) 'The Idea of Nature and the Nature of Distributive Justice', in A. Dobson and P. Lucardie (eds).
Wright, E.O. (1978) *Class, Crisis and the State*, London: New Left Books.
—— (1985) *Classes*, London: Verso.
—— (1991) 'The Conceptual Status of Class Structure in Class Analysis', in S.G. McNall *et al.* (eds.).
Zeldin, T. (1995) 'An Intimate Future of Time', *Demos Quarterly*, 5, 35–6.
Zizek, S. (ed.) (1994), *Mapping Ideology*, London: Verso.

INDEX